IMAGES
of Modern America

Golf in Broome County

Jim Maggiore and Michael J. McCann

ARCADIA
PUBLISHING

ISBN 978-1-4671-2365-5

Published by Arcadia Publishing
Charleston, South Carolina

Printed in the United States of America

Library of Congress Control Number: 2014958702

For all general information, please contact Arcadia Publishing:
Telephone 843-853-2070
Fax 843-853-0044
E-mail sales@arcadiapublishing.com
For customer service and orders:
Toll-Free 1-888-313-2665

Visit us on the Internet at www.arcadiapublishing.com

This work is dedicated to all the tournament volunteers who have worked at En-Joie, especially Alex Alexander and Johnny Hart.

Contents

ACKNOWLEDGMENTS

As with the En-Joie tournaments, this work needed many volunteers, including those who offered comments on drafts: Joseph McCann; Alice Maggiore, who was a great copy editor; and Susan McCann. Thanks also to those at the offices of Broome County Community Charities, especially John Karedes and Liz Klein, for opening their archives to us and answering countless questions. Thanks to Maureen Radzavicz, communications director for the Champions Tour, and to Gene Null and Mike Norman for sharing some of their many stories.

All photographs in this book are from the authors' collection, unless otherwise noted. The following sources of photographs are identified with abbreviations: Broome County Historical Society (BCHS), Broome County Community Charities (BCCC), and the private collections of Ken Barber (KB), Leo Hubik (LH), Frank Micalizzi (FM), and Kathleen Wolfe (KW).

In addition to numerous interviews, the following sources of information were used to gather material: *Binghamton Press & Sun Bulletin*; Dick's Sporting Goods website (dsgopen.com); PGA Tour website (www.pgatour.com); and scrapbooks from Alex Alexander's collection, courtesy of the Broome County Historical Society.

INTRODUCTION

In golf, humility, patience, and sportsmanship are the primary principles at play. Unlike boxing, football, and hockey, golf has no violence. Unlike baseball, there is no hubris of delivering a "high, hard one." Nor is there any screaming at an official, as often happens on other courts. Golfers are their own judges and scorers, their every shot a measure of integrity, with the stationary ball ensuring no one strikes out. The links demand respect and gentlemanly behavior from fans and players alike, with the pastoral "whack" of a club reminding all that every shot is an opportunity for success. This book captures golf at its finest and illustrates its history in Broome County, tracing the development of the present-day Dick's Sporting Goods Senior Open (DSGO) from the BC Open, which was held from 1971 to 2006.

The BC Open began in 1971 as the Broome County Open, a one-day golf tournament. It expanded to two days in 1972, and in 1973, it was accepted as a four-day PGA tournament. In naming the event, organizers showed their creative genius in selecting the mundane "BC Open," as the "BC" stood for Broome County. How can both "mundane" and "creative genius" be used to describe the tourney's name? Well, the illustrator behind the advertisements for the tournament was none other than the creator and illustrator of the comic strip *B.C.*, Endicott native Johnny Hart. Even after achieving national fame as a syndicated columnist, he remained a lifelong resident of Broome County. Hart was also instrumental in producing a unique trophy for the PGA Tour: winners of the BC Open took home a bronze statue of Thor, a character from his comic strip. So in naming the tournament the "BC Open," Endicott was also able to honor a native son.

Following the 2006 tournament, the directors opted to accept a spot on the Champions Tour (previously known as the Senior PGA Tour). It was fitting for Dick's Sporting Goods to become the title sponsor of this tournament, as the Pittsburgh-based company got its start in the neighboring city of Binghamton, in the basement of the home of founder Richard "Dick" Stack.

Over the years, the golfers who have passed through the En-Joie golf course have praised the tournament organizers because the event has been run so well, with all golfers receiving equal treatment, whether they were a hall of famer or a struggling tour player. The tournaments have always offered a number of events and activities for the golfers that weren't in most other, larger PGA tournaments. The B.C. Open hosted annual 9-ball billiards tournaments, charity softball games, and various golfing contests, including the "King is a Fink" shootout and short-shot contests. The "King is a Fink" short-shot contests included a mix of professional golfers paired with famous cartoonists to try their hands at trick shots, and was named after a famous refrain from the B.C. comic strip. Besides Johnny Hart, who also created the Wizard of ID strip, some of the other participating cartoonists included Jim Davis of Garfield, Dean Young of Blondie, and Mike Peters of Mother Goose and Grim.

For both the B.C. Open and the DSGO, clearly the biggest attraction besides the golf has been the Friday night concert, which has been free for all fans attending the first round of golf. The concert started off on a small scale, with a local national recording star, Rochester native Chuck Mangione, but has grown to become an enormous event. The recent musical guests have been major recording artists, including Tim McGraw, Huey Lewis and the News, Hootie and the Blowfish, Maroon 5, and the Zac Brown Band. While music fans love listening to the music, the golf fans are amazed at how quickly the 18th hole transforms from a spot off the 18th fairway to a concert stage—and back again—in time for tournament play by eight the next morning!

In this book, readers, whether golf enthusiasts or not, will get a feel for the rich history of professional golf at En-Joie. Chapters two and three target the golf fan, illustrating the winners at En-Joie, while also sharing stories of those who have chased championships on its undulating greens and tight fairways. And for readers who might think of a bogey as Sam Spade's favorite drink in the film-noir classic *The Maltese Falcon*, they, too, will find the book informative. For this is a story of how a community has rallied around a golf tournament and served one million volunteer hours to ensure golfers relish their sojourn to Endicott. The "can-do" and resilient attitude of Endicott and its surrounding community is the not-so-subtle theme of chapter one, "A Million Hours, $14 Million, and Counting." Finally, for those looking to catch glimpses of celebrities at work and play, the "Beyond the Golf" chapter is for them.

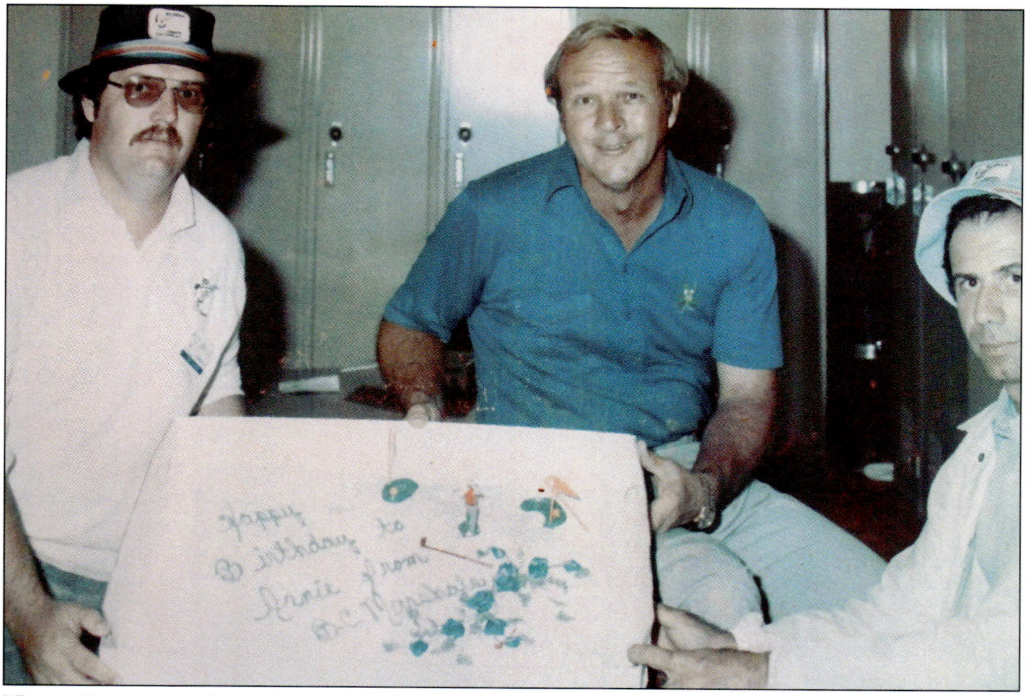

HAPPY BIRTHDAY, ARNIE! Arnold Palmer celebrated his 48th birthday at the BC Open in 1977. Palmer finished 22nd in the tournament, with a score of 283 over four rounds of golf.

One

A Million Hours, $14 Million, and Counting

In 1925, George F. Johnson, chairman of the Endicott-Johnson Corporation, commissioned the building of the En-Joie Golf Course in Endicott, New York. It was America's first corporate-built golf course, symbolizing Johnson's commitment to philanthropic practices. In 1971, Alex Alexander, En-Joie's golfing director, envisioned the course becoming a stop on the PGA Tour. After running two "satellite" tournaments in 1971 and 1972, he was instrumental in getting the PGA to accept Endicott as a stop on its tour in 1973.

The Broome County Chamber of Commerce ran the event for the first three years, but, as the event grew, it became apparent that a separate organization was needed to run the tournament. Consequently, Broome County Community Charities (BCCC) was incorporated in 1974 to operate the golf tournament and distribute the proceeds to charitable organizations within the community. Today, more than 40 years later, the primary mission of BCCC remains the same: run the Dick's Sporting Goods Open (DSGO) and distribute proceeds to the community.

The theme of "giving back" is evident in every step in running today's tournament. Hundreds of neighboring businesses contribute money and resources, with Dick's Sporting Goods Corporation purchasing the naming rights. Just as important as these contributions are the thousands of hours donated annually by community residents. Every year, over 1,600 volunteers donate a minimum of 12 hours to work for over 20 committees, which involve such jobs as drivers, leaderboard workers, marshals, standard-bearers, and security personnel. Add in the hours from local Rotary and Lions clubs to run the concession stands, and over one million hours have been donated to the tournament since its inception. In return, the BCCC has donated over $14 million to the community since the first tournament!

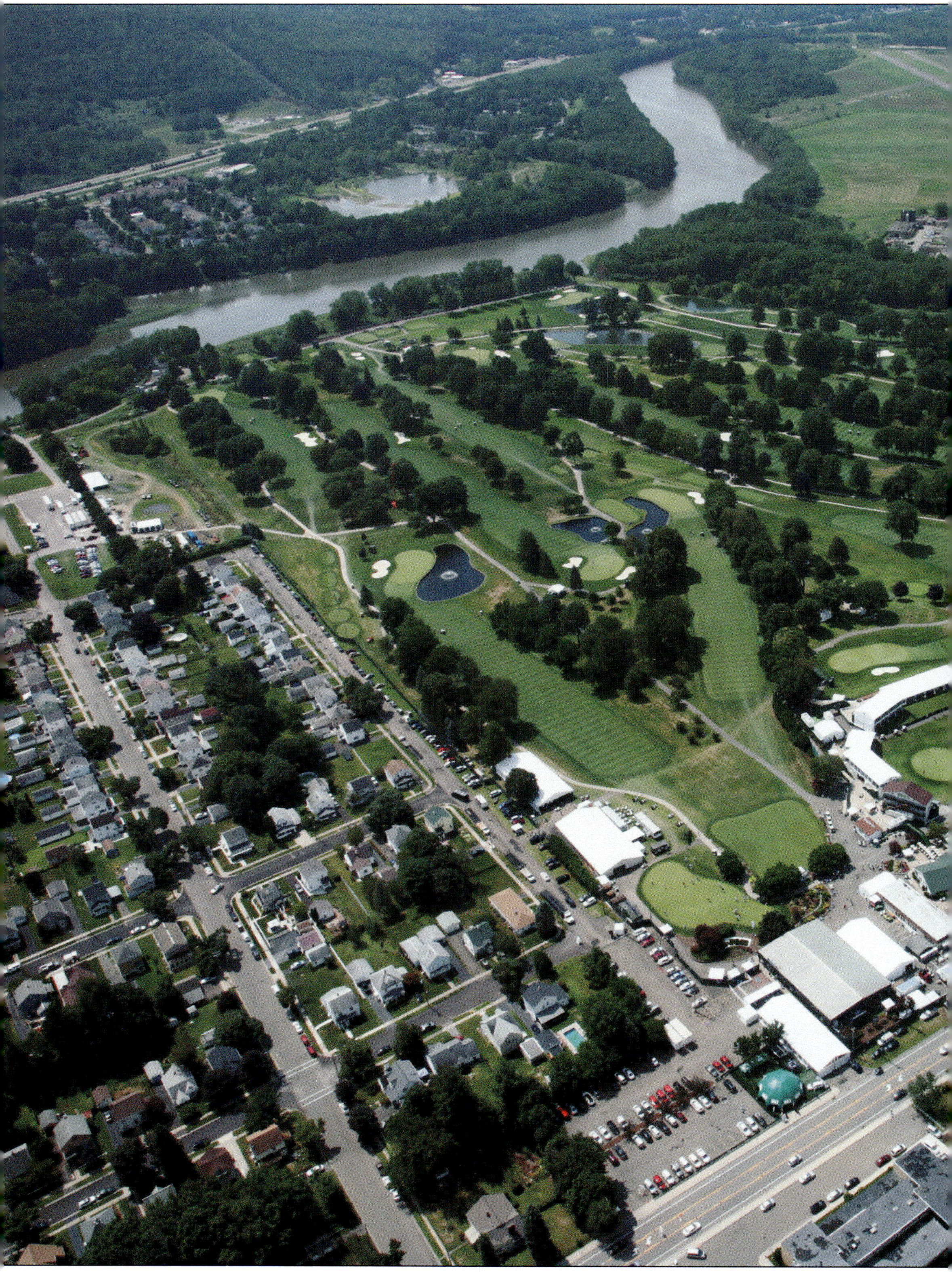

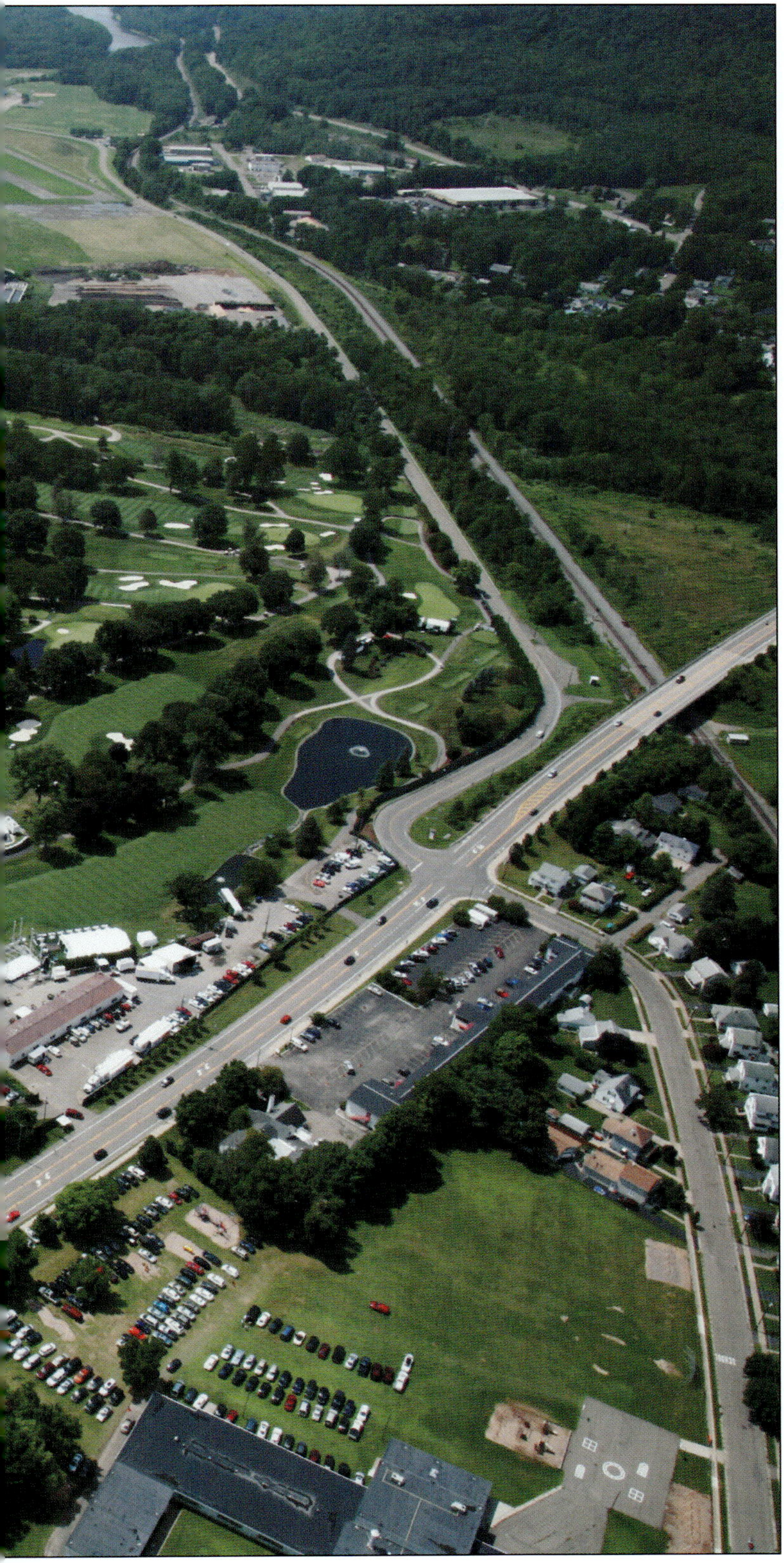

SMALL TOWN, BIG-TIME GOLF. This aerial photograph shows En-Joie nestled within the community of Endicott. Main Street (Route 17C) is at lower right, with the course's parking lot to its left. The course is bordered on the south by the Susquehanna River, on the north by Main Street, on the east by homes originally built by the Endicott-Johnson Corporation for its employees, and on the west by the Tri-Cities Airport. (Courtesy of BCCC.)

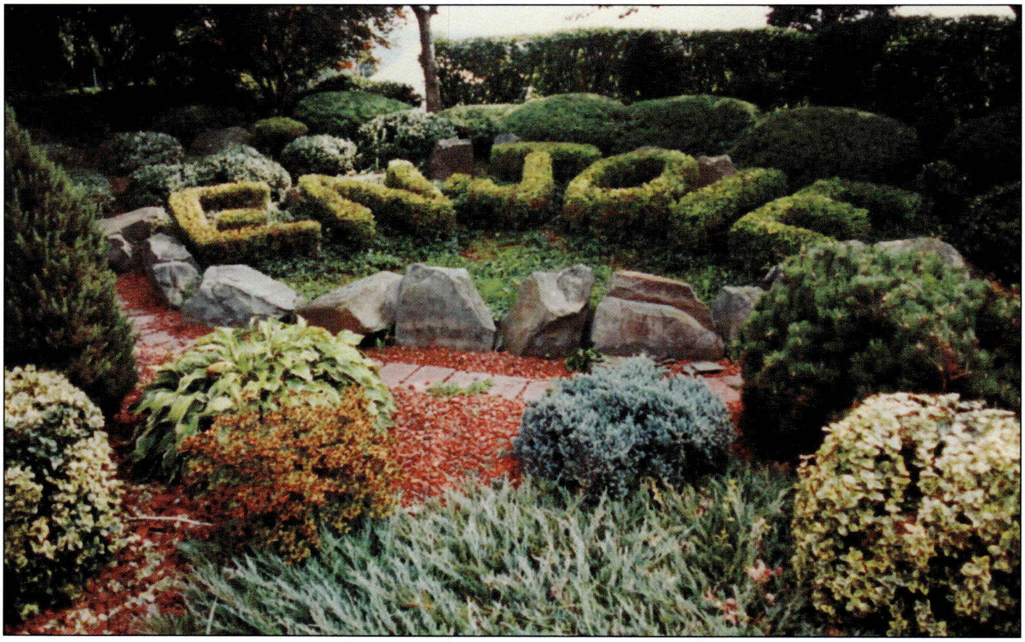

"Enjoy" Golf at En-Joie. The En-Joie Golf Club opened its doors to the public in 1927, laying claim to be the first golf course built by a corporation in America. George F. Johnson, CEO and president of the Endicott-Johnson Corporation, felt strongly that his employees should have a golf course on which they could take up the growing sport. (Courtesy of BCCC.)

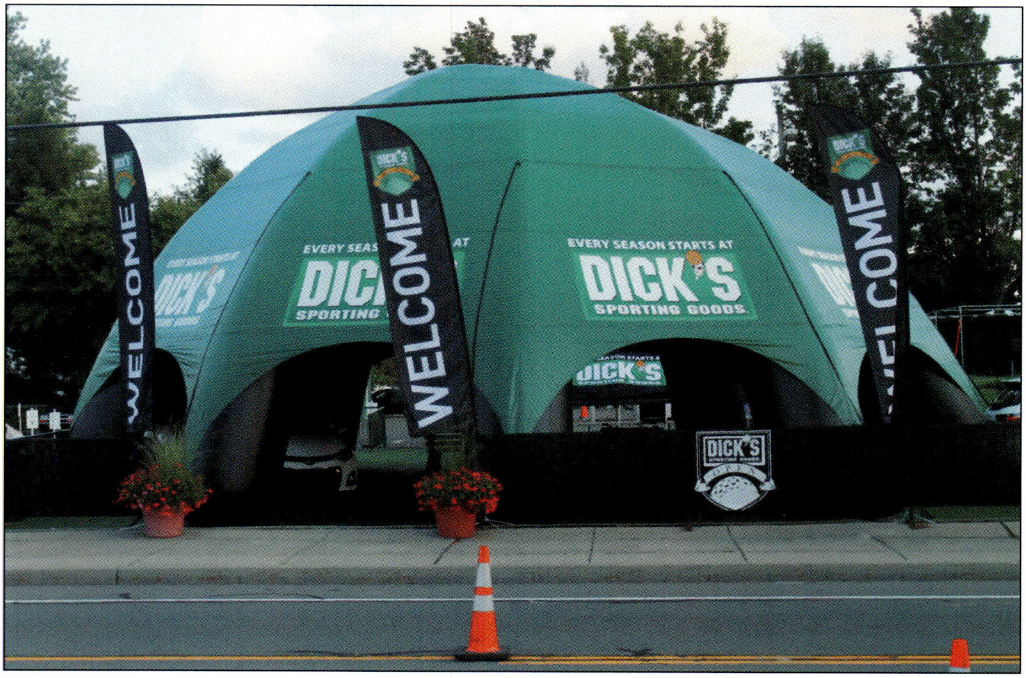

Meet Me Under the Tent. The spectator entrance to En-Joie is marked by a huge umbrella-like tent that serves as a beacon for golfing enthusiasts during the week of the DSGO. Besides being a meeting place, the front gate is an invitation for all to come in and experience the thrill of a golf tournament.

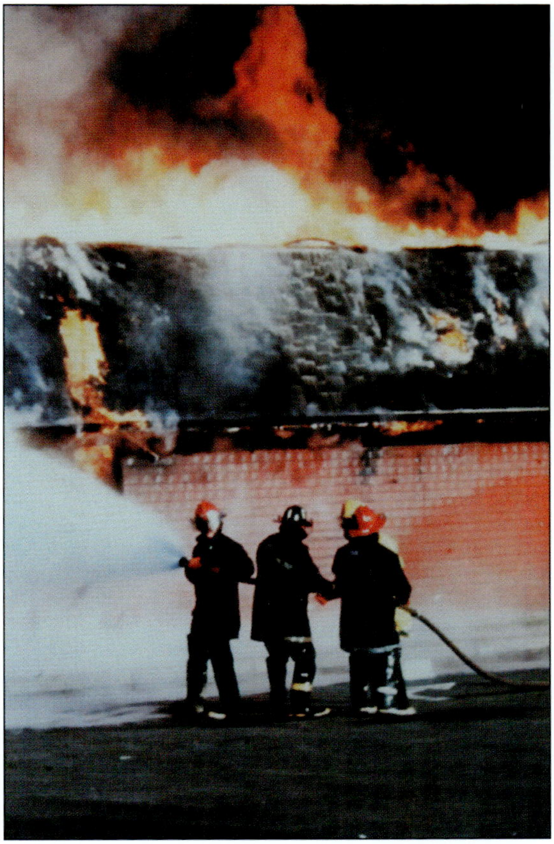

First a Fire, Then a Tornado! The public golf course has been a symbol of the resiliency of its community, as in 1974 when a fire destroyed the clubhouse. The course, however, was unaffected, so the tournament went on as scheduled. In the photograph at right, note that the water spraying out of the hose has turned to steam. In 1975, scoreboard operators used an oxymoron to describe what ravaged the course (below). Over 500 volunteers pulled together to get the course playable in time for the pro-am! (Both, courtesy of BCHS.)

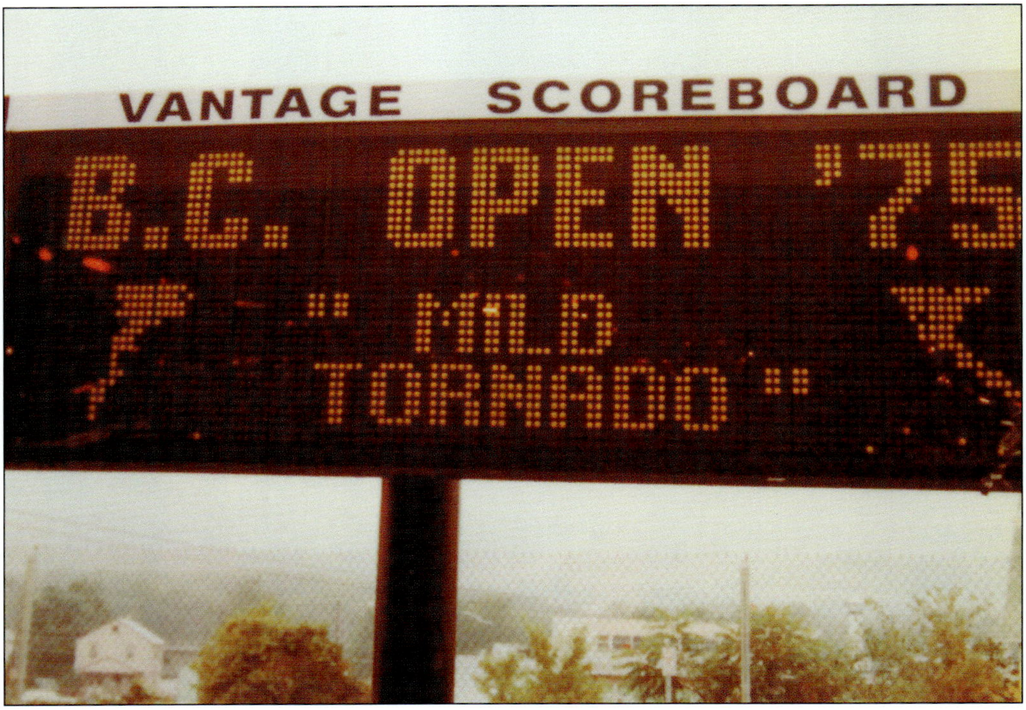

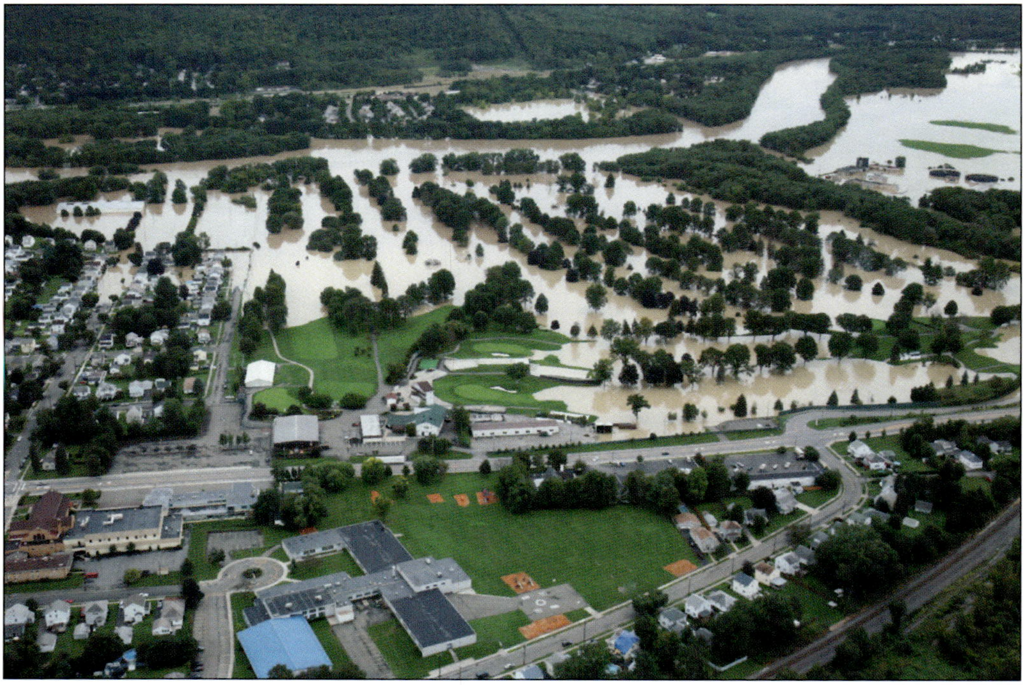

Air or Land, It's All Water. In both 2006 and 2011, the area experienced major flooding. In 2006, the BC Open was moved to Verona, New York, at the Turning Stone Resort and Casino. Above, the Susquehanna River has overflowed to the brink of Main Street in some spots. Nearly the entire course was under water. Below, the sixth fairway is a river. (Both, courtesy of BCCC.)

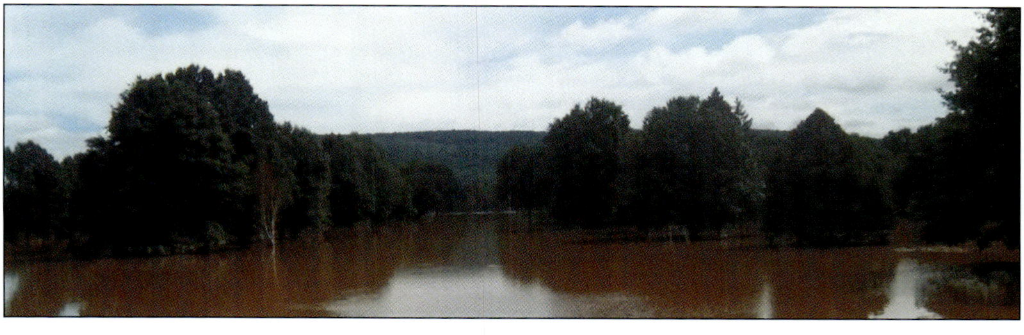

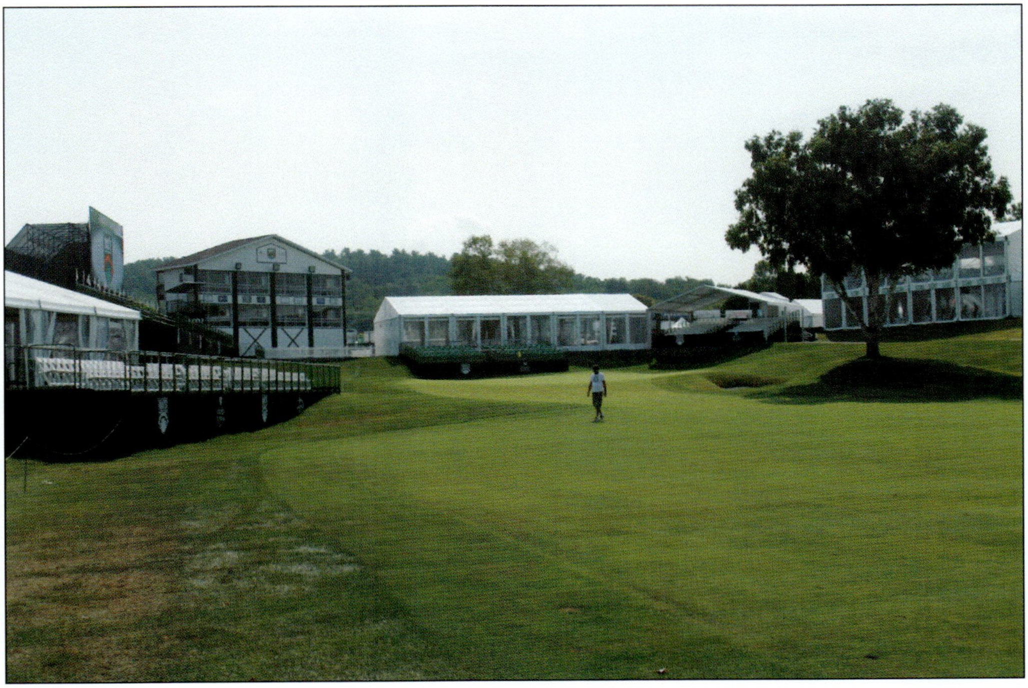

It Ends Here. Before the start of play, the entire course is thoroughly inspected. Above, one of the final reviews of the 18th hole is being conducted. Below, the 18th green is the center of activity. Note the marshals surrounding the green, dressed in orange polo shirts and holding signs asking for quiet from the gallery. Mark O'Meara, elected to the World Golf Hall of Fame in 2014, is in the center of the green, about to putt.

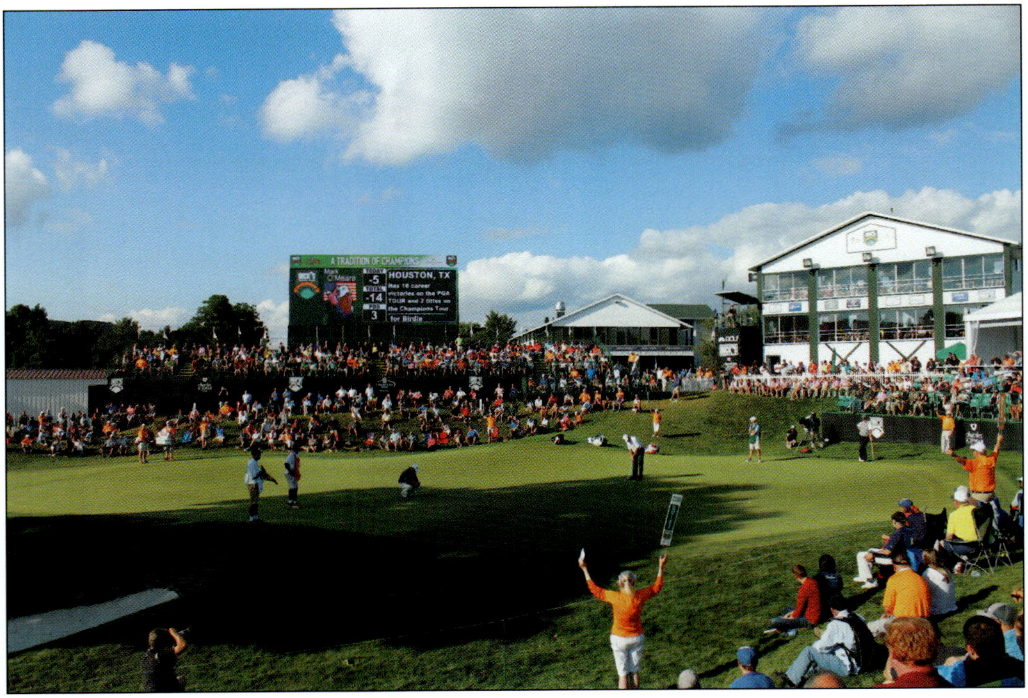

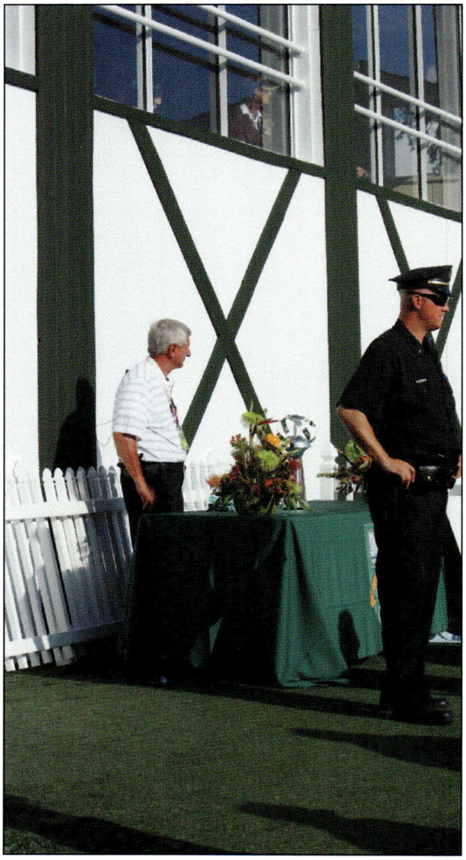

Guarding the Goods. Lt. Steven Noyes of the Endicott Police Department guards the coveted trophy, while tournament committee member Ron Dahulich covers the rear. During the days of the BC Open, the trophy was a bronze statue of Thor, a character from the comic strip *B.C.* Today, the trophy is a sterling silver masterpiece from the Tiffany Company.

Serving the Media. Maureen Radzavicz and Phil Stambaugh, members of the media staff for the Champions Tour, work in the media room at En-Joie during the 2014 tournament. Radzavicz, who grew up in neighboring Vestal, told the *Binghamton Press & Sun Bulletin* in 2014: "There's a genuinely warm feeling about this tournament in particular—I don't know what it is. . . . It makes me proud to be from Broome County."

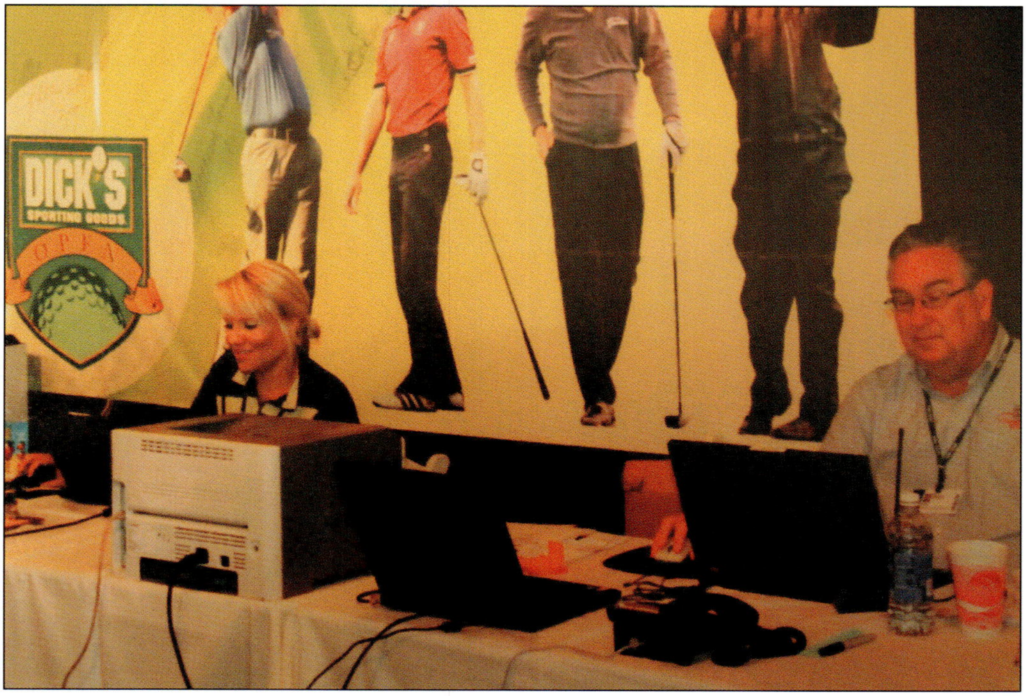

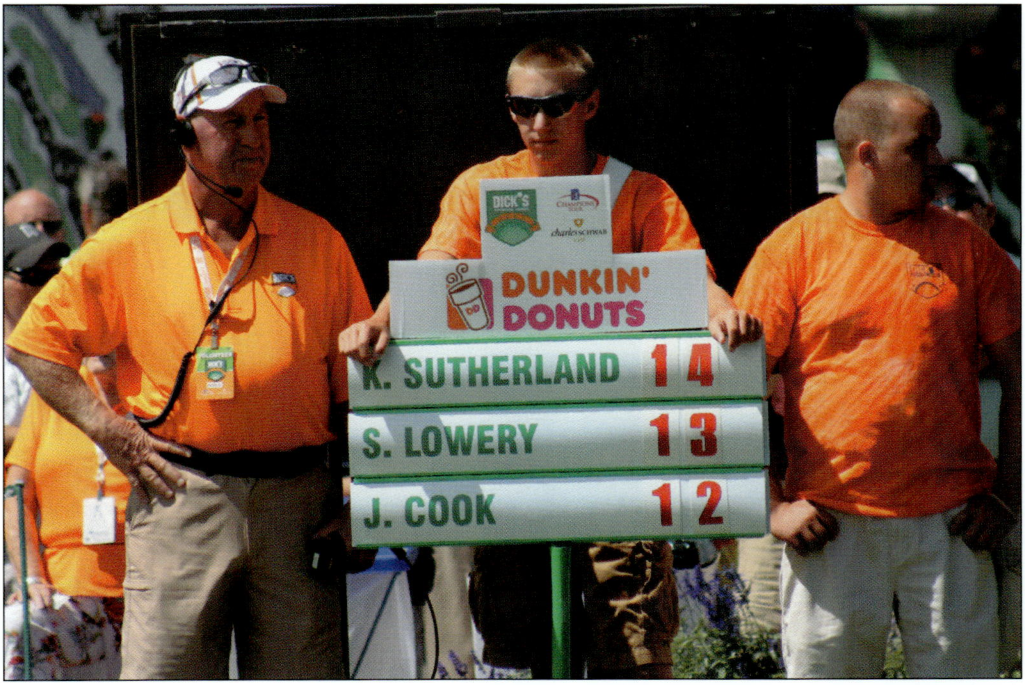

TEE TIME FOR THE LEADERS. Going into the final round of the 2014 DSGO, Kevin Sutherland, John Cook, and Steve Lowery were leading the field. The standard-bearer views the activity behind sunglasses as he waits for the players to get things started on the first tee. Standard-bearers play the key role of carrying the scores of the threesome to which they are assigned.

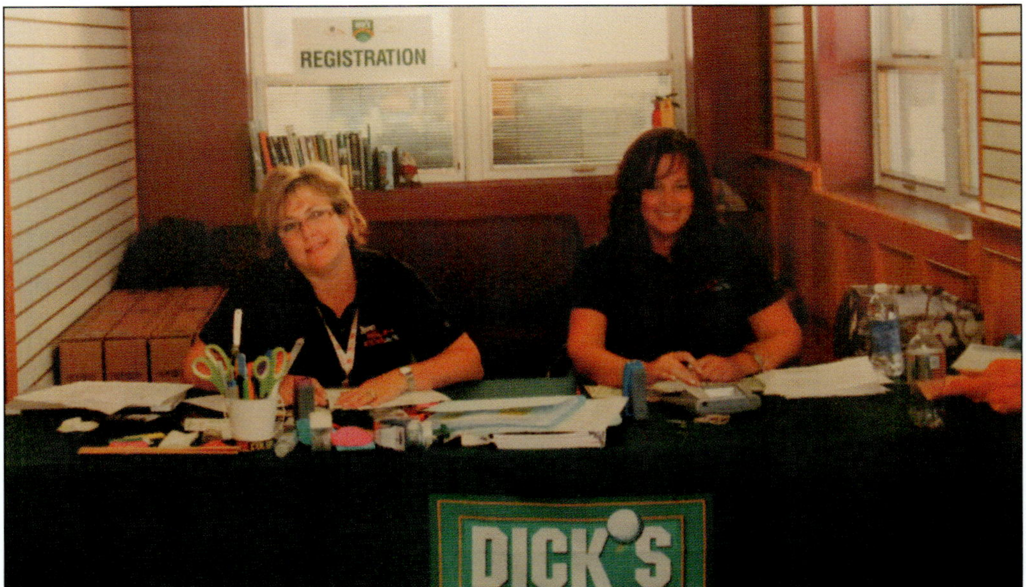

UBIQUITOUS VOLUNTEERS. Volunteers are needed in virtually every nook and cranny of the golf club, not just on the field of play. Michelle Miller (left) and JoAnn Smith (right) collect team revenue for Wendy's Walk for Kids while also serving as sentinels for access to the player's locker room and dining area. Wendy's Walk for Kids, sponsored by Wendy's restaurants, is a nonprofit organization that uses its proceeds to support local children's charities.

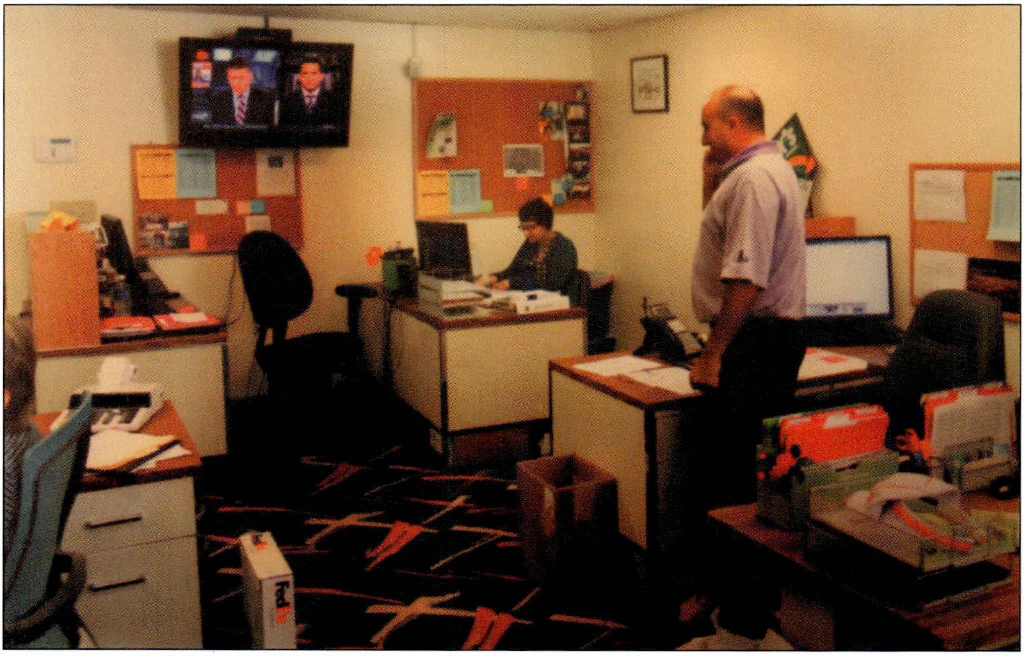

The Director Never Rests. Being tournament director of the DSGO is a full-time job. John Karedes has served in this post since 2008. He is shown here working the phones. The offices of the BCCC, open year-round, are located in Vestal, New York, just a few miles from En-Joie.

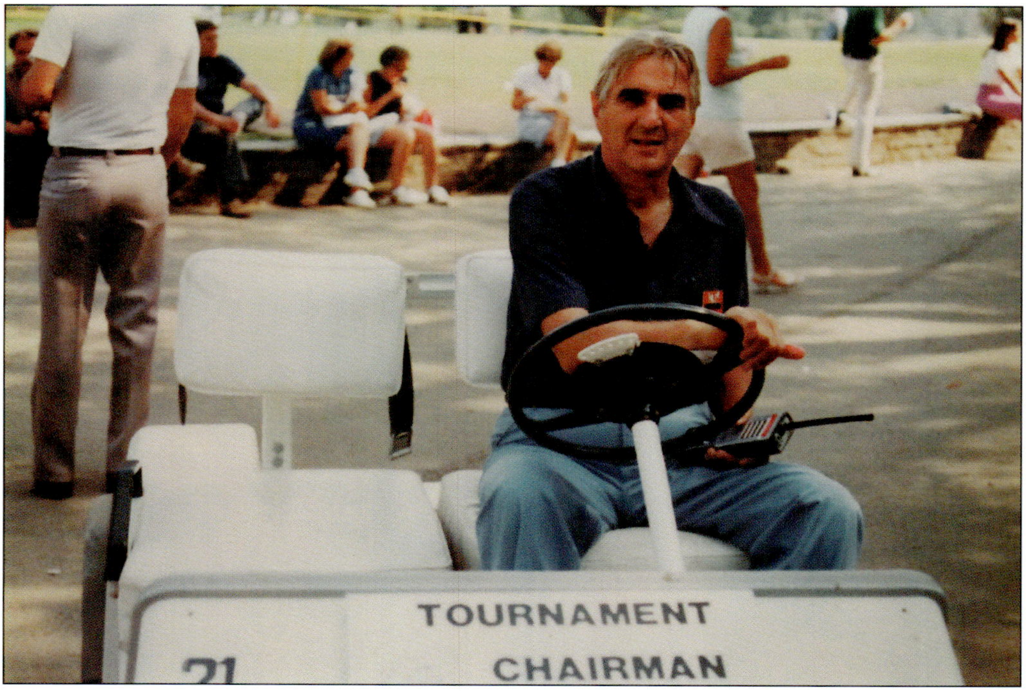

Founding Father. Alex Alexander was the first tournament director at En-Joie and longtime executive director of Broome County Community Charities. He was the driving force behind convincing the PGA that Endicott could be a tour stop and was the director of the tournament from its inception until 1996. (Courtesy of BCHS.)

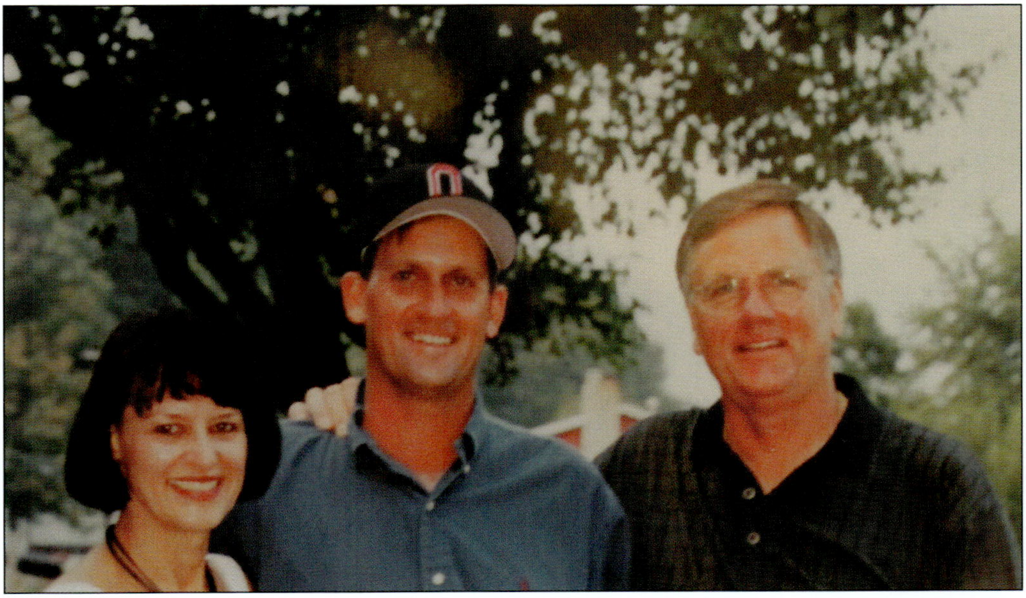

Passing the Torch. In 1996, Alex Alexander passed the reigns of tournament director to Mike Norman, shown on the right with his wife, Linda, a former newspaper reporter, and golfer Chris Perry. Norman started at the BC Open as a marshal and moved to the leaderboard, then to sales, before ultimately succeeding Alexander. (Courtesy of Mike Norman.)

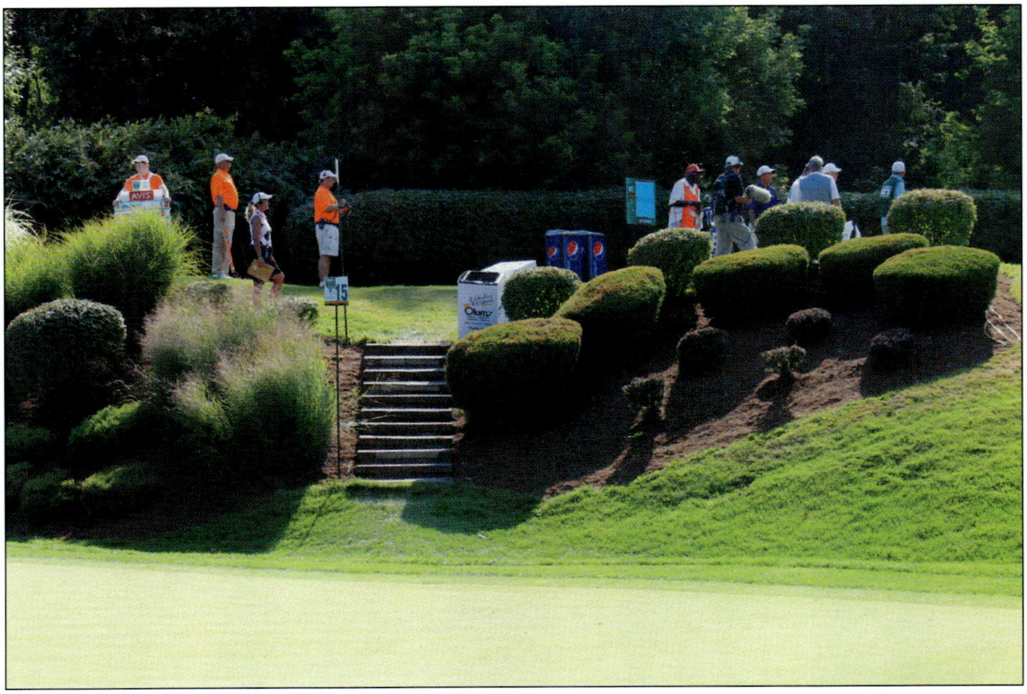

You're Surrounded! The tee on the 16th hole shows the network of volunteers and workers that follow the golfers. To the left of the stairway are the standard-bearer, the marshals, and the scorer. At right are the golfers and caddies, as well as the sound technician for the Golf Channel.

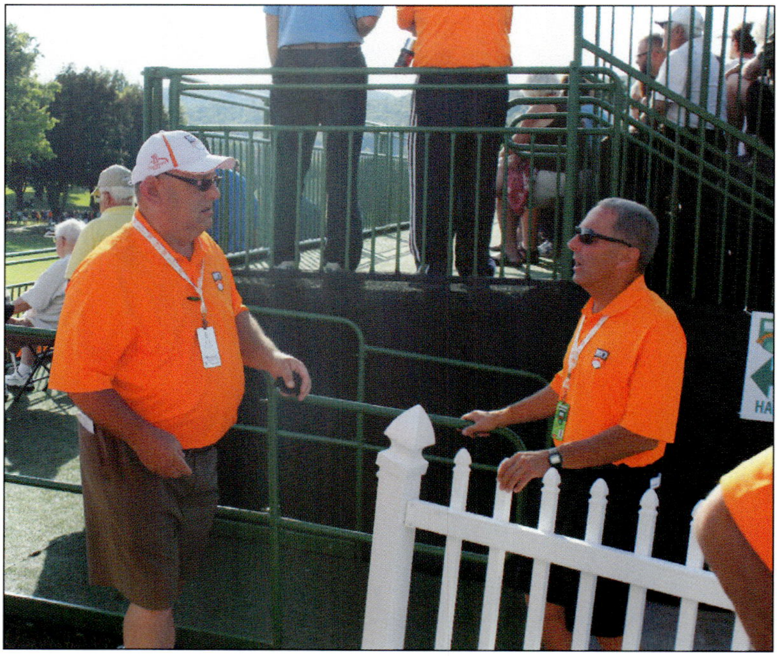

Don't Forget the Bibs. Keith Zulko (left), the current caddy master at the DSGO, has been involved with the tournaments at En-Joie for more than half of his life. Here, he makes sure his staff knows to collect the bibs from all of the caddies as they exit the 18th green.

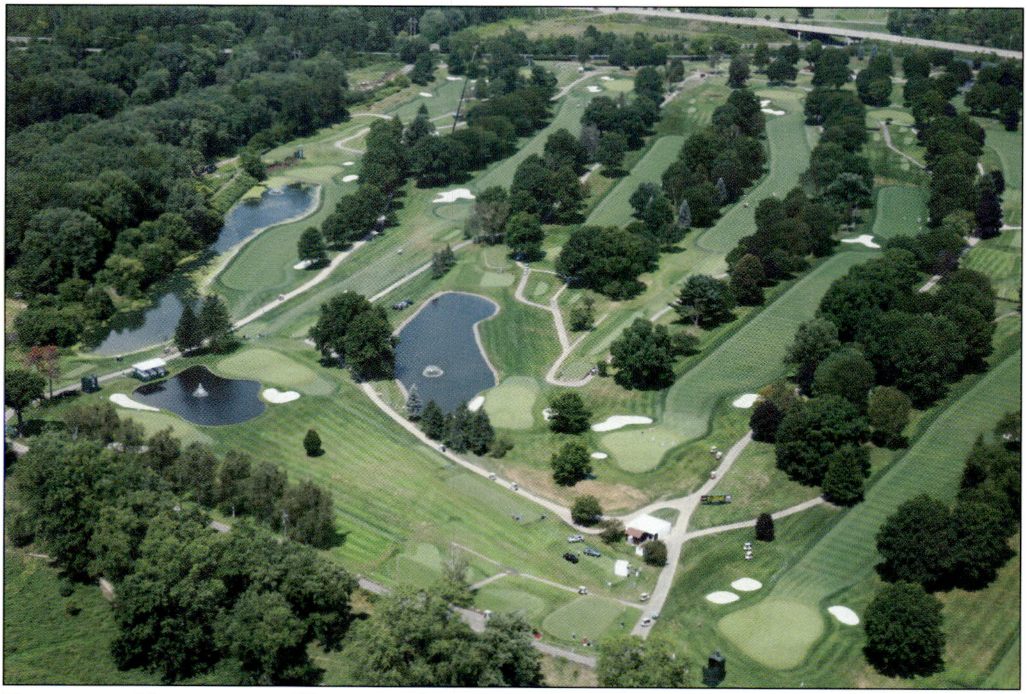

Tight and Undulating. These are the two words used most often to describe the layout of En-Joie, due to its narrow fairways and sloping greens. This aerial photograph, with the 15th hole at far left, shows the lack of forgiveness of En-Joie's fairways. The holes and their respective pars are as follows: 1(4), 2(4), 3(5), 4(3), 5(5), 6(4), 7(3), 8(5), 9(4), 10(4), 11(4), 12(5), 13(4), 14(3), 15(4), 16(4), 17(3), and 18(4). (Courtesy of BCCC.)

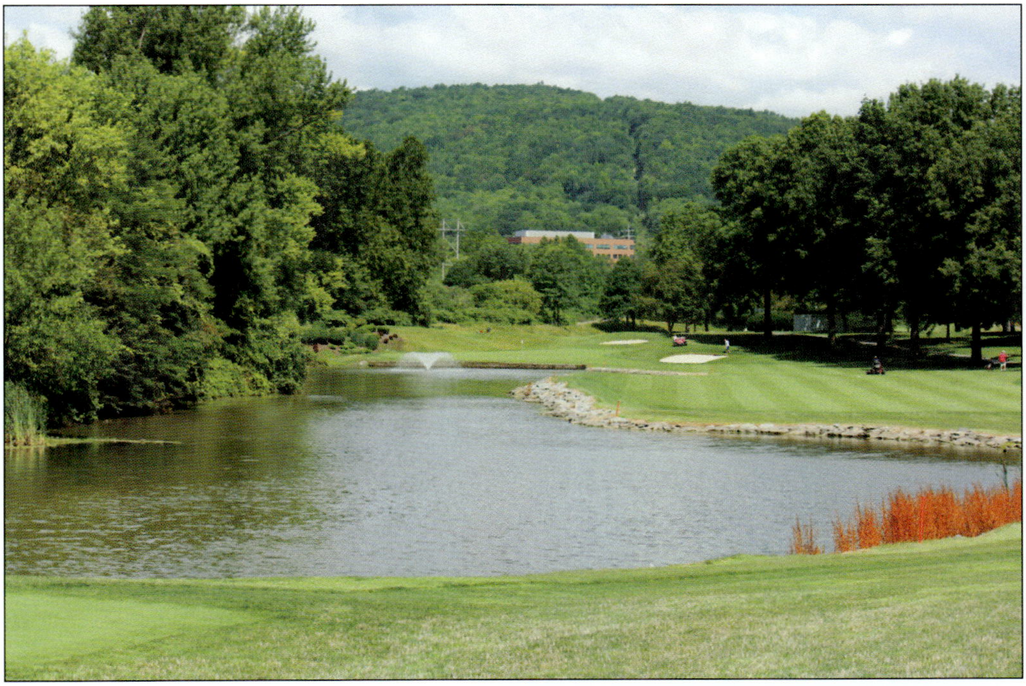

Talk about a Water Hazard. The 15th hole at the En-Joie golf course has always been one of the tougher holes. The 150-yard pond is in front of a green that slants back into the water. Most tee shots land to the right because putting a ball in the water makes it almost impossible to make par.

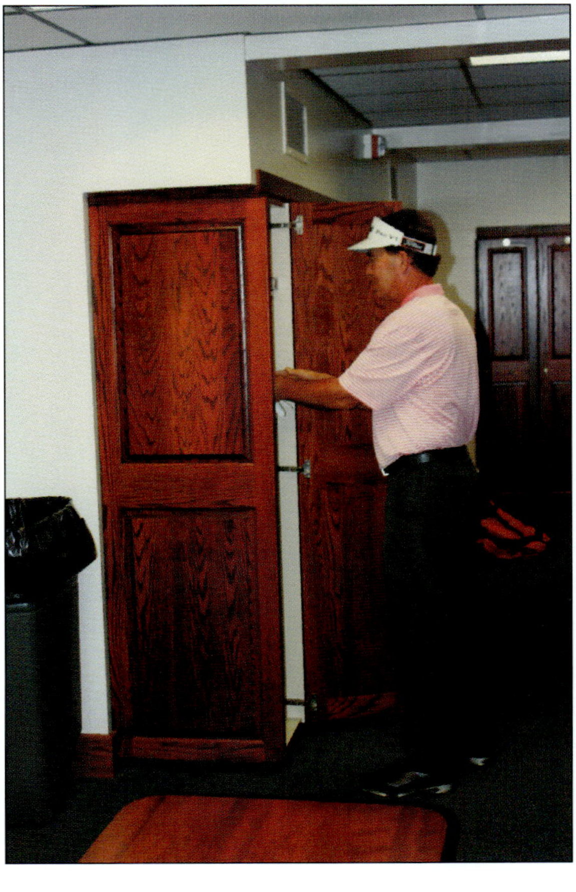

Sizing Up His Chances. Longtime pro Dick Mast gets ready for his final round of golf in 2014 DSGO by gathering a few things from his locker. He entered the final round within striking distance of the leader, Kevin Sutherland, trailing by five strokes. Mast ended his day with a 69, tying for seventh place at 12 under par and winning $54,020 in prize money.

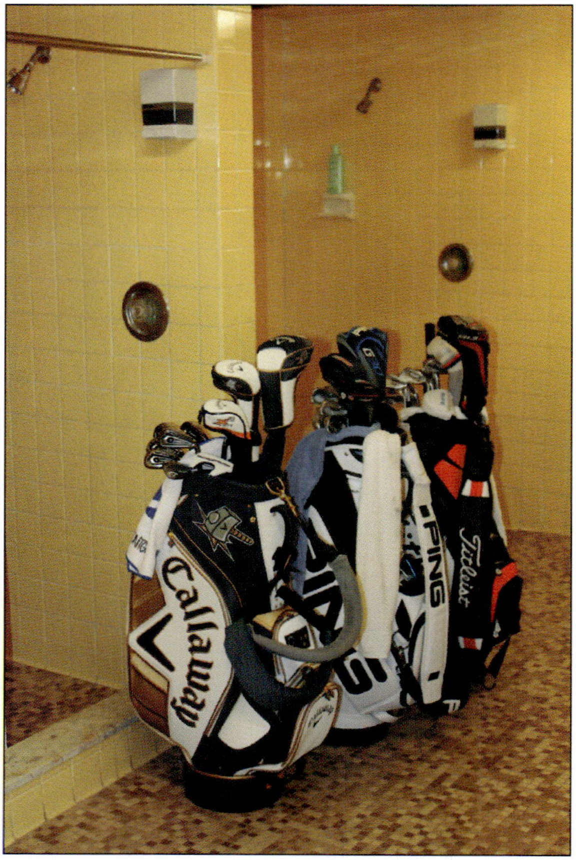

Would Hitchcock Have Filmed Here? During a tournament, pro golfers are so consumed with their work, they take their clubs everywhere, even the locker-room showers. Though this "shower scene" cannot compete with the classic one in the Alfred Hitchcock thriller *Psycho*, it is a reminder that pros and their caddies are constantly cleaning their tools of the trade.

Setting Up Shop. The media room is a center of activity for journalists, who use the space to set up shop. The room also allows golfers to meet with the media after their respective rounds are complete. In the foreground is Roger Neel, broadcaster for local radio station WNBF. Neel is also a member of the Southern Tier Broadcaster's Hall of Fame.

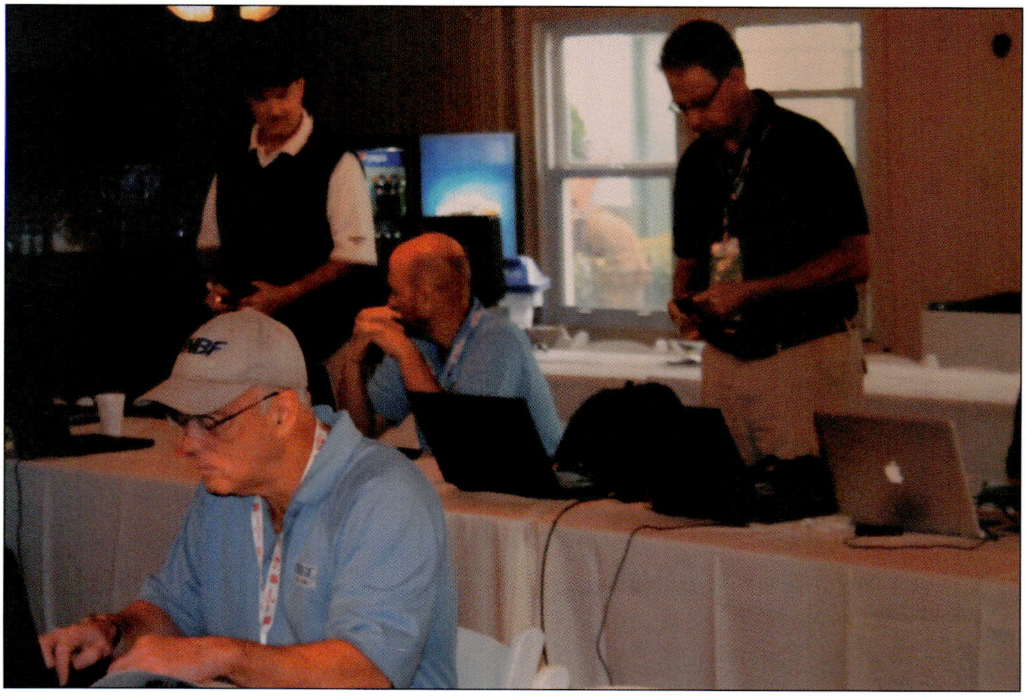

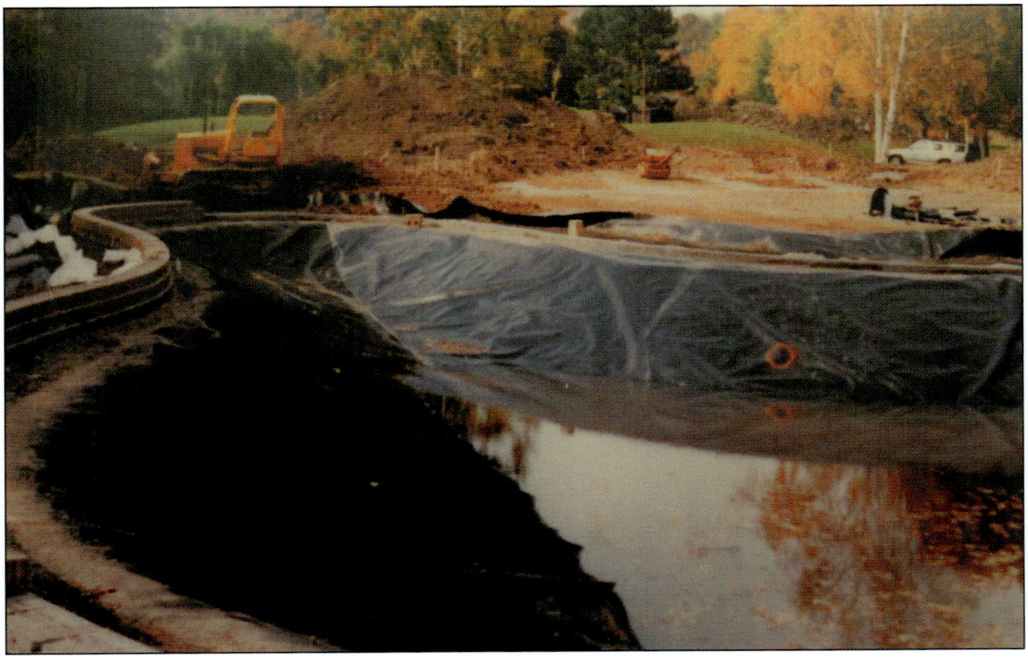

Ongoing Work. The second hole's pond is shown under construction in the above photograph. The completed pond is shown below. After each tournament, the BCCC, besides distributing the proceeds to the community, almost immediately starts lining up the next year's sponsors and volunteers. It also oversees any offseason improvements to the golf course. (Both, courtesy of BCHS.)

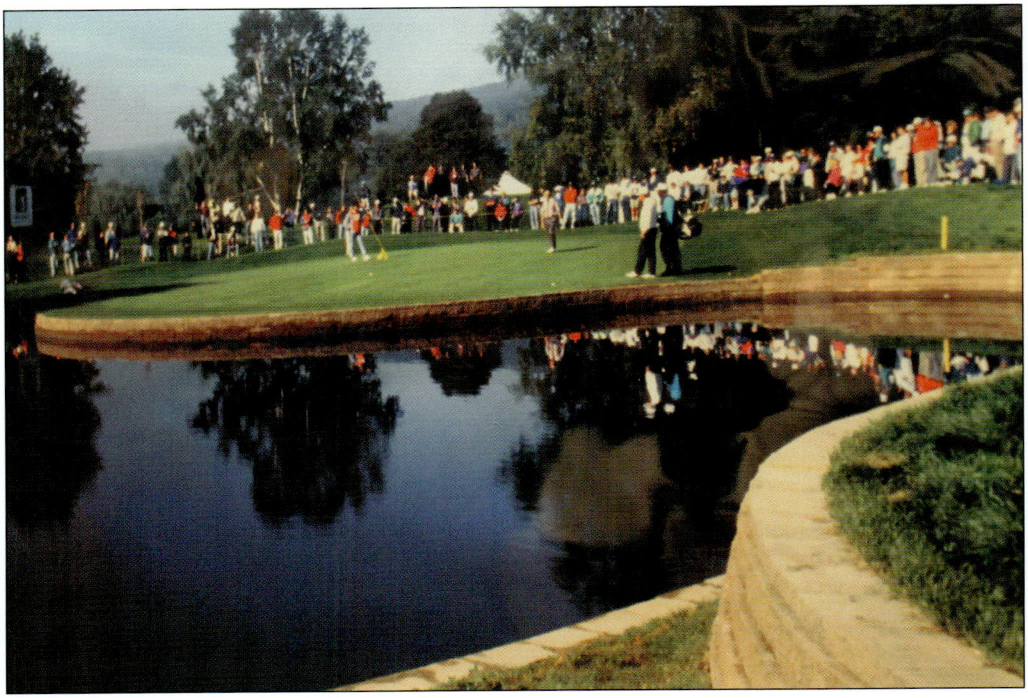

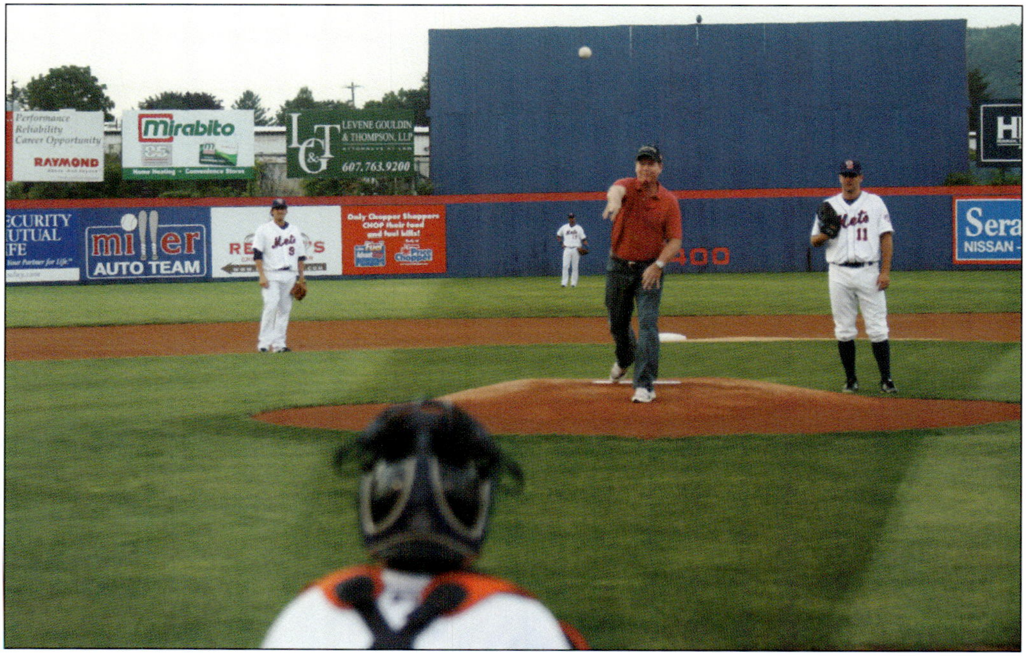

Watson on the Diamond and in a Frame! Hall of Fame golfer Tom Watson delivers the first pitch at a Binghamton Mets game in 2012 (above) on the day before the start of the DSGO. Starter Mark Cohoon (right) admires Watson's form. Watson won 39 PGA Tour events and was inducted into the World Golf Hall of Fame in 1988. In 2003, he donated the entire $1 million he won on the Champions Tour to ALS research. His caddy for three decades, Bruce Edwards, passed away from the disease in April 2004. Below, golf enthusiast and weekend hacker John Castelli checks out some of the items available in the charity auction, including signed memorabilia from Watson, Arnold Palmer, and Tiger Woods. (Above, courtesy of Binghamton Mets.)

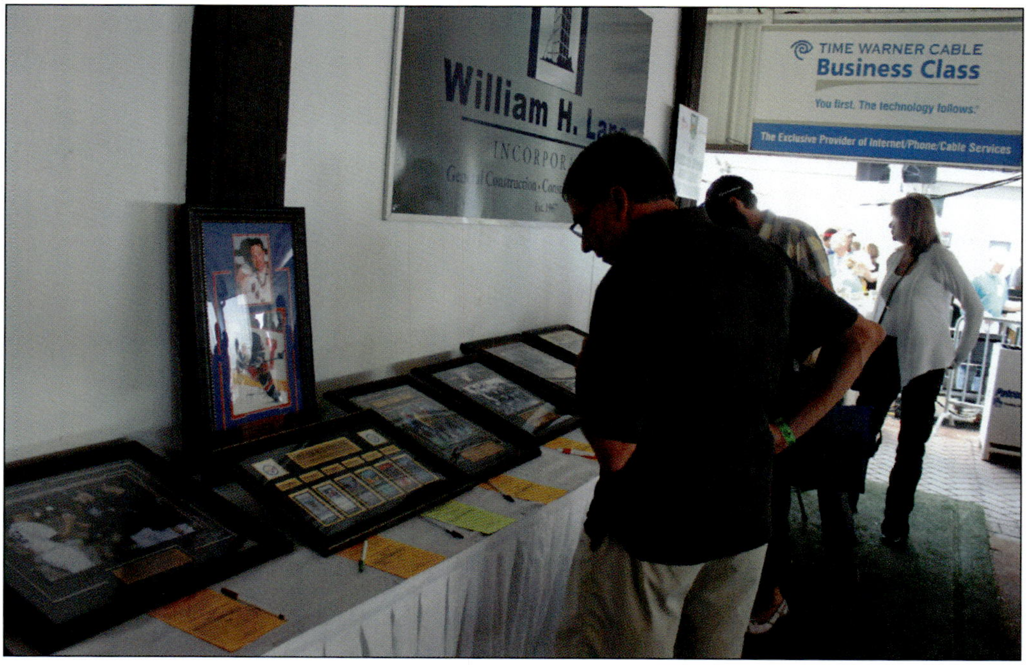

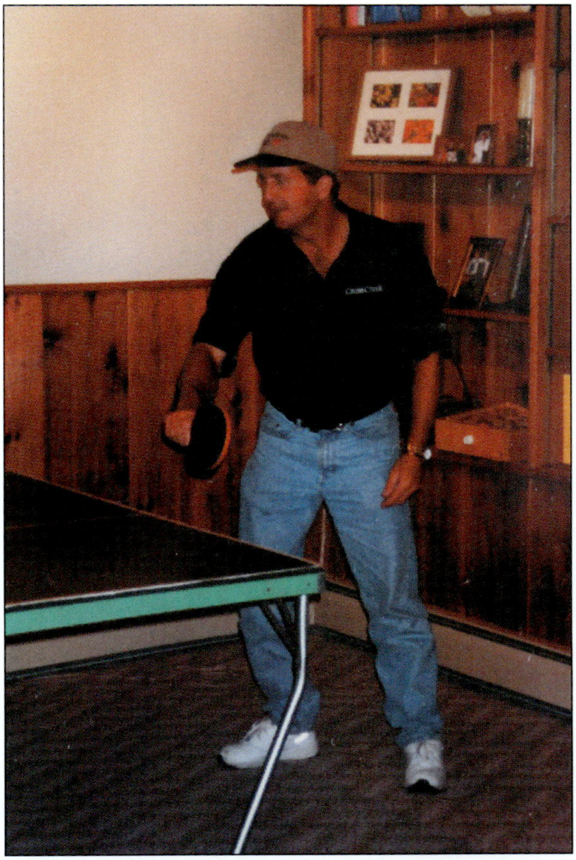

Funky House Guest. Volunteers come in all shapes and sizes. Right, Fred Funk plays ping-pong at Ken and Cindy Barber's home in neighboring Vestal. When Funk was trying to break onto the PGA Tour, expenses were high and money low. While golfing in the BC Open, he finished a hole and tossed his ball to a young Drew Barber, sitting with his father, Ken. The Barbers followed the new golfer and had him sign the ball after his round was over. Ken offered to have Funk stay at his house if he returned to En-Joie the following year. Funk accepted the generous offer, and the Barbers and Funk have been great friends ever since. Shown below are, from left to right, Ken Barber, Funk, Drew Barber, Cindy Barber, and Kyla Barber. (Both, courtesy of KB.)

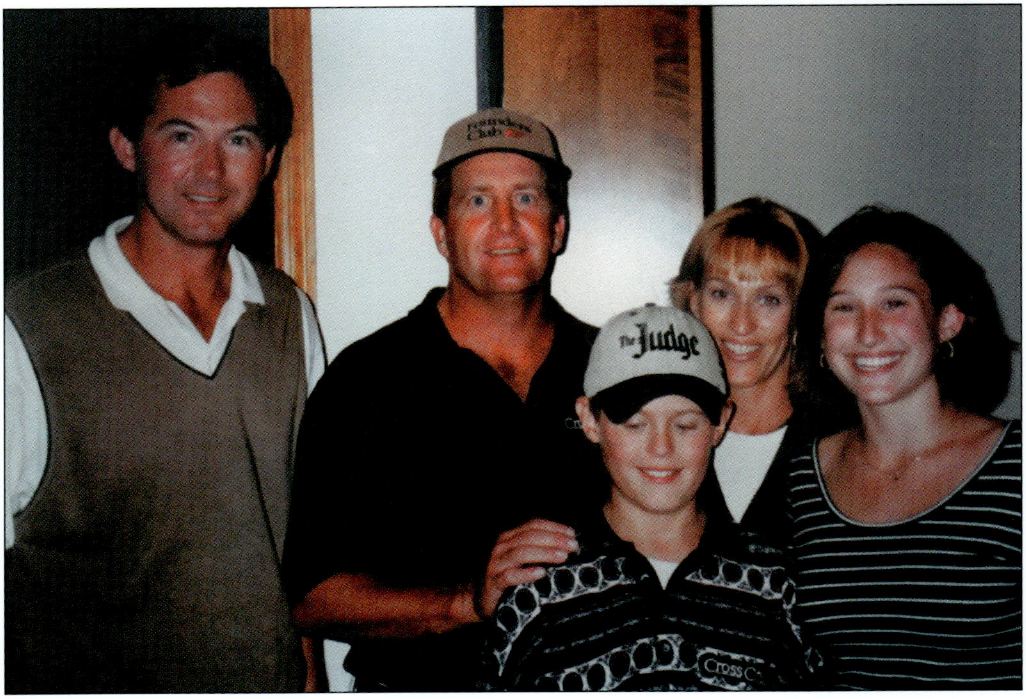

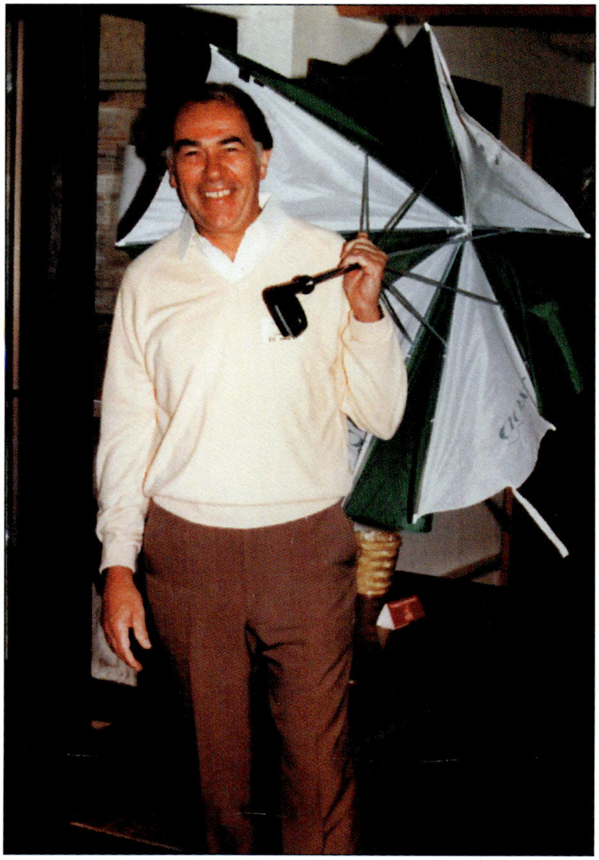

Smiling in the Rain. Gene Null has been a longtime volunteer for the tournaments. In 2010, a number of golfers were competing in Canada after their stint in Endicott, so they drove rental cars to the nation to the north. However, the rental car company did not have any offices in Canada, so Null had to arrange for 65 area volunteer drivers to be bused to Canada to drive the rental cars back to Endicott! Below, a rainbow provides a dome over En-Joie, perhaps providing a catalyst for Null's smiling face. (Both, courtesy of BCHS.)

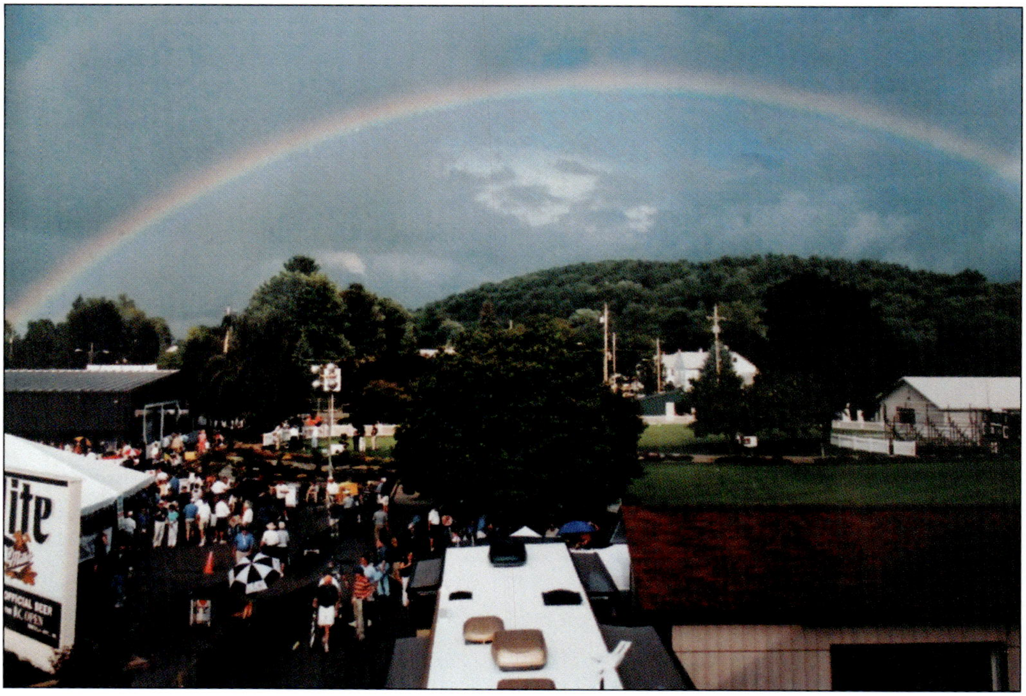

Two

Champions of En-Joie

There have been 42 different champions of the 44 tournaments at En-Joie (Joey Sindelar and Brad Faxon have each won twice). All the winners from the BC Open and DSGO are shown in this chapter, complete with their winning scores. Despite playing host to a large number of hall of famers, including Hale Irwin, Sandy Lyle, Phil Mickelson, Mark O'Meara, Colin Montgomerie, Arnold Palmer, Gary Player, and Tom Watson, En-Joie has proven to be a challenging course to conquer for the all-time greats.

The event's winners are as follows: Butch Harmon (1971), Bob Payne (1972), Hubie Green (1973), Richie Karl (1974), Don Iverson (1975), Bob Wynn (1976), Gil Morgan (1977), Tom Kite (1978), Howard Twitty (1979), Don Pooley (1980), Jay Haas (1981), Calvin Peete (1982), Pat Lindsey (1983), Wayne Levi (1984), Joey Sindelar (1985 and 1987), Rick Fehr (1986), Bill Glasson (1988), Mike Hurlbert (1989), Nolan Henke (1990), Fred Couples (1991), John Daly (1992), Blaine McCallister (1993), Mike Sullivan (1994), Hal Sutton (1995), Fred Funk (1996), Gabriel Hjertstedt (1997), Chris Perry (1998), Brad Faxon (1999 and 2000), Jeff Sluman (2001), Spike McRoy (2002), Craig Stadler (2003), Jonathan Byrd (2004), Jason Bohn (2005), John Rollins (2006), R.W. Eaks (2007), Eduardo Romero (2008), Lonnie Neilsen (2009), Loren Roberts (2010), John Huston (2011), Willie Wood (2012), Bart Bryant (2013), and Bernhard Langer (2014).

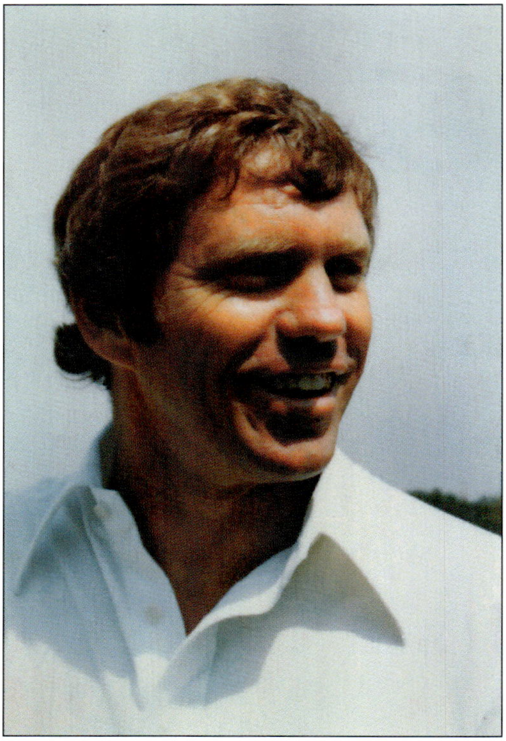

Like Father, Like Son. The inaugural winner at En-Joie was Claude Harmon Jr., who grew up in New Rochelle, New York. Affectionately known as "Butch," Harmon is the son of legendary Masters champion Claude Harmon Sr. Butch played on the PGA Tour for two years; his sole win was the 1971 BC Open [-4 (68)], which was a single round with a winner's purse of $2,000. Harmon later became a premier golf coach for PGA players. (Courtesy of BCHS.)

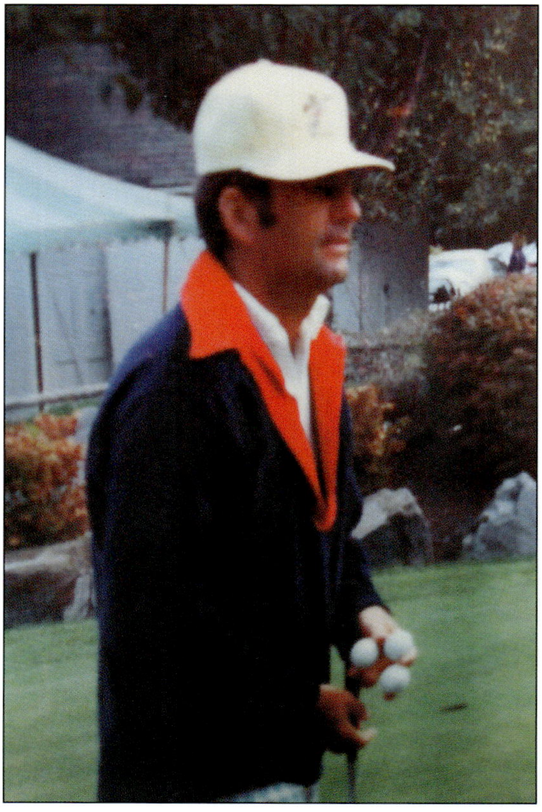

Two Rounds in 1972. Bob Payne was a professional golfer from 1970 to 1985, with career earnings totaling $99,086. A portion of that money was gained winning the 1972 BC Open. The tournament was still considered a satellite event and would not be accepted as a regular PGA event until 1973. Payne won the BC Open with a score of -8 (71-65-136). (Courtesy of BCHS.)

Nothing but 60s in the 1970s. The year 1973 marked the first time the BC Open was considered a full PGA tournament. Hubie Green won by six strokes [-18 (69-65-65-67-266)] over Dwight Nevil. Green won 18 PGA tournaments, including two majors, the 1977 US Open and the 1985 PGA Championship. Green was inducted into the World Golf Hall of Fame in 2007. (Courtesy of FM.)

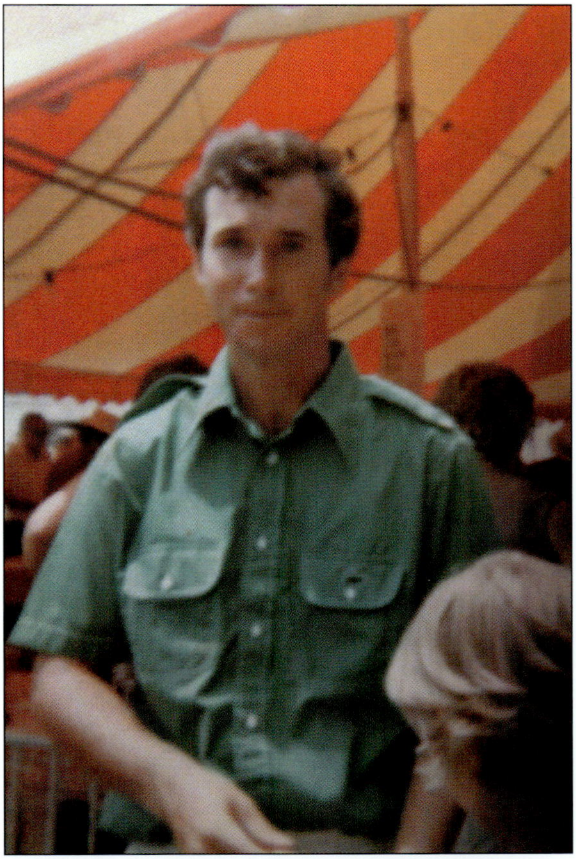

Local Kid Scores Big. Richie Karl (foreground) practices his putting and shows his prescience as he gets ready to play in the 1974 BC Open. Karl grew up along the 10th fairway of En-Joie and became the club pro at his home course. In 1974, playing on a sponsor's exemption, Karl sank a 35-foot putt on the first playoff hole to beat Bruce Crampton and capture the title [–11 (70-67-68-68-273)]. (Courtesy of BCHS.)

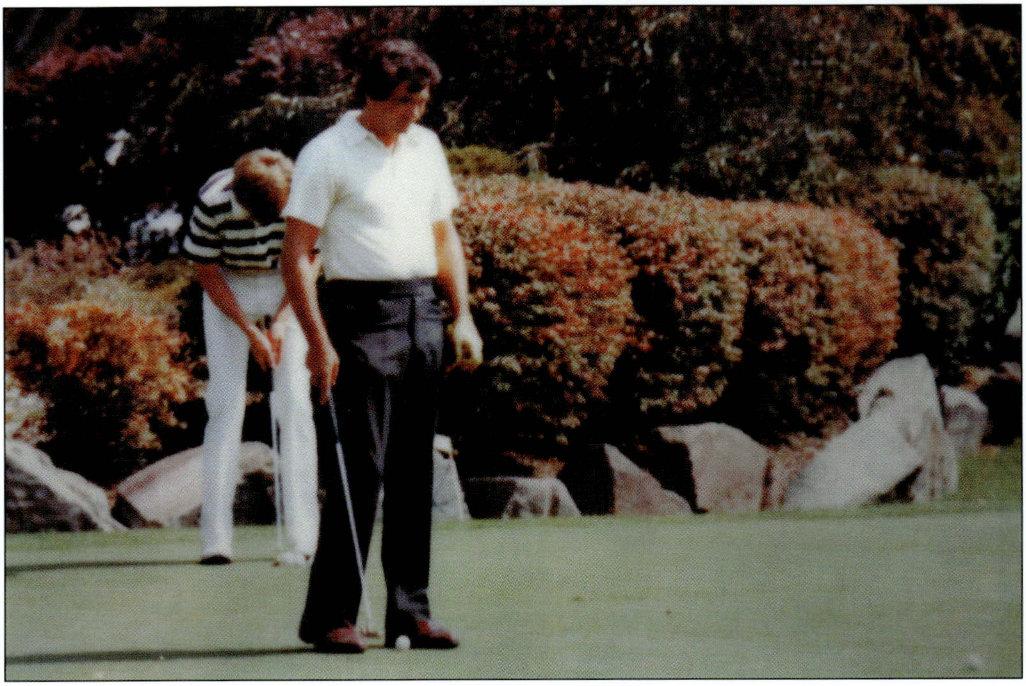

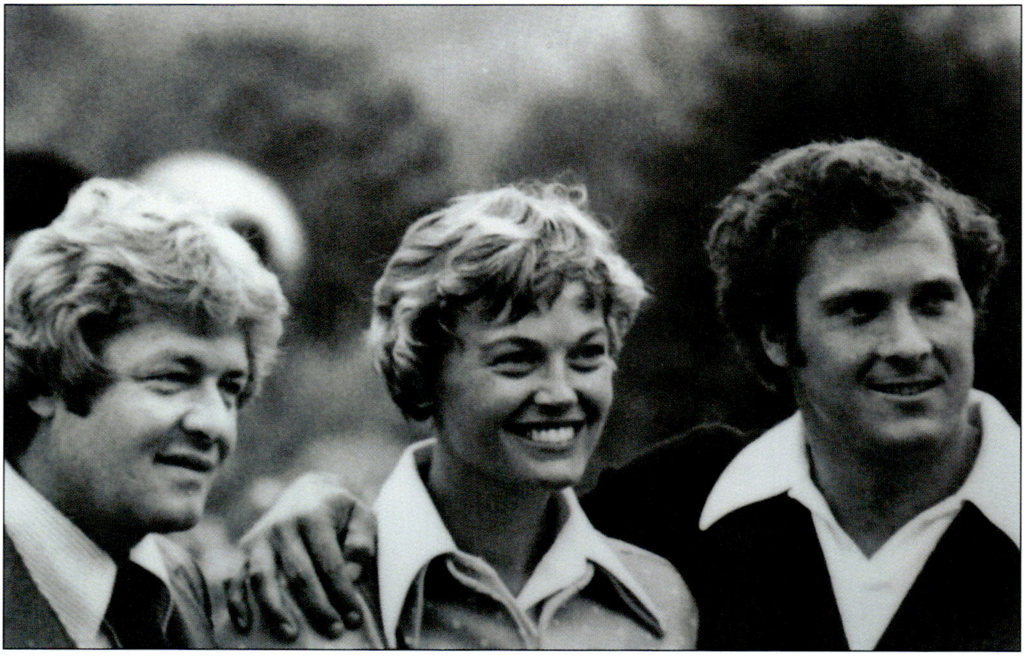

Lone PGA Wins. Don Iverson, pictured above at right, with his wife and Johnny Hart, graduated from the University of Wisconsin–La Crosse in 1963. He toured as an amateur, winning six times in Wisconsin before turning pro in 1968 and joining the PGA Tour from 1971 to 1979. His only PGA win came at the 1975 BC Open [-10 (66-69-71-68-274)]. Below, Bob Wynn (right, black shirt) turns in his scorecard with fellow golfers Pat Fitzsimons (left) and Leonard Thompson (center). A final round of 69 was good enough for Wynn to capture the 1976 BC Open [−13 (65-71-66-69-271)]. (Above, courtesy of LH; below, courtesy of FM.)

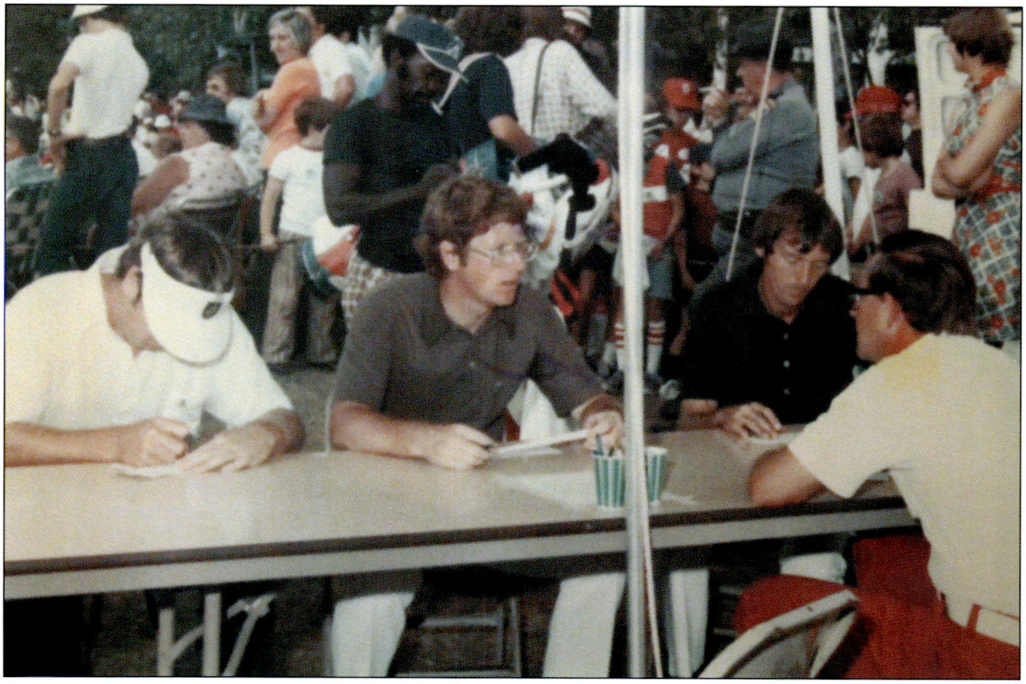

WHAT'S UP, DOC? Dr. Gil Morgan, a graduate of East Central State and the Southern College of Optometry, turned pro in 1972. His first professional win came at the 1977 BC Open, where he beat Lee Elder by five strokes [-14 (67-65-69-69-270)]. Here, Morgan (right) checks in his golf ball with the starter. (Courtesy of LH.)

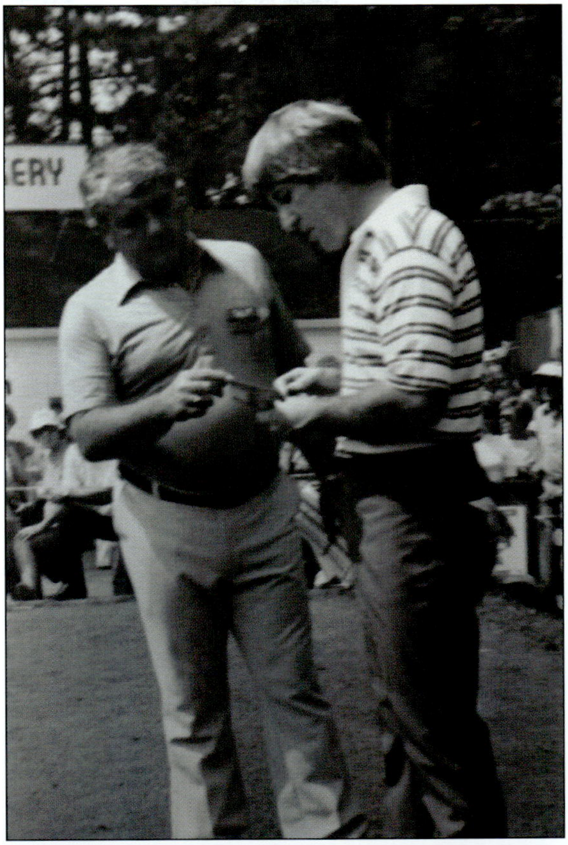

KITE WINS BY FIVE. Tom Kite won the BC Open in 1978 [-17 (66-65-68-68-267)] by five strokes over Mark Hayes. Kite accumulated 19 PGA Tour victories and held a top-10 ranking in the golf world for 175 weeks between 1989 and 1994. He was elected to the World Golf Hall of Fame in 2004. (Courtesy of BCHS.)

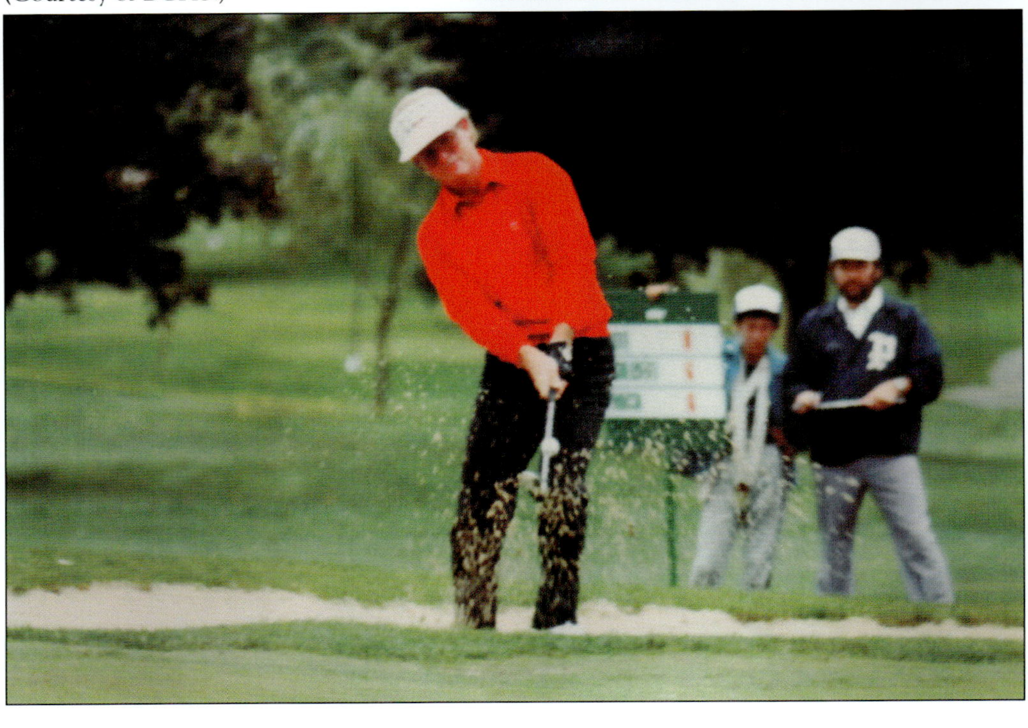

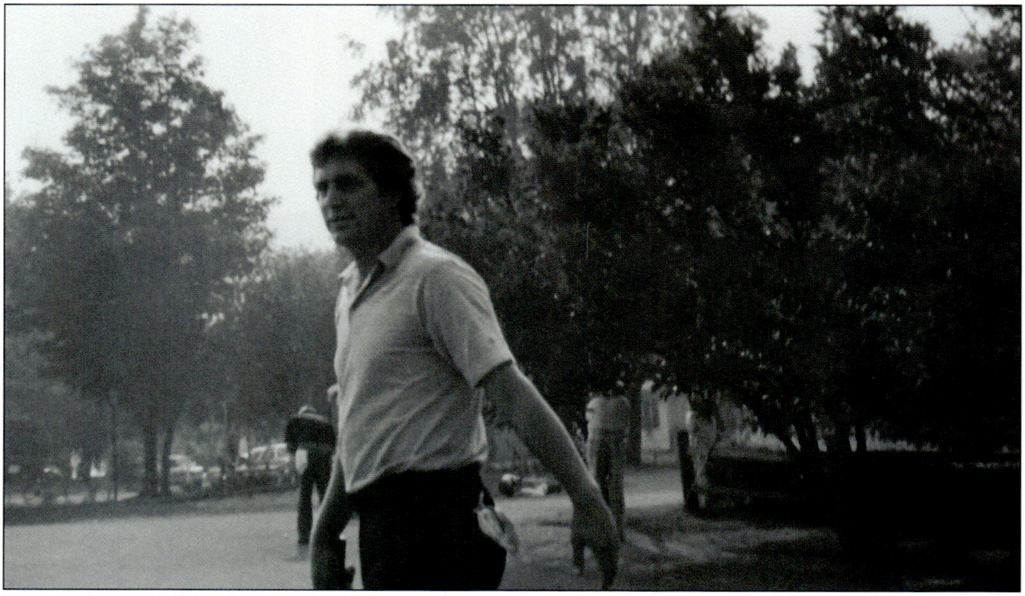

Twitty Bird! The 1979 BC Open gave Howard Twitty his first PGA Tour win [-14 (69-70-64-67-270)] when he beat Tom Purtzer by one stroke. His other two wins on tour came in two different decades, as he won the 1980 Sammy Davis Jr. Greater Hartford Open and the 1993 United Airlines Hawaiian Open. (Courtesy of LH.)

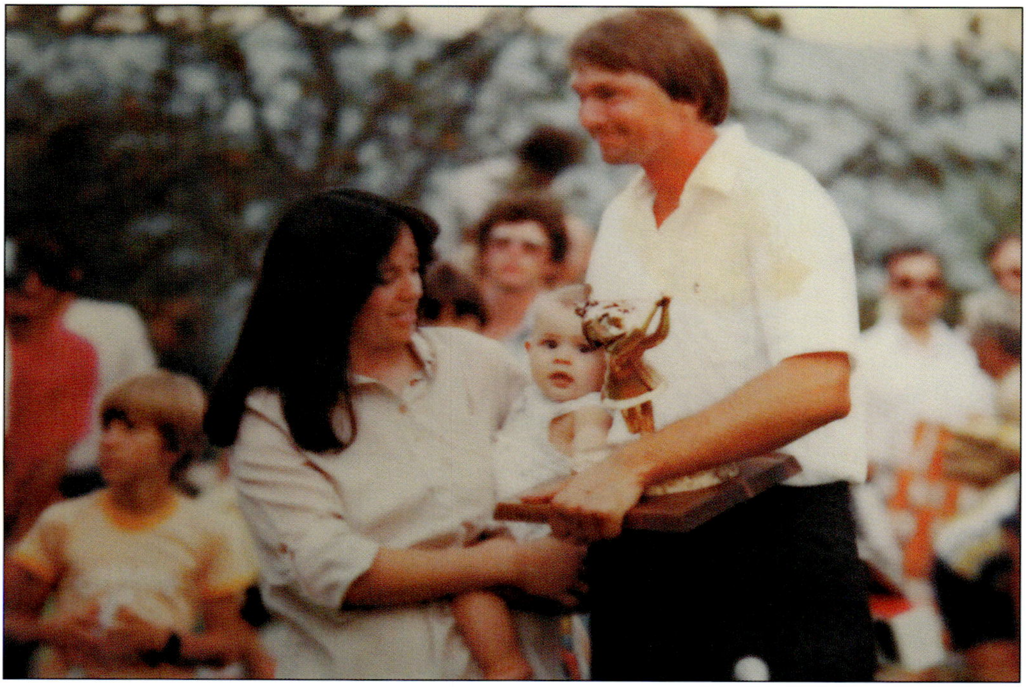

Another Tour First. Don Pooley shows off the spoils of his first PGA Tour win to his wife and child in 1980 [−17 (68-69-66-68-271)]. In 2012, Pooley had a cancerous prostate gland removed, and he continues to be a vigorous advocate for prostrate screening. "It's a surprise when someone says you've got cancer, but my dad died of prostate cancer, so it wasn't totally unexpected," Pooley told the *Arizona Daily Star* in 2012. (Courtesy of BCHS.)

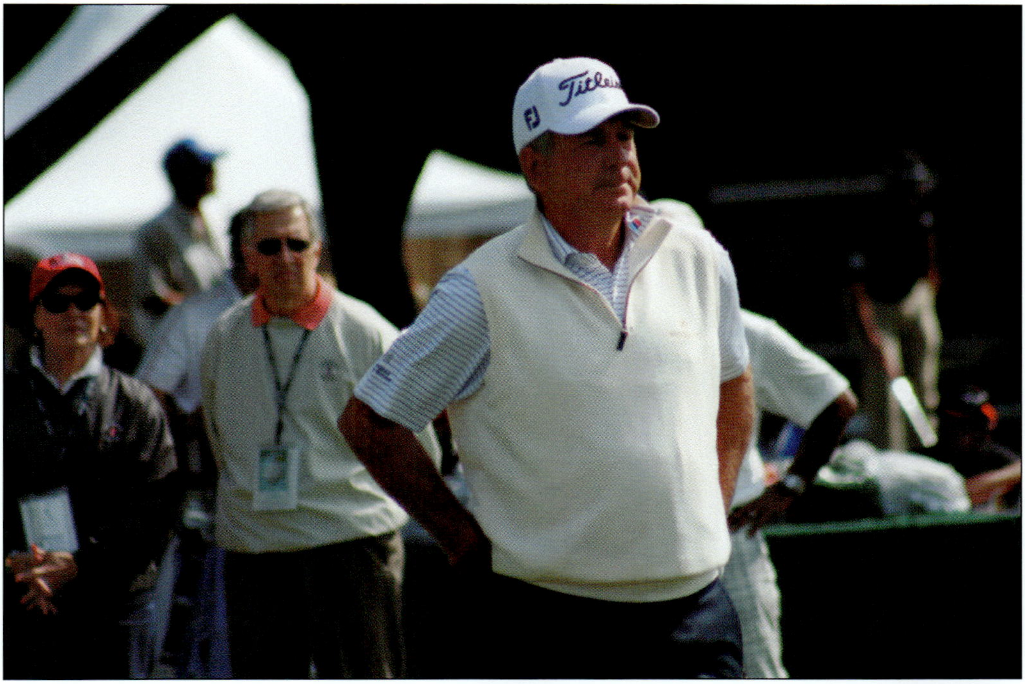

Nothing Matches Being a Senior! Jay Haas won the 1981 BC Open by three strokes [-14 (67-65-69-69-270)] over Tom Kite. At Wake Forest University, his teammates included Curtis Strange and Bob Byman. Haas has twice been named Player of the Year on the senior circuit while capturing two Charles Schwab Cups, which carry a $1 million bonus prize.

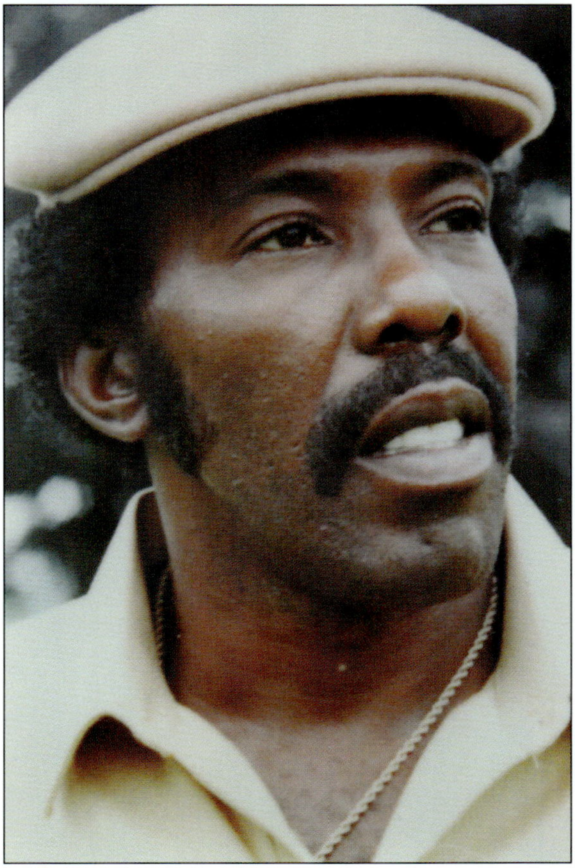

Late Start. Calvin Peete did not pick up a golf club until he was 23! He learned the game of golf in Rochester, New York, playing at the public Genesee Valley Park. He fell in love with the game, worked tirelessly at it, and turned pro in 1973. He won 12 PGA tournaments, including the 1982 BC Open [−14 (69-63-64-69-265). (Courtesy of BCHS.)

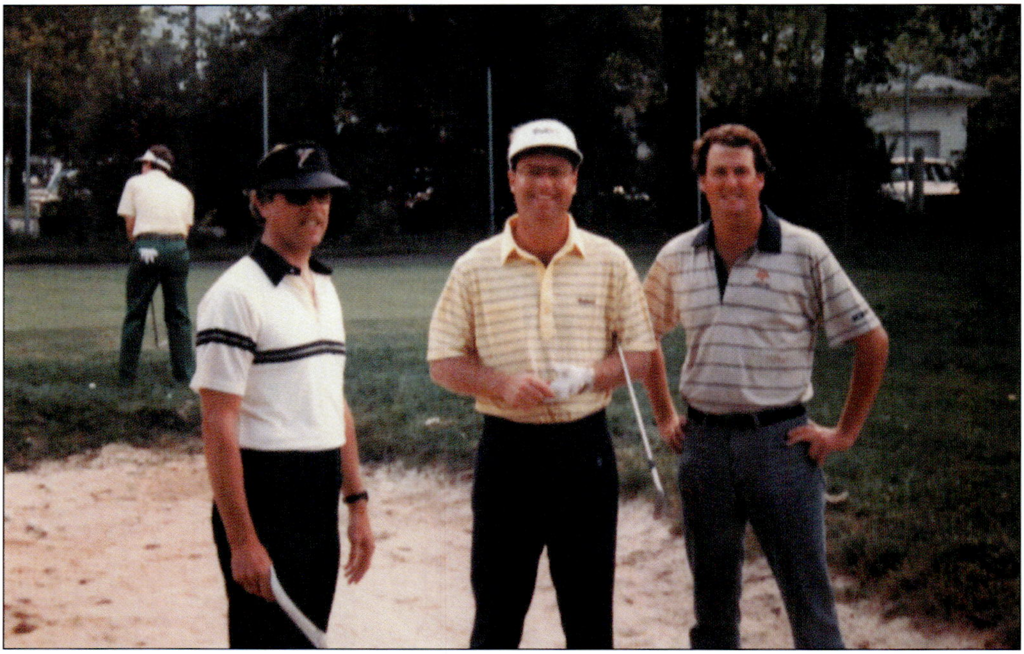

54K in 1983! Pat Lindsey (center) graduated from the University of South Florida in Tampa in 1975. He traveled on mini-tours and as a club pro for four years until joining the PGA Tour in 1979. His only PGA victory came at the 1983 BC Open [-16 (71-64-65-68-268)]. (Courtesy of FM.)

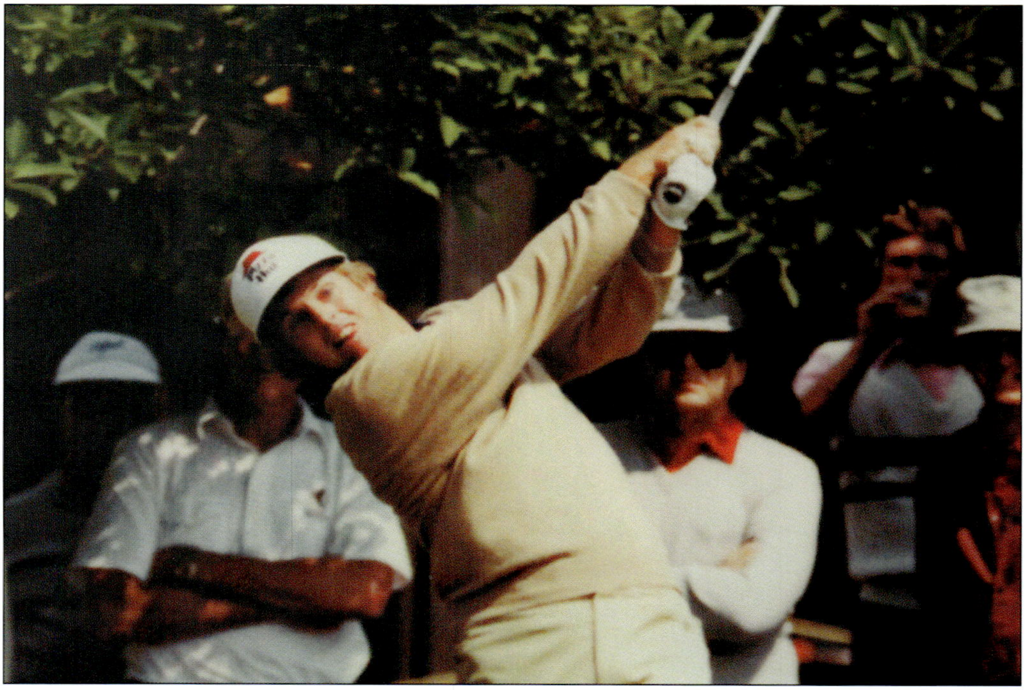

SUNY Oswego is a Golf School? Wayne Levi won the BC Open in 1984 [- 9 (67-71-71-66-275)] by one stroke over Hal Sutton. He turned professional in 1973 after attending SUNY Oswego and the University of South Florida. Levi was born in Little Falls, New York, and grew up in Herkimer, New York. (Courtesy of BCHS.)

Sindelar Sizzles in 1985 and 1987. Joey Sindelar grew up in Horseheads, New York, and was a childhood friend of fellow BC Open winner Mike Hulbert. Sindelar won the 1985 tournament [-10 (66-71-69-68-274)], as well as a second BC Open title in 1987 [-18 (65-63-69-69-266)]. Including the two BC Open wins, Sindelar won seven PGA titles. (Courtesy of GN.)

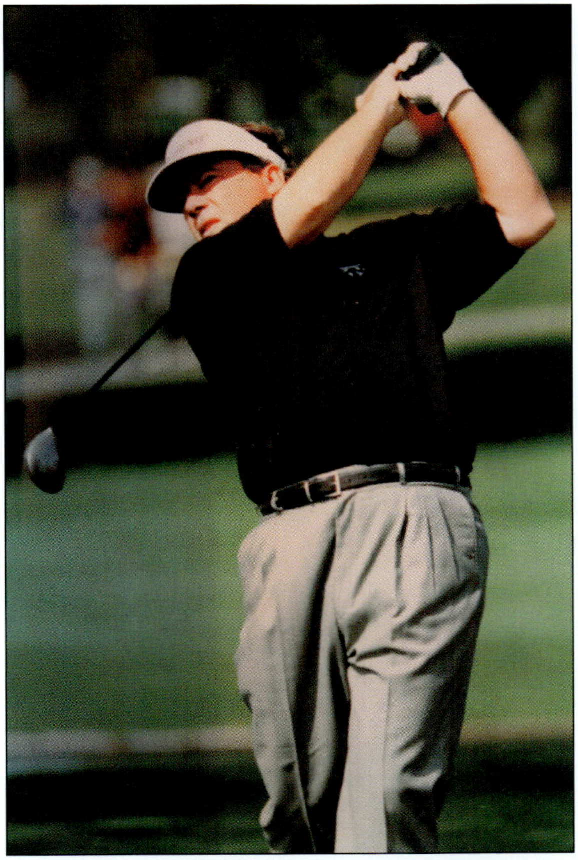

Still Playing En-Joie After All These Years. Rick Fehr won the BC Open in 1986 by two strokes over Larry Mize [-17 (65-66-67-69-267)]. Here, he closes out his second round of golf in 2014 at En-Joie by sinking a 12-foot putt. After this round, he was tied for fourth, but he slumped on Sunday, finishing 16th in the tournament.

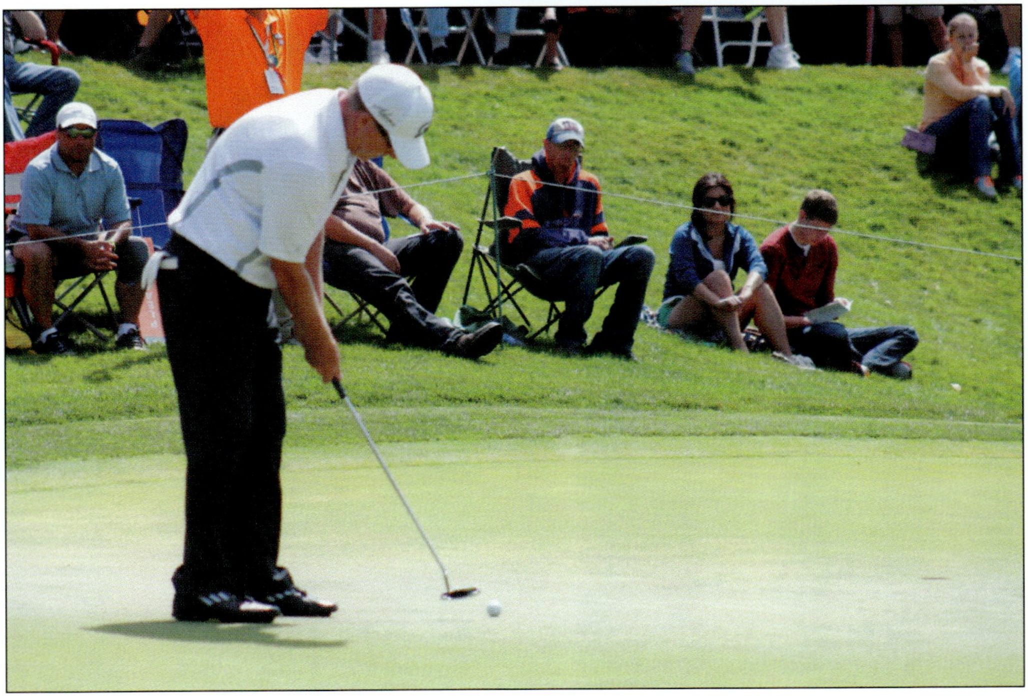

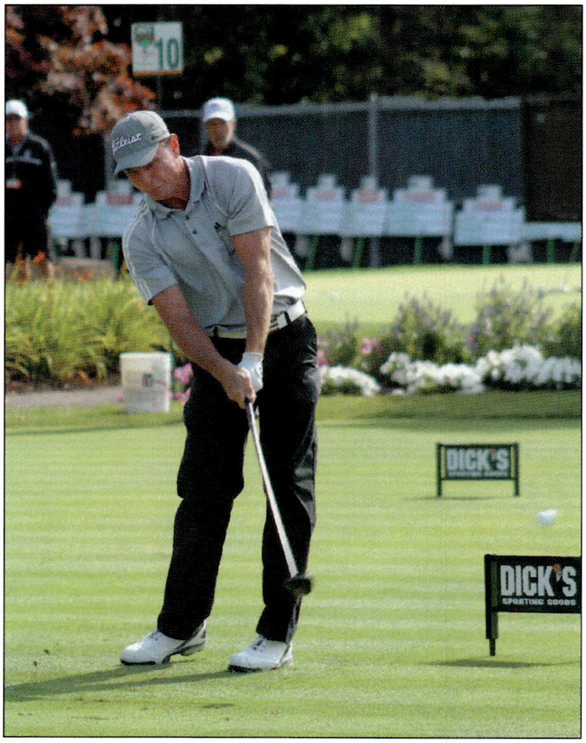

Advil, Anyone? Bill Glasson has just started his round of golf with this shot off the first tee in the 2014 DSGO. The ball is seen taking flight at lower right. Glasson won the BC Open in 1988 [-16 (66-68-65-69-268)]. In 1994, referring to the numerous surgeries he has undergone, Glasson quipped, "For me, breakfast is a bowl of Advil."

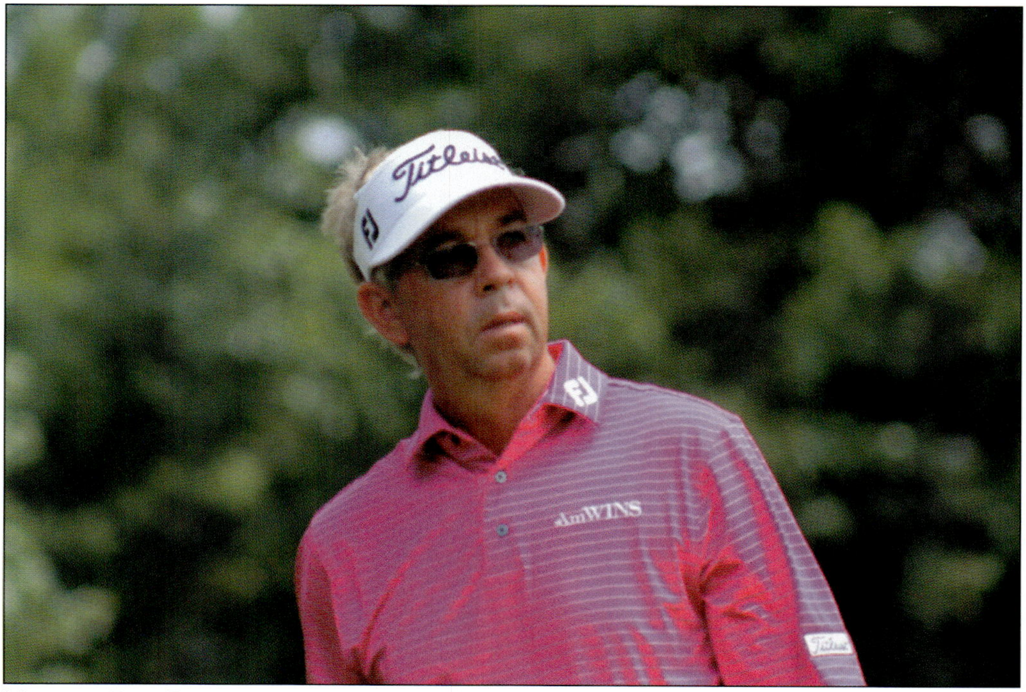

Nothing Like Beating Your Buddy! Mike Hulbert won the BC Open in 1989 [-16 (69-66-68-65-268)], but his first PGA Tour win came in the Federal Express St. Jude Classic in 1986, when he beat his hometown buddy, Joey Sindelar, by one stroke. Hulbert joined the tour in 1985 and won over $4 million during his PGA career.

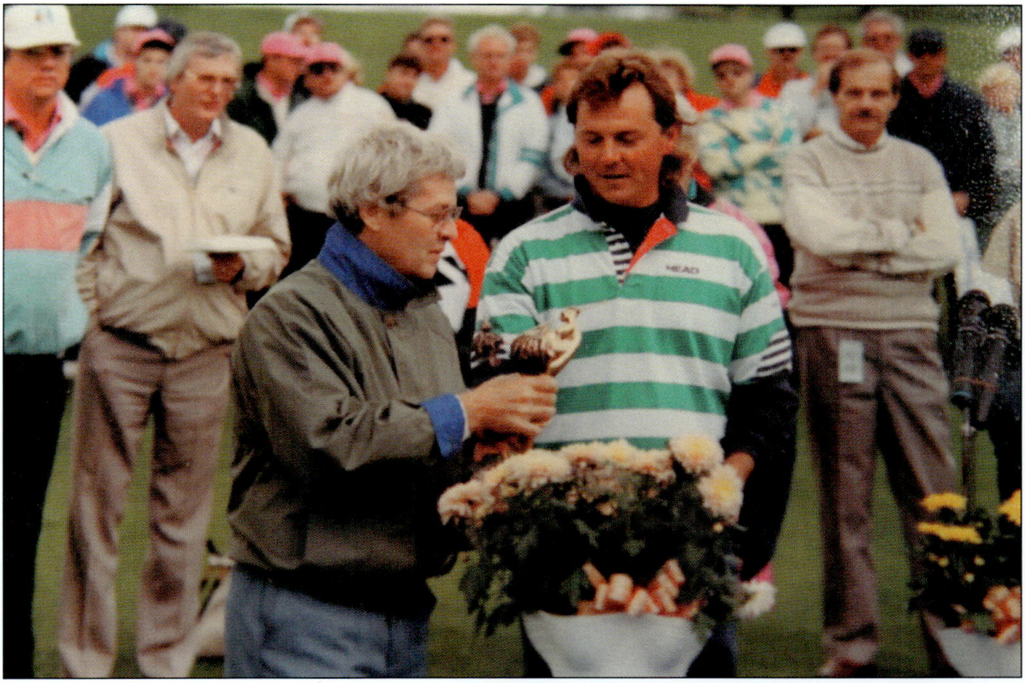

Henke's First Win. Like many golfers before him, Nolan Henke enjoyed his first PGA Tour victory in Endicott. His inaugural win came in the 1990 BC Open [-18 (66-64-70-68-268)], as he beat Mark Weibe by three strokes. Henke captured two more PGA titles, the 1991 Phoenix Open and the 1993 Bell South Classic. (Courtesy of BCHS.)

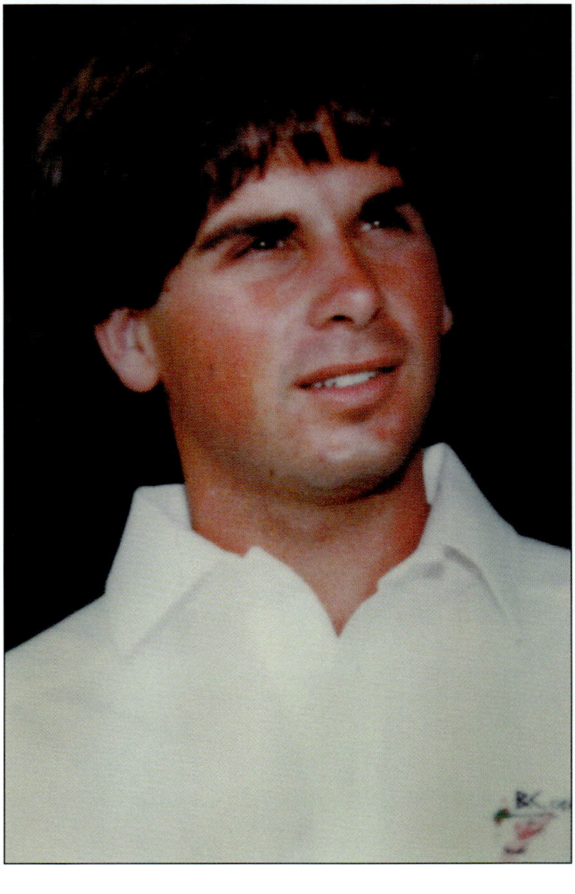

FC Wins the BC. On September 22, 1991, Fred "Boom Boom" Couples sealed his three-stroke victory [-15 (66-67-68-68-269)] over Peter Jacobsen with a final round of 68 for his fifth of what would be 15 PGA Tour wins. He was inducted into the World Golf Hall of Fame in 2013. Couples's nickname came courtesy of his outstanding driving ability. (Courtesy of BCHS.)

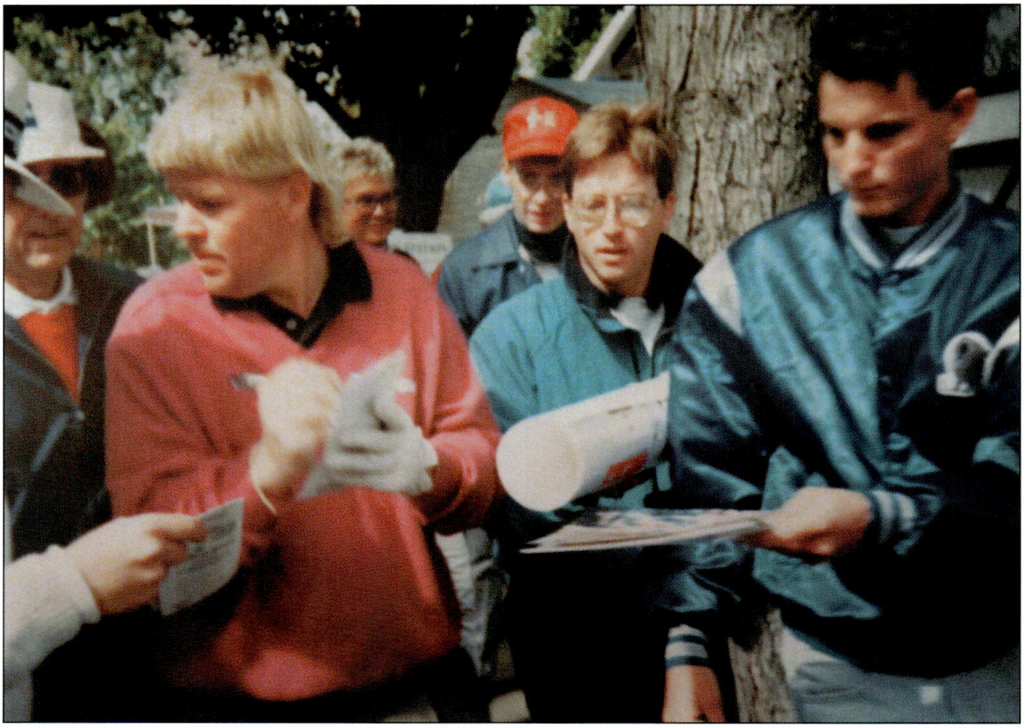

LONG JOHN. John Daly (left), winner of the 1992 BC Open, joined the tour in 1991 and promptly won his first tournament, the PGA Championship, at the famous Crooked Stick Golf Club in Carmel, Indiana. He entered the tournament as a ninth alternate, but stormed into stardom with a three-stroke win over Bruce Lietzke. He captured the 1992 title in Endicott [-22 (65-66-67-68-266)].

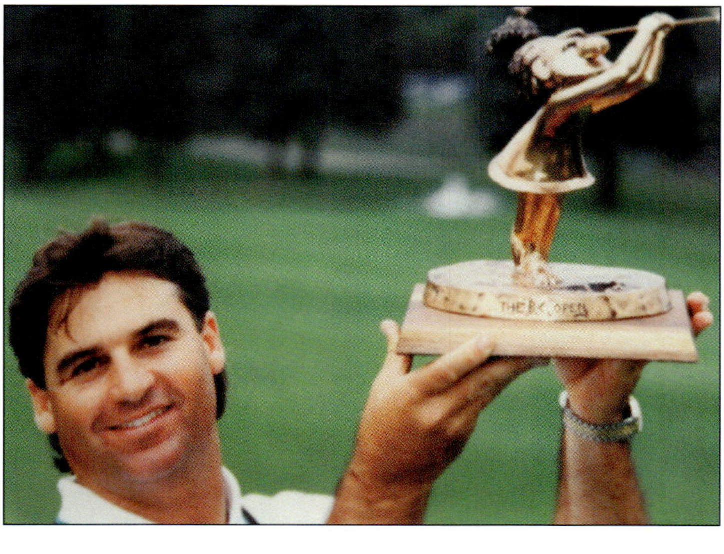

BLAINE WHO? The 1993 BC Open winner [−13 (68-71-65-67-271)], Blaine McCallister, roomed with his future PGA colleague and World Golf Hall of Famer Fred Couples, and CBS Sports anchor Jim Nantz while attending the University of Houston. McCallister won five PGA titles, with his final victory coming at En-Joie. (Courtesy of BCHS.)

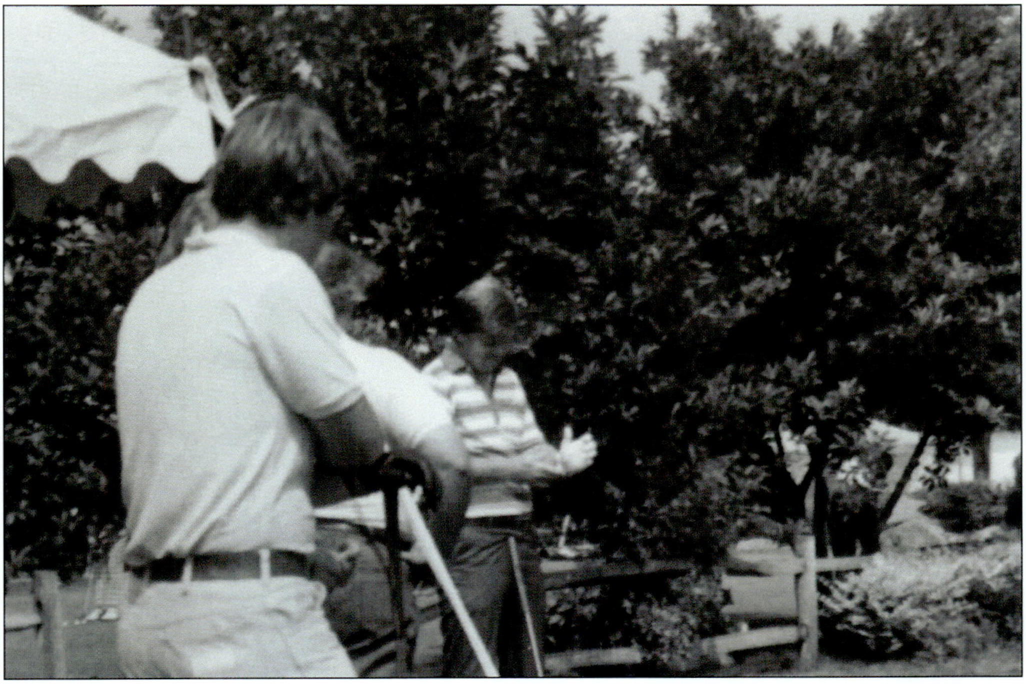

From Sullivan to Sutton. After only a brief time on the Florida Gators golf team, 1994 BC Open winner Mike Sullivan [–18 (65-67-68-66-266)] turned pro in 1976. "Sully" (above, right) won three PGA tournaments and was the first golfer to commit to play in the 2007 DSGO. Below, Hal Sutton (left) and his wife pose with tournament director Alex Alexander after Sutton won the BC Open in 1995 [-15 (71-69-68-61-269)] by one stroke over Jim McGovern. Sutton won 14 PGA titles, including the 1983 PGA Championship. (Both, courtesy of BCHS.)

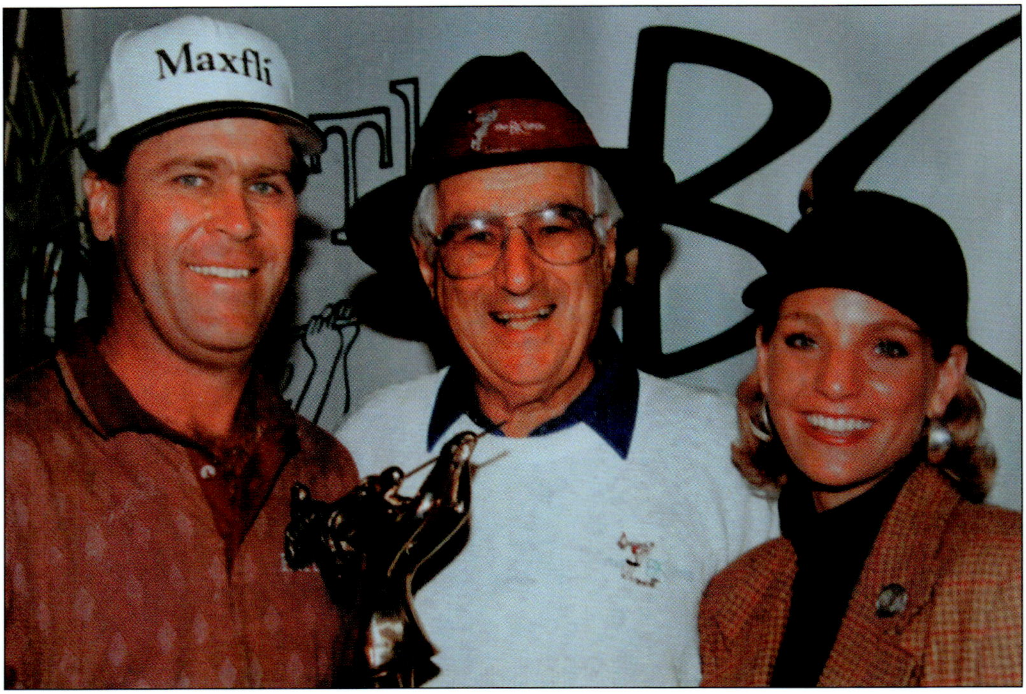

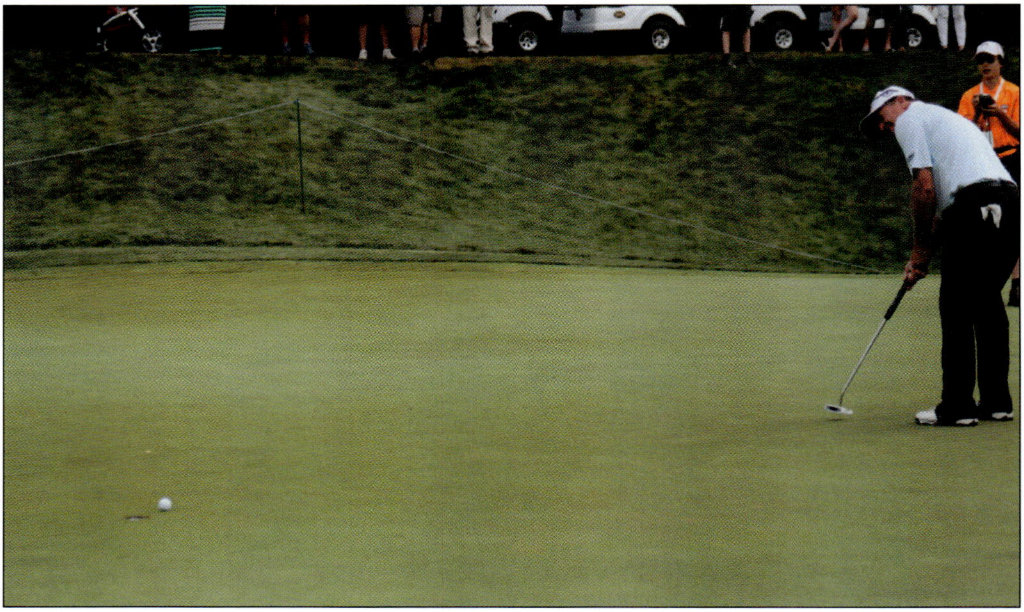

Looking Good? Fred Funk won the 1996 BC Open in a one-hole playoff over Pete Jordan [-16 (68-66-63-197)], as weather shortened the tournament to three rounds. Here, he just misses his putt on the 18th hole in the 2014 pro-am. Funk started his professional career in 1981, but he did not make the PGA Tour until 1989. Funk graduated from the University of Maryland in 1980, majoring in law enforcement.

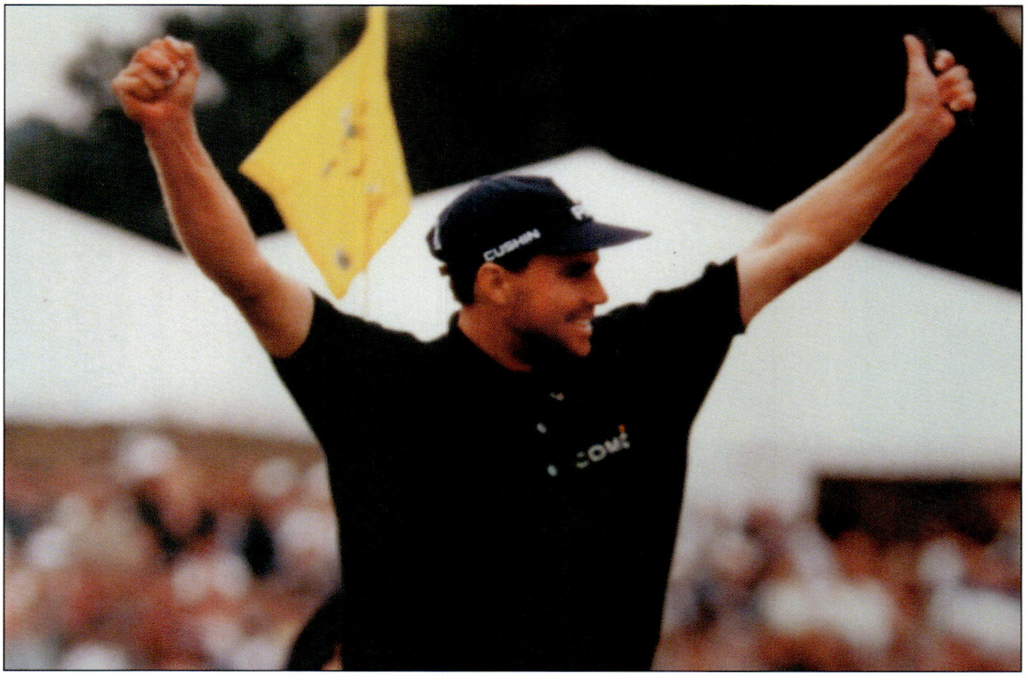

It's Pronounced Yet-shted! A first-place finish at the 1997 BC Open [-13 (70-69-66-70-275)] allowed Gabriel Hjertstedt to become the first Swede to win on the PGA Tour. Known primarily for its chocolate and watches, Sweden could finally be known for golf! Hjertstedt beat Andrew Magee, Chris Perry, and Lee Rinker by one stroke.

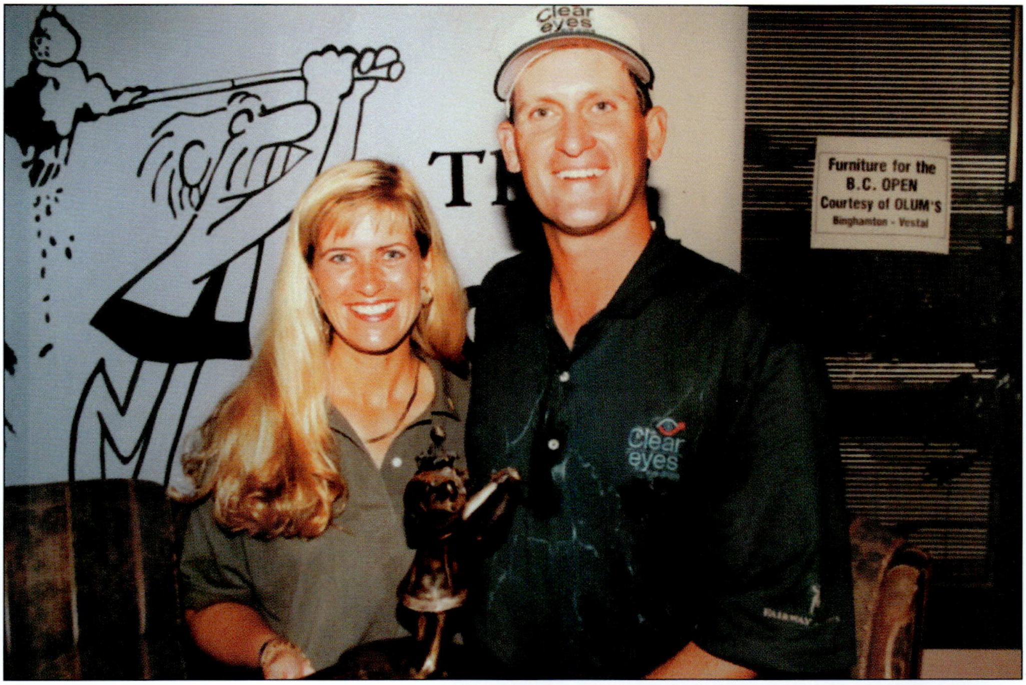

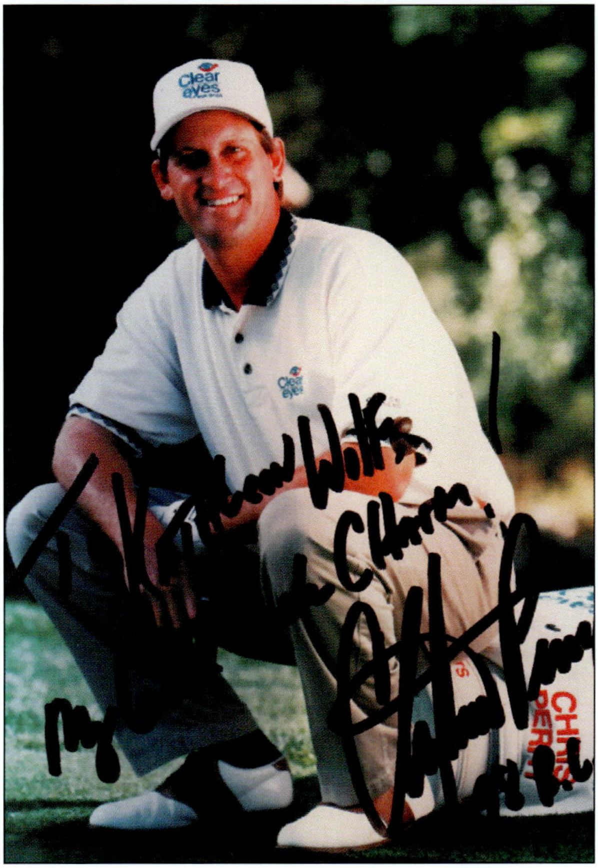

A Lucky Charm! Above, Chris Perry poses with Kathleen Wolfe, who was his walking scorekeeper during his second and final rounds of the 1998 BC Open. Perry requested Wolfe to be his scorekeeper during his final round, as he felt she was his good-luck charm. He was right. He shot a final-round score of 67 to clinch his first PGA Tour victory [-15 (67-70-69-67-273)] by three strokes over Peter Jacobsen. "Chris was fun to watch, he had a great pre-shot routine, a beautiful swing and he was so focused," recalls Wolfe, who has been a volunteer at En-Joie since 1985. Perry and his family still keep in touch with Wolfe today. (Both, courtesy of KW.)

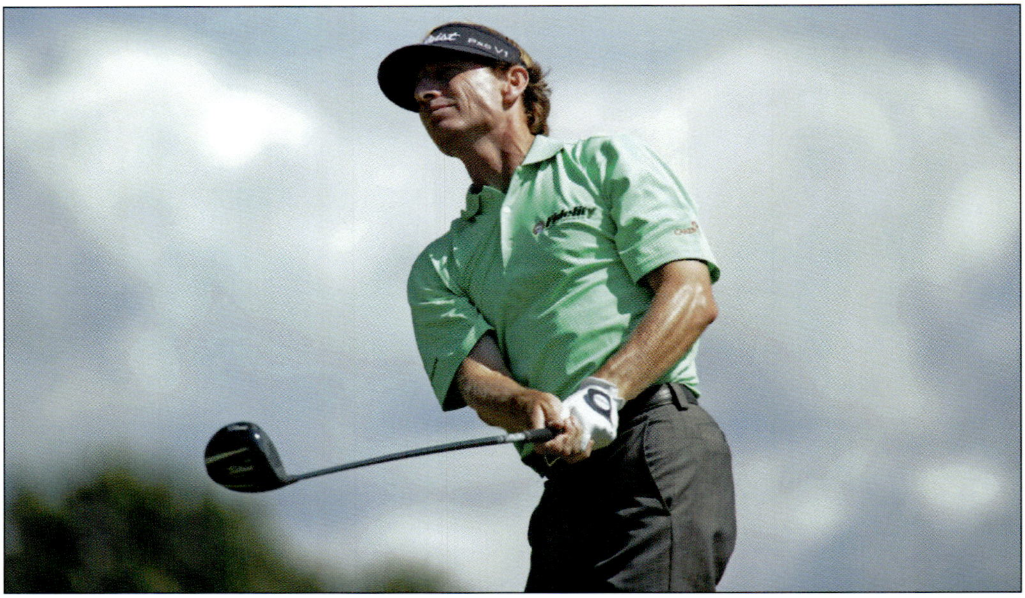

BACK-TO-BACK: Brad Faxon won the BC Open in 1999 [-15 (69-67-70-67-273)] and successfully defended it in 2000 with an even better score [-14 (68-66-68-68-270)], making him the only golfer in En-Joie's history to win back-to-back titles. Faxon's strength is putting: "I just try to hit every putt as if I've just made a million in a row." (Courtesy of BCCC.)

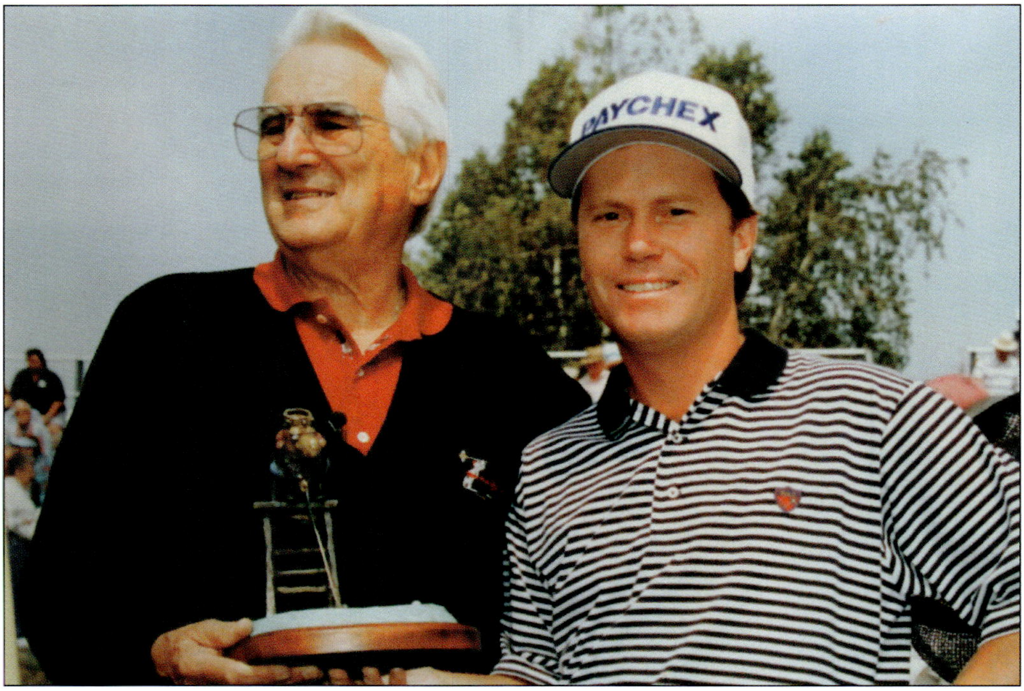

I LOVE NEW YORK. Jeff Sluman (right), shown here with Alex Alexander, was born and raised in Rochester and won the BC Open in 2001 [-22 (67-68-65-66-266)] in a playoff against Paul Gow. Sluman (right), born on September 11, 1957, graduated from Greece Arcadia High School. He won six PGA events and won the PGA Championship in 1988 by three strokes over Paul Azinger. (Courtesy of BCHS.)

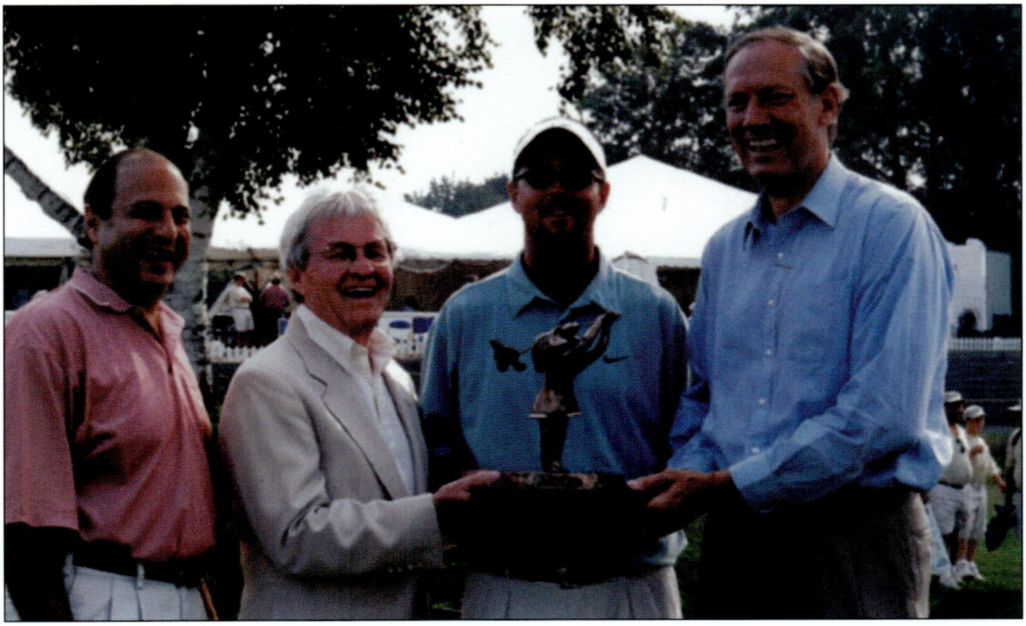

Roll Tide! University of Alabama graduate Robert "Spike" McRoy, shown here with state senator Tom Libous (left), Johnny Hart (second from left), and New York governor George Pataki (right), won seven tournaments in his professional career. His only PGA victory came at the 2002 BC Open [-19 (70-65-69-65-269)]. (Courtesy of BCCC.)

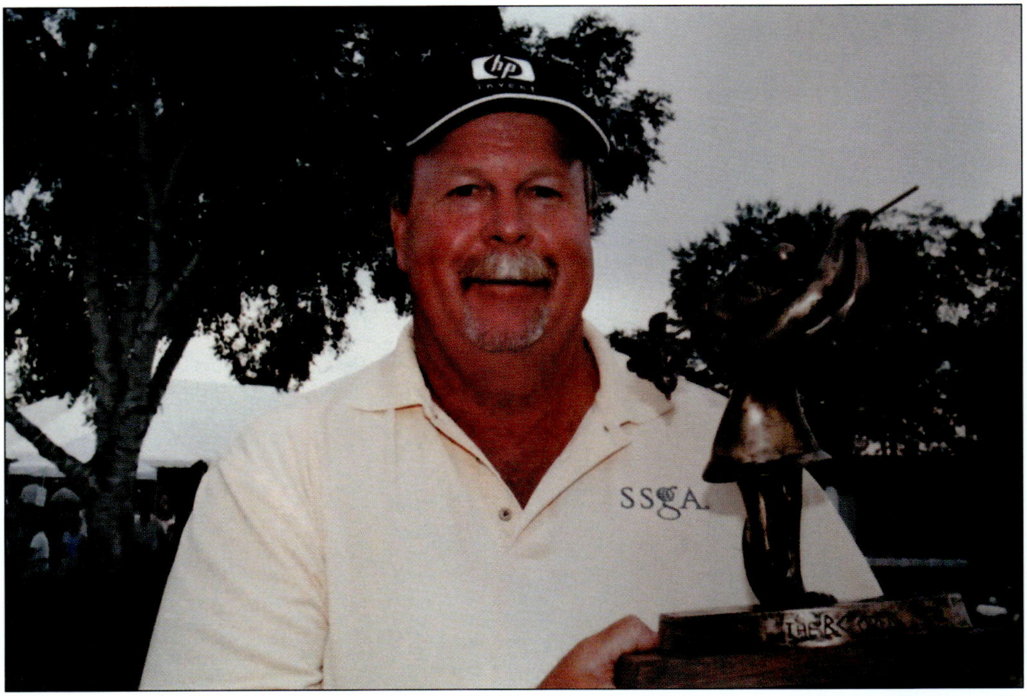

Twenty-One Under Wins by One. Craig Stadler won the BC Open in 2003 [-21 (67-69-68-63-267)] by one stroke. Here, he proudly poses with Thor. Stadler actually won the BC Open shortly after he became eligible for the Champions Tour, celebrating his 50th birthday on June 2, 2003. (Courtesy of GN.)

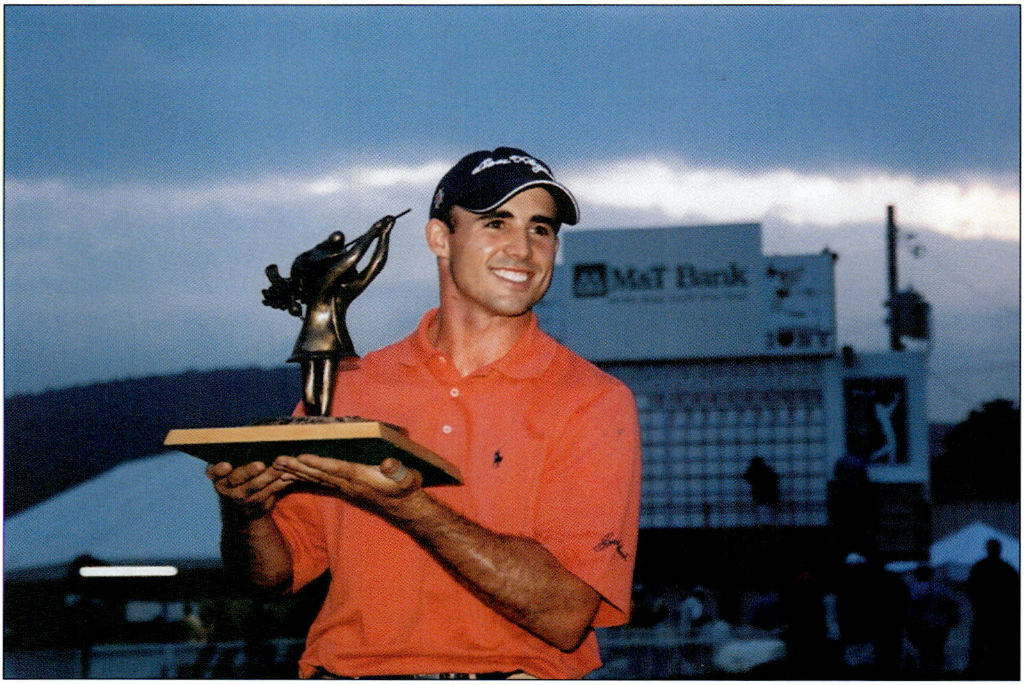

What a Way to Win $540K! The 2002 Rookie of the Year, Jonathan Byrd, has captured five PGA titles, including the 2004 BC Open. Byrd beat Ted Purdy by one stroke [-20 (67-65-68-68-268)]. The win earned him $540,000—not bad for a week of work! Byrd's career earnings through 2014 were over $17 million. (Courtesy of BCCC.)

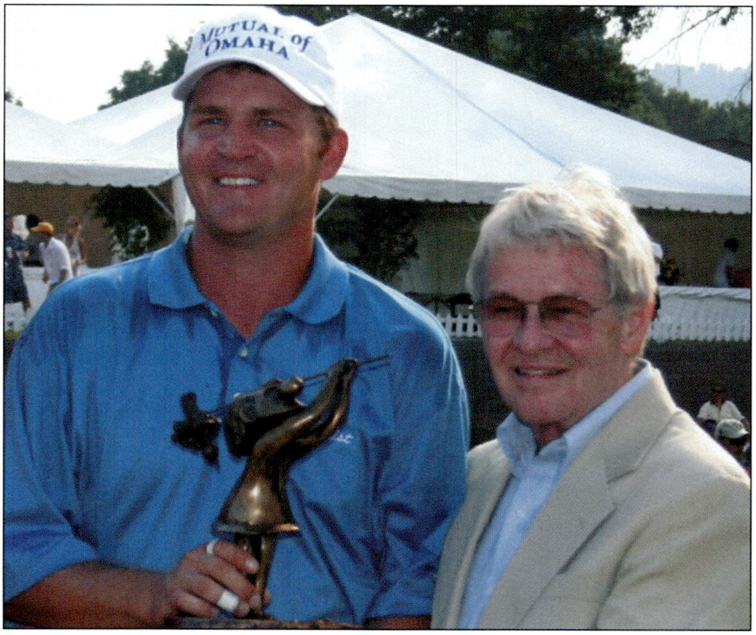

One for a Million. The 2005 winner, Jason Bohn (left), poses with Johnny Hart after his victory. In 1992, Bohn hit a hole-in-one in a charity fundraiser to earn $1 million. Because he was in college at the time (on the University of Alabama golf team), he had to turn pro in order to collect the money. His score in 2005 [-24 (64-68-66-66-264)] is the best four-day total in BC Open history. (Courtesy of BCCC.)

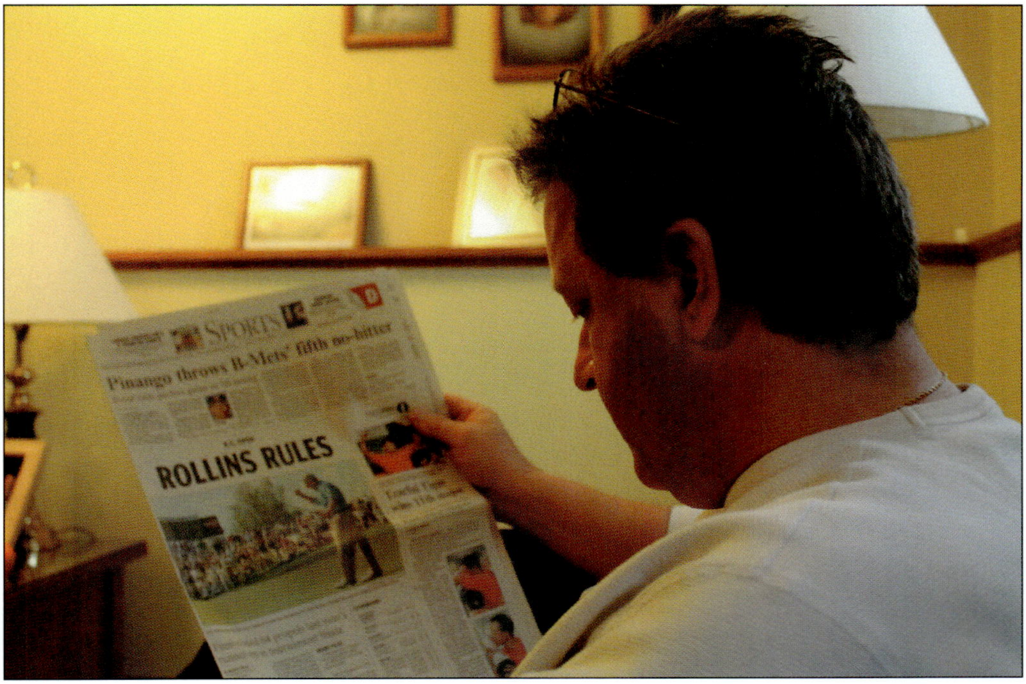

The Finale! Not many people from Broome County remember who won the final BC Open in 2006. That is because it was played in Verona at the Turning Stone Resort and Casino due to a flood at En-Joie. John Rollins [-19 (67-70-68-64-269)] beat Bob May. Here, coauthor Mike McCann researches the events in 2006.

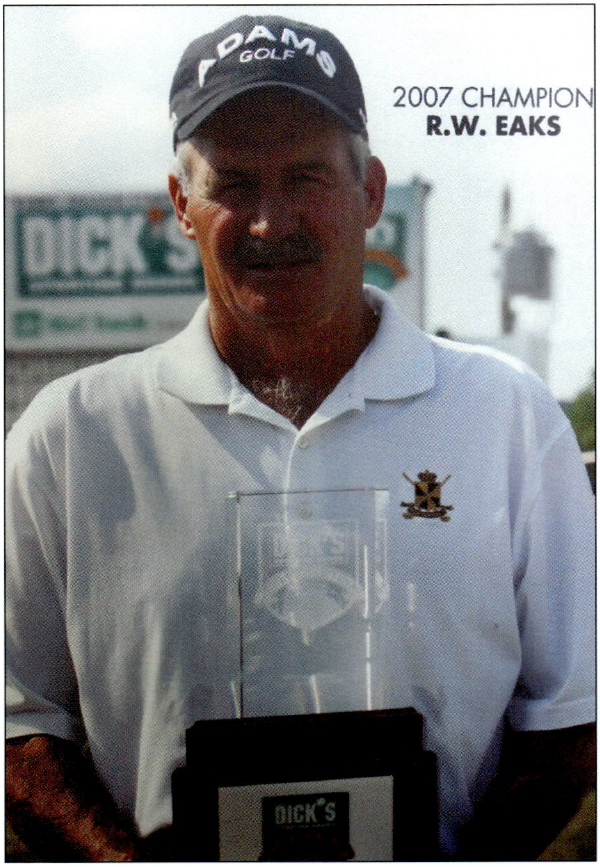

Now 1 for 91! The DSGO champion in 2007, R.W. Eaks, ended a long drought with his win [-17 (71-62-66-199)]. He had been winless in 77 PGA Tour events over a dozen years, as well as going 0-for-90 in six years on the Champions Tour entering to the 2007 tournament at En-Joie. His only prior wins had been on the Nationwide Tour. (Courtesy of BCCC.)

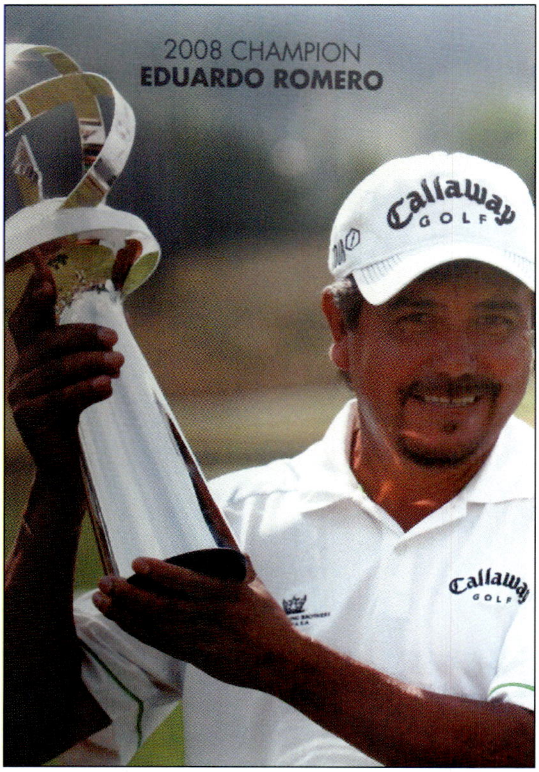

"EL GATO," THE CHAMP. Eduardo Romero won the 2008 tournament by one stroke with a score of 199 [-17 (65-65-69-199)]. Romero, from Argentina, accumulated 8 European Tour wins and 44 Argentine Tour wins after turning professional in 1982. He is affectionately known as "El Gato" (the cat). (Courtesy of BCCC.)

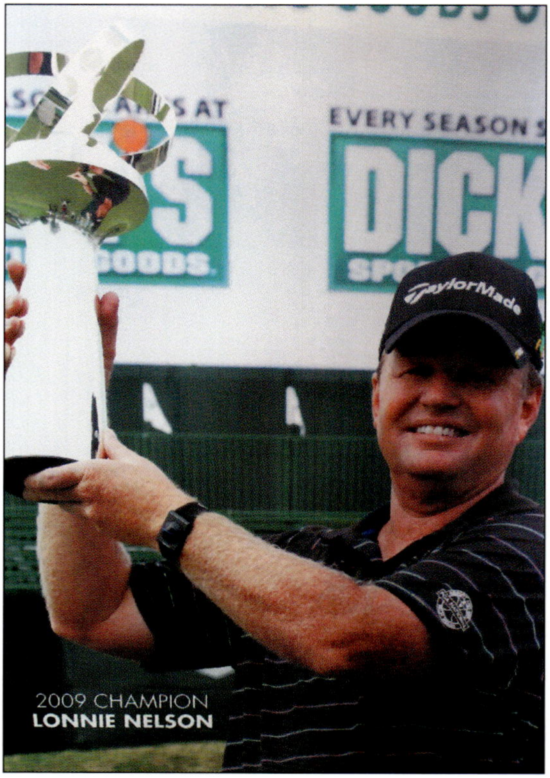

BEATING FUNK IS FINE! Lonnie Neilsen, a native of Iowa, finished the 2009 event with a final round of 63 to overcome his three-stroke deficit to Fred Funk [-21 (66-66-63-195)]. Neilsen has won two times on the Champions Tour and works with Golf for Injured Veterans Everywhere (GIVE), which provides a structured golf program for Iowa veterans. (Courtesy of BCCC.)

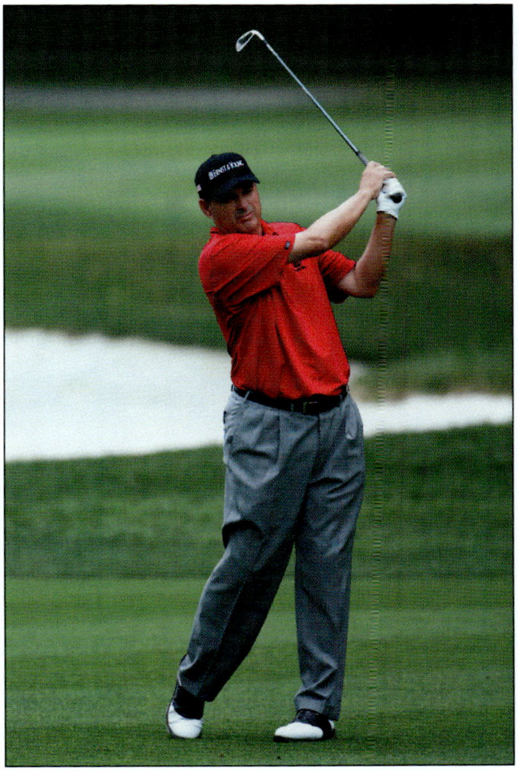

Beating Funk Again Is Even Finer. Not to be outdone by Neilsen, 2010 champion Loren Roberts [-15 (68-68-65-201)] also bested Funk. His 201 score was good for a one-stroke victory. Roberts had eight PGA Tour wins before he embarked on his Champions Tour career in 2005. (Courtesy of BCCC.)

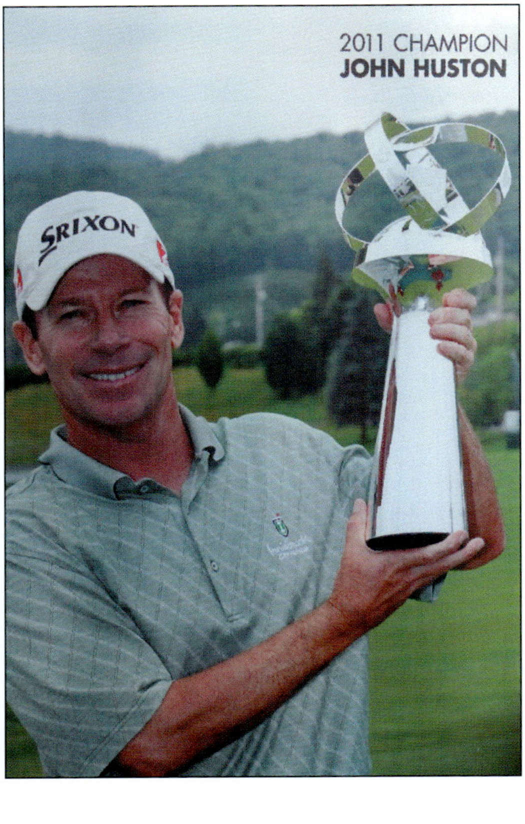

An Early Win. John Huston [-16 (65-70-65-200)] did not have to wait long for his first win on the Champions Tour—he was only 25 days past his 50th birthday when he won the 2011 DSGO tournament by three strokes over Nick Price. Huston's seven PGA wins did not give him the same notoriety that his namesake received as an actor, director, and screenwriter. (Courtesy of BCCC).

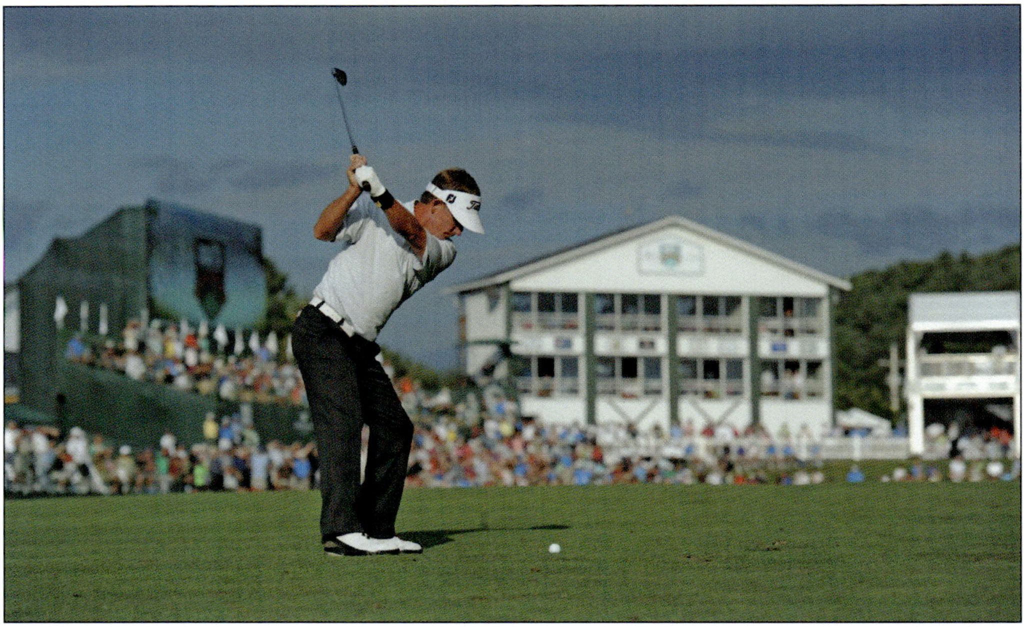

Back-to-Back Wins. Willie Wood [-13 (68-67-68-203)] won by one stroke in a one-round playoff with Michael Allen in 2012 to garner his first Champions Tour win at the DSGO. Wood got his second Champions Tour win the very next month, doubling his number of PGA Tour wins! (Courtesy of BCCC.)

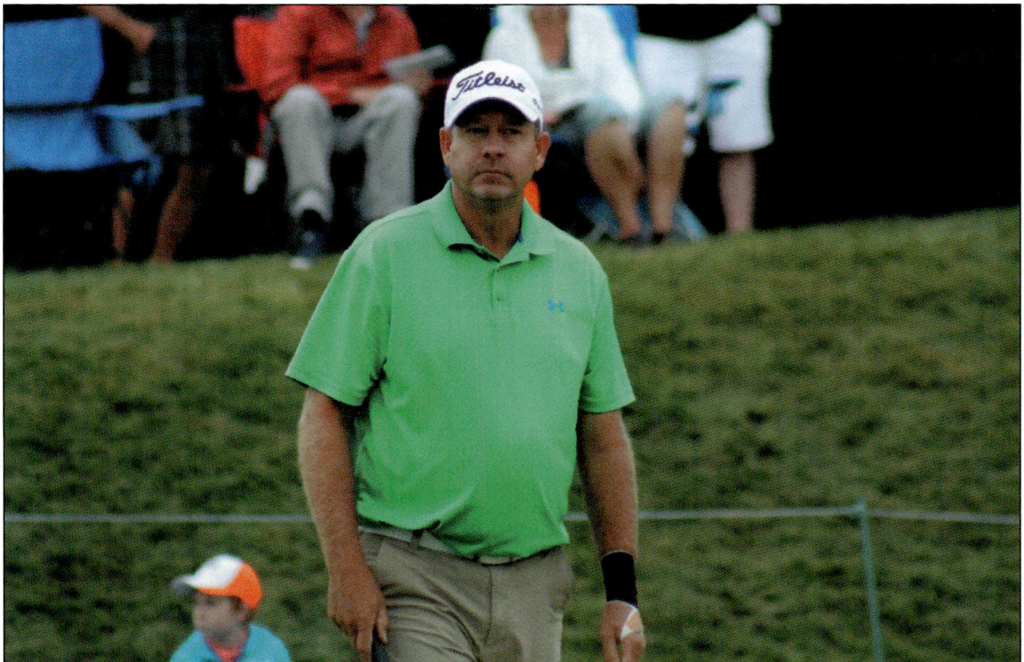

A Thousand Winners. Bart Bryant [-16 (66-62-72-200)] won in 2013 by one stroke over Corey Pavin and Russ Cochran. His win at the 2013 event also gave him the distinction of being the 1,000th overall winner on the Champions Tour. His older brother Brad also won on both the PGA and Champions Tours. (Courtesy of BCCC.)

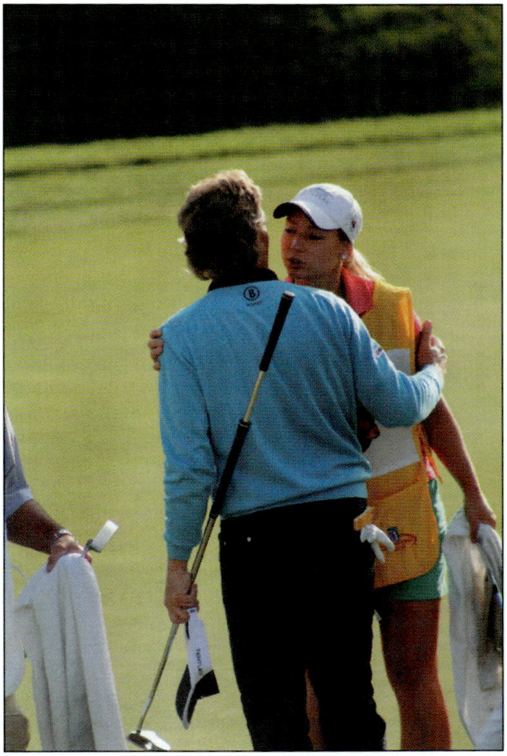

A Victory Kiss. Bernhard Langer [-16 (67-67-66-200] had his daughter as a caddy in the 2014 DSGO. At right, Langer gets a kiss from her after finishing his first round. Below, he celebrates his 2014 championship at En-Joie after finishing his round of 66, which allowed him to edge out Woody Austin and Mark O'Meara by one stroke for the tournament win. Langer was elected to the World Golf Hall of Fame in 2001. At the end of 2014, he had 23 wins on the Champions Tour.

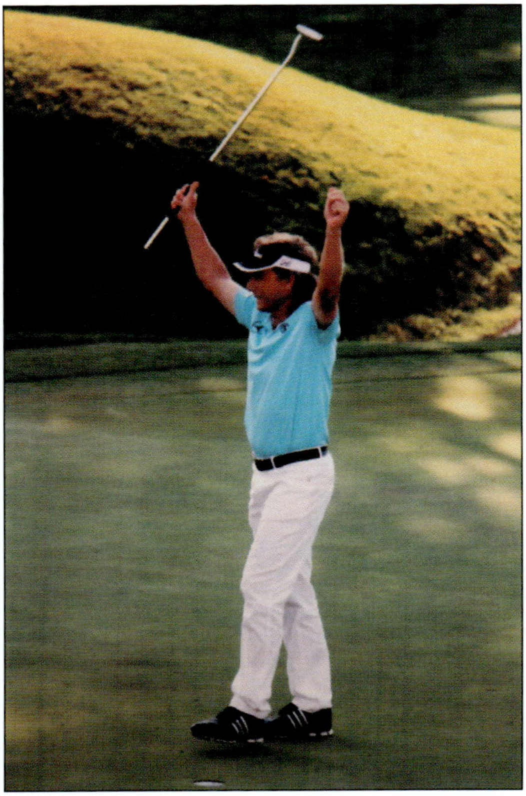

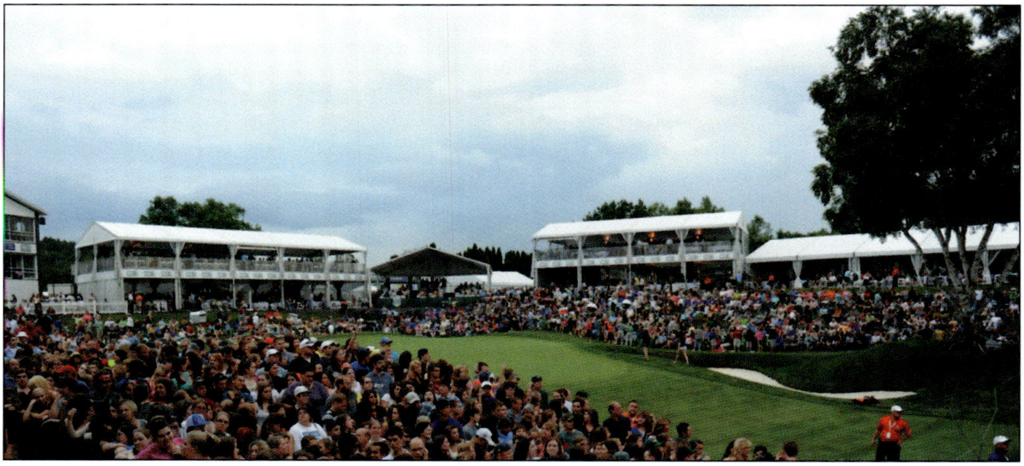

Champs All the Way. The golfers who take home the first-place prize money are not the only winners of the Endicott tournaments. Due to the efforts of the Broome County Community Charities, as well as the thousands of fans and volunteers who visit En-Joie each year, over $14 million has been distributed throughout the community since 1971. Here, spectators enjoy golf during the day (above) and a concert under a periwinkle sky (below). (Both, courtesy of BCCC.)

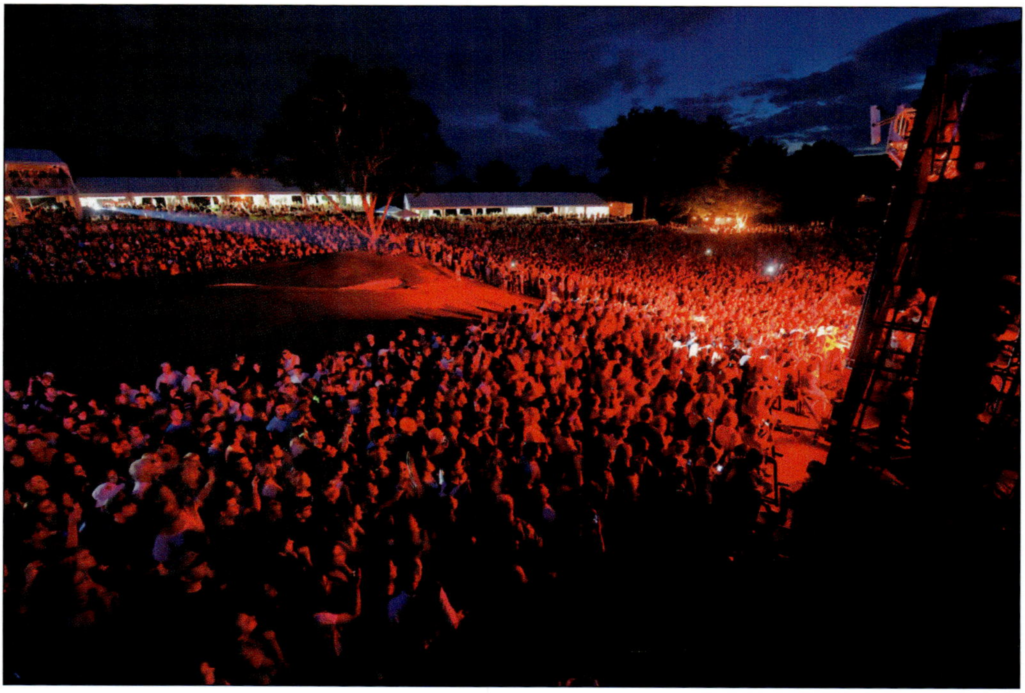

Three

I Wish I Had Shot 58!

In this chapter, the camera captures emotions, reminding the reader that golf is a great equalizer. No matter how talented a golfer may be, the game is always humbling. The photographs in this chapter are not discriminating, treating World Golf Hall of Famers such as Colin Montgomerie and Mark O'Meara in the same manner as the sport's "grinders," such as Doug Garwood and Mike Goodes. Bunker shots, divots, fist pumps, forlorn visages, and a smile or two fill these pages.

Though no one in this chapter has won a championship in Endicott, the subjects nevertheless represent greatness, on and off the course. The success Montgomerie and O'Meara have seen on the links speaks volumes, but the work ethic for golf that Goodes discovered in time for the Champions Tour is a lesson on wasted opportunity. While Tom Byrum has won only one PGA Tour event and has yet to notch a win on the Champions Tour, his dedication and commitment to chasing a championship have provided him with the joy of competing at a game he loves.

In these pages, readers will be a witness to greatness, as they see how Kevin Sutherland joined only six other golfers in the history of the PGA to shoot a 59: Al Geiberger (1977 Danny Thomas Memphis Classic), Chip Beck (1991 Las Vegas Invitational), David Duval (1999 Bob Hope Chrysler Classic), Paul Goydos (2010 John Deere Classic), Stuart Appleby (2010 Greenbrier Classic), and Jim Furyk (2013 BMW Championship). The closing pages of the chapter highlight golfers who have played bit roles in various movies. Hollywood, like Endicott, has had an affinity with the links.

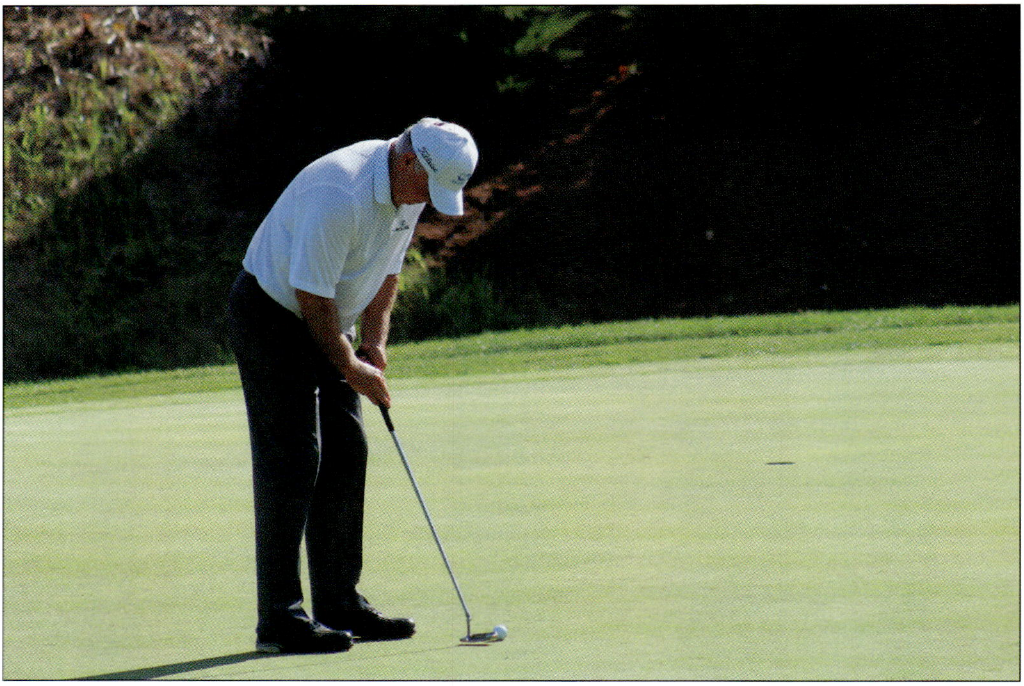

Close, but No Cup. Mark O'Meara watches his putt roll downhill toward the cup on the 15th green during the 2014 DSGO. O'Meara won 16 PGA tournaments as well as four events on the European Tour before joining the Champions Tour in 2007. He was elected to the World Golf Hall of Fame in 2014. Below, he stares down the ball, as there is nothing left to do but watch in disappointment as it just misses the cup. He played too short, miscalculating the softness of the green.

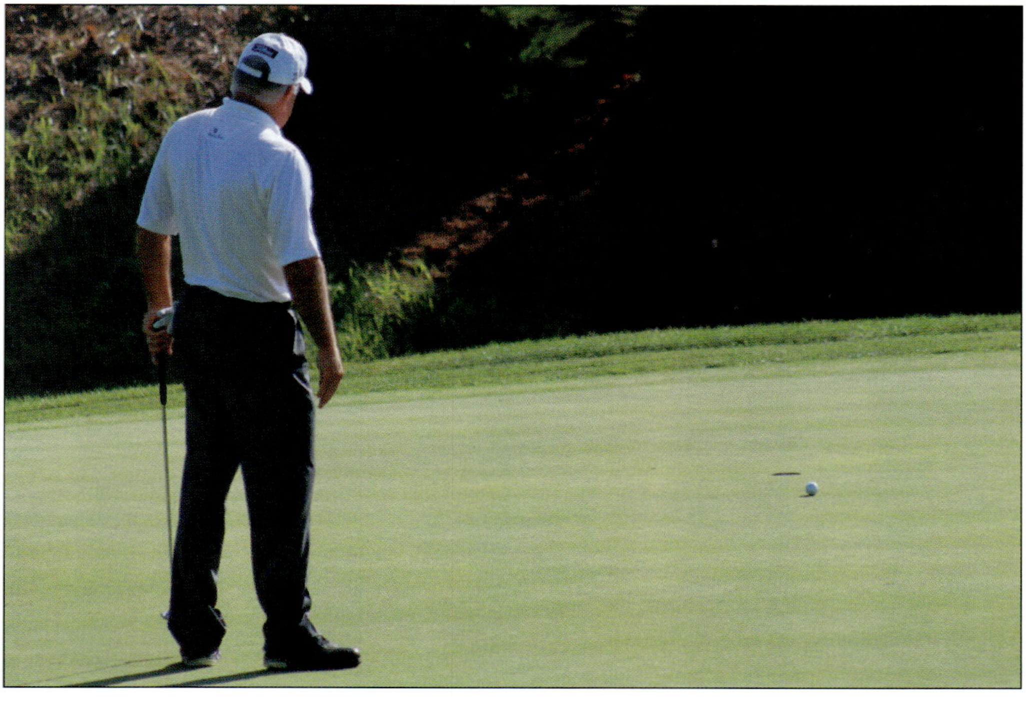

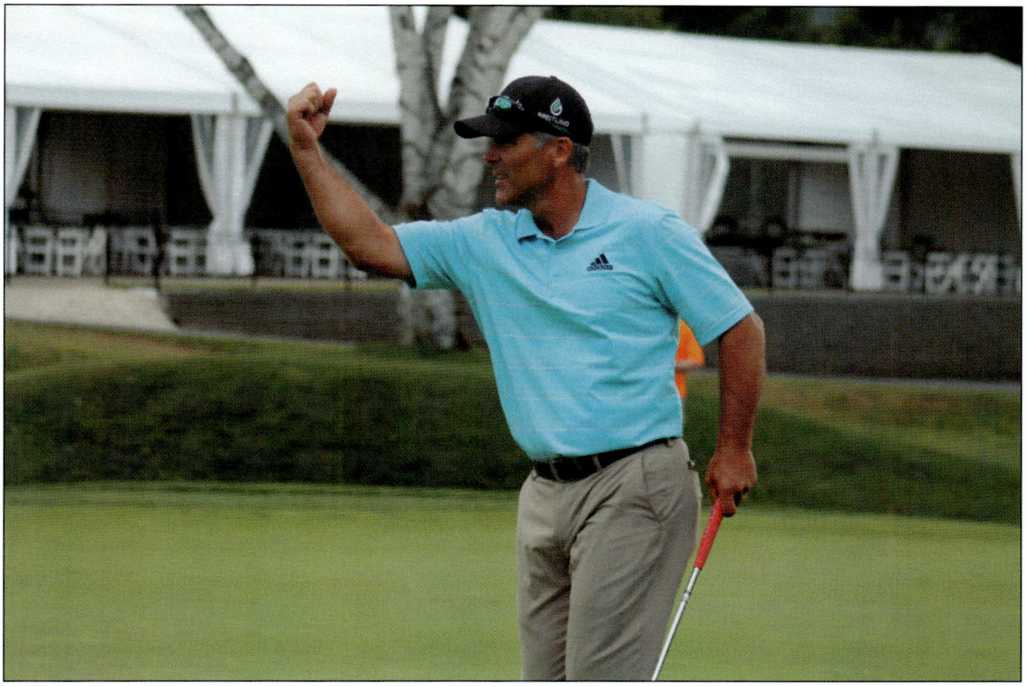

Oh, Yeah! Tom Byrum pumps his fist in elation as he sinks a long putt from the edge of the 18th green in the pro-am for the 2014 DSGO. Byrum joined the PGA Tour in 1984. He joined the Champions Tour in 2011, after turning 50 on September 28. Though playing in over 500 PGA Tour events, his only win came in the 1989 Kemper Open in Bethesda, Maryland.

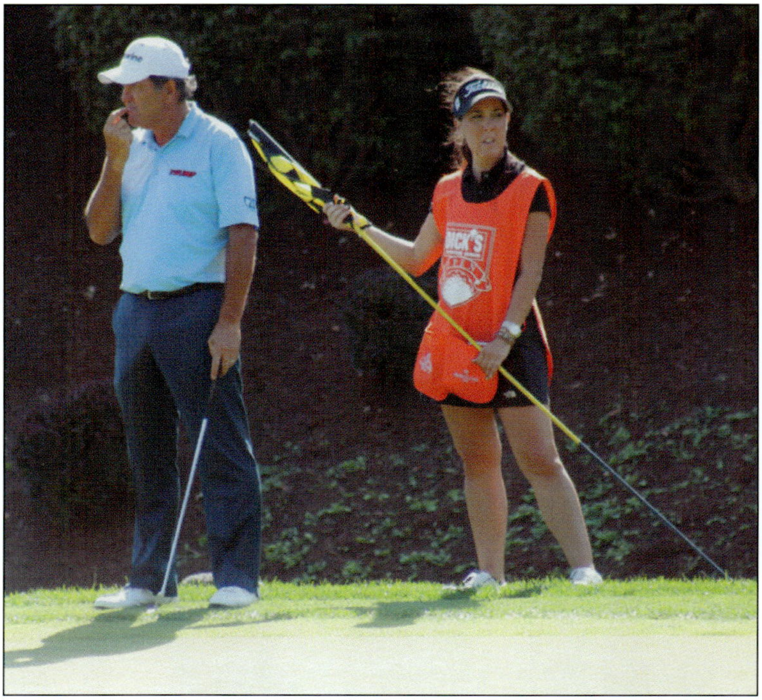

Lifetime Guarantee. David Frost's daughter was his caddy on the Champions Tour in August 2014. Years ago, while playing in the BC Open, after Frost broke the nose piece on his Bolle sunglasses, he gave them to a young fan, Clarke Giblin, who had the ingenuity to call the sunglass manufacturer. Giblin was informed that those sunglasses had a lifetime guarantee, so he received a new pair in the mail!

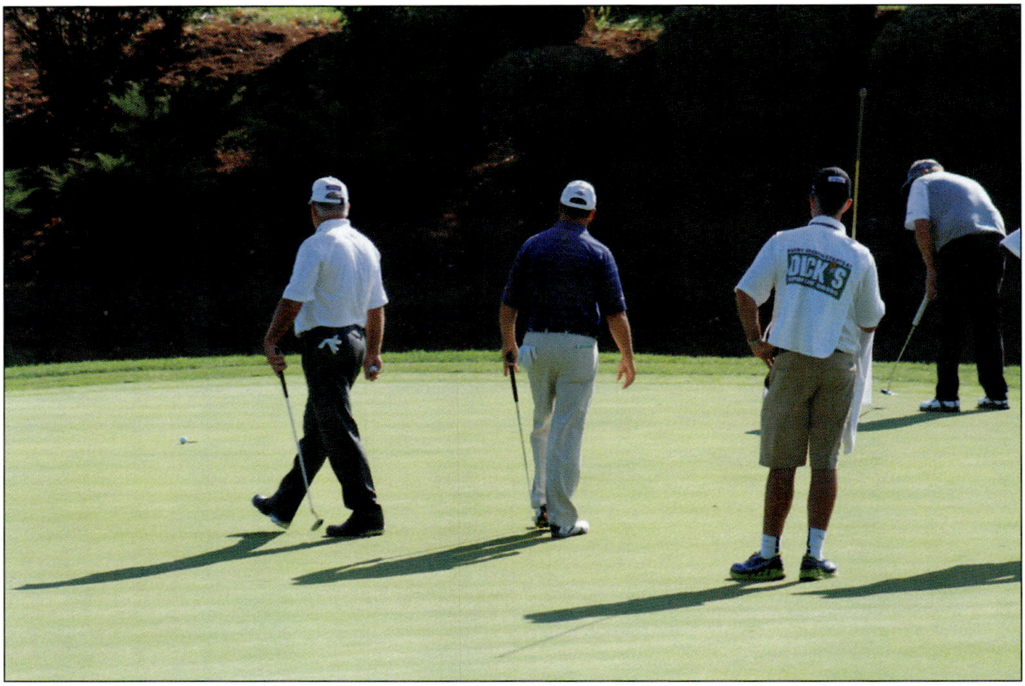

I Came Here for This? Colin Montgomerie (above, right), elected to the World Golf Hall of Fame in 2013, misses a putt by the slimmest of margins. The ball rims the hole as Mark O'Meara (left) and Olin Browne (center) look on. Below, Montgomerie shows his frustration by burying his head in his hat. He finished his 600th tournament on the European Tour in November 2014 when he played in the Turkish Airlines Open, which was played on a course he designed, the Montgomerie Maxx Royal course in Antalya.

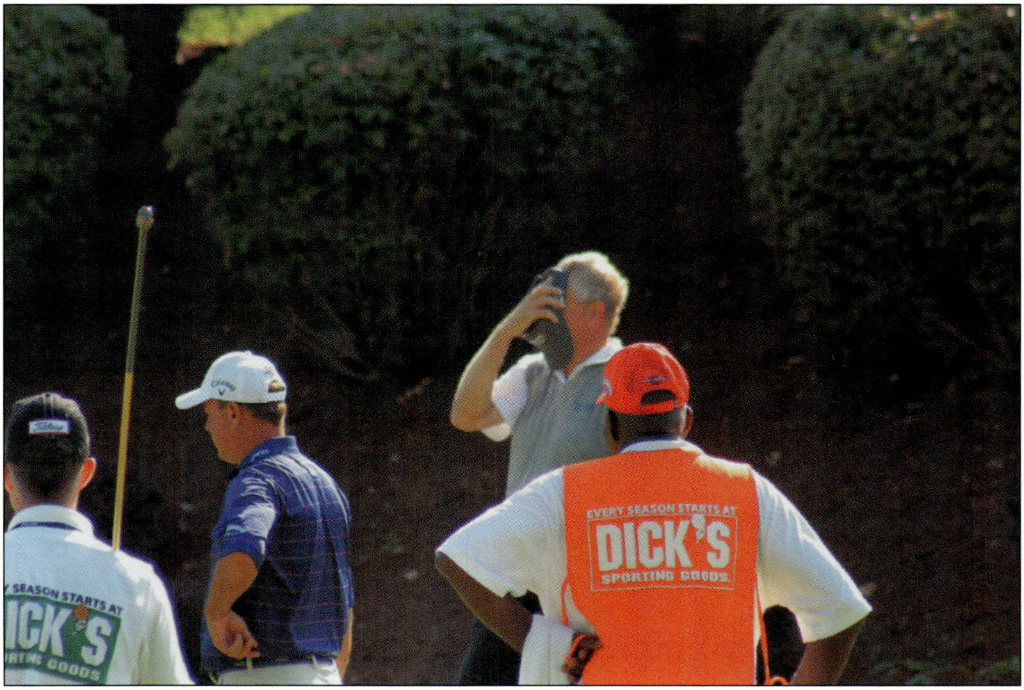

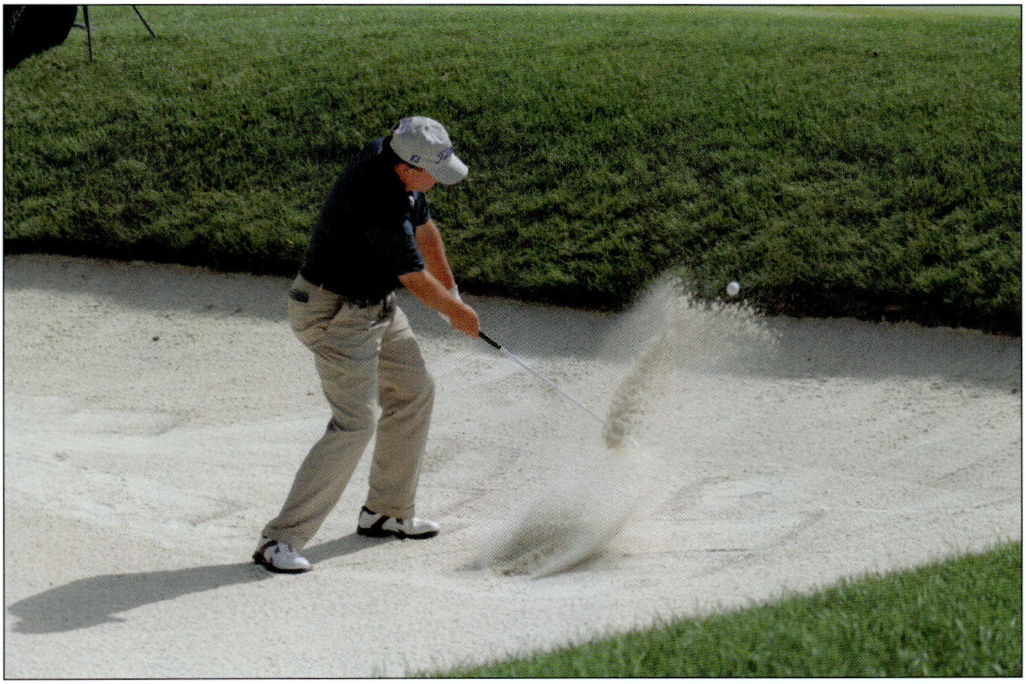

Anyone Have a Beach Blanket? Perseverance and a self-deprecating sense of humor have marked Woody Austin's career. He did not get a PGA Tour card until he was 30 years old. He jokes that he is named after actor Woody Harrelson, who is only three years older than he is. Seen on this page, Austin is slightly under the ball as he generates a burst of sand with his shot. In 1997, while playing a tournament at Hilton Head, South Carolina, he banged his putter against his head in disgust so many times, he bent the putter's shaft!

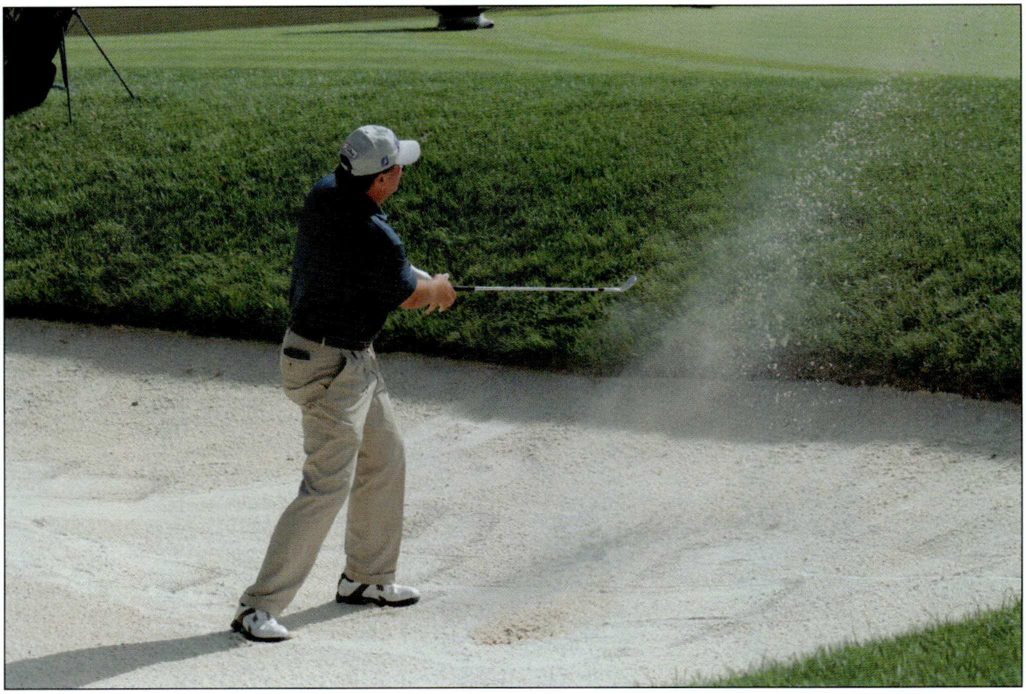

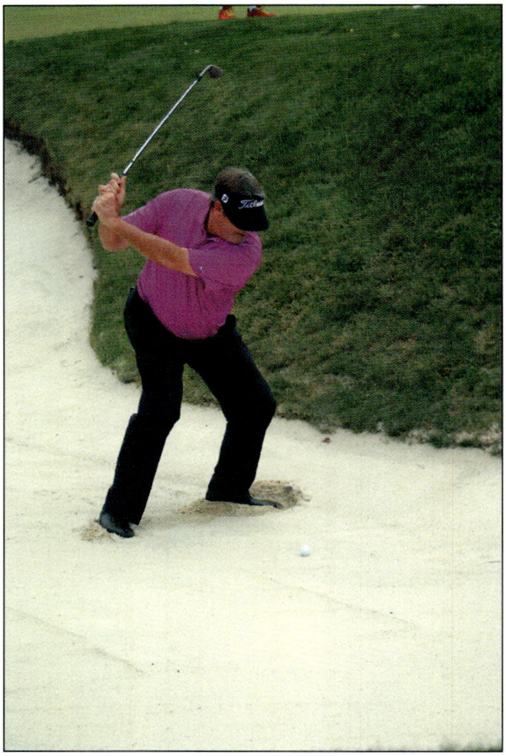

Sand, but No Seagull. Steve Lowery uses a big swing to get out of the sand on the 14th hole in the second round of the DSGO in 2014, sending the ball toward the green with a tail of sand. Heading into 2015, Steve was still looking for his first win on the Champions Tour. In 1998, in the Players Championship Tournament, Lowery had his successful approach shot to the island green on the 17th hole stolen by a seagull (which then dropped his ball into the adjacent water hazard). Under PGA rules, Lowery was allowed to replace his ball with no penalty.

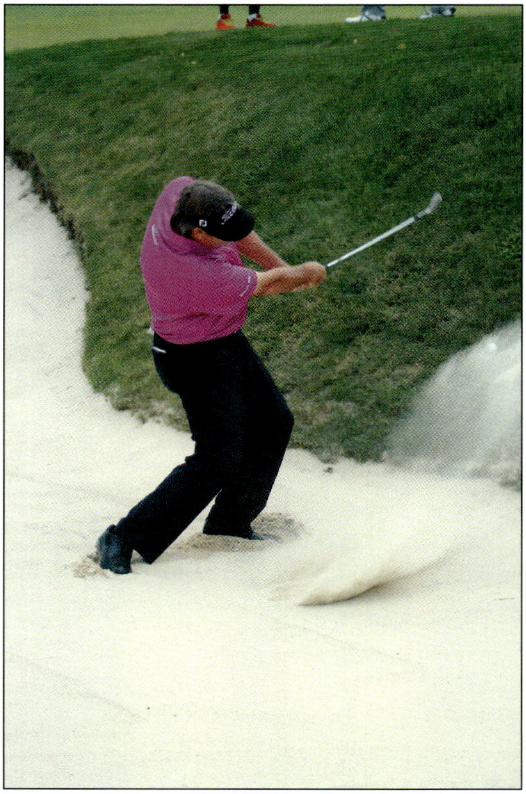

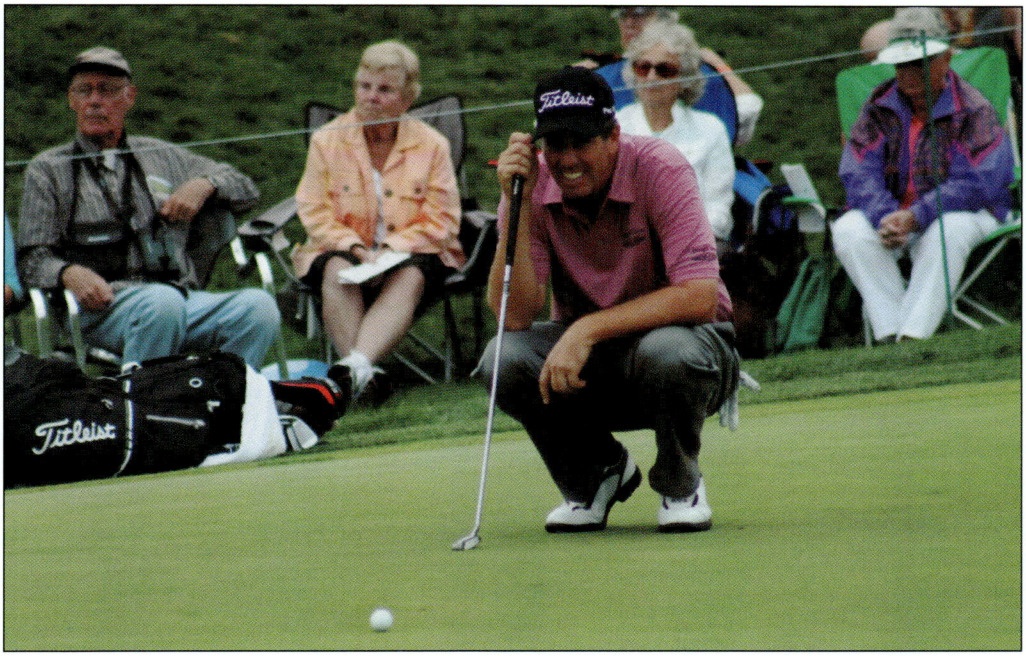

This Senior Life is Good. Doug Garwood lines up his short putt on the 18th green. Garwood is a rare specimen on the Champions Tour, as he never played a single round of PGA golf before finding success on the Champions circuit, which he joined in 2013. While playing in the DSGO in 2014, he told the *Binghamton Press & Sun-Bulletin*, "It's pleasing obviously, to have the success that I've had on the Champions Tour. I just think playing against my age, it's been more conducive to success." Garwood won over $700,000 in 2014 on the tour. Below, his body language shows he just missed the cup.

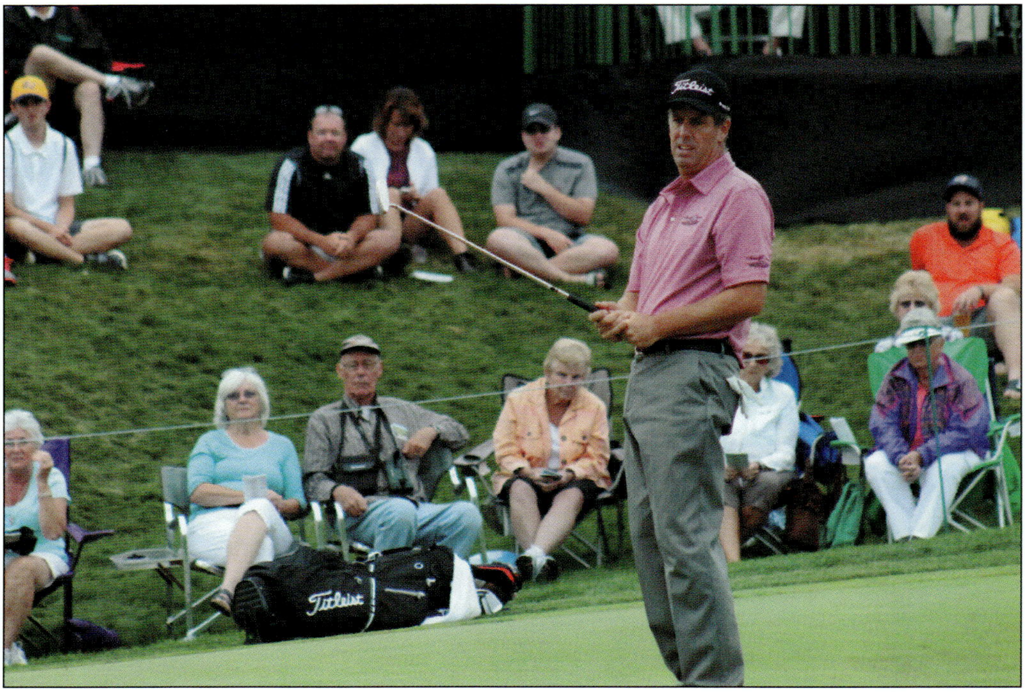

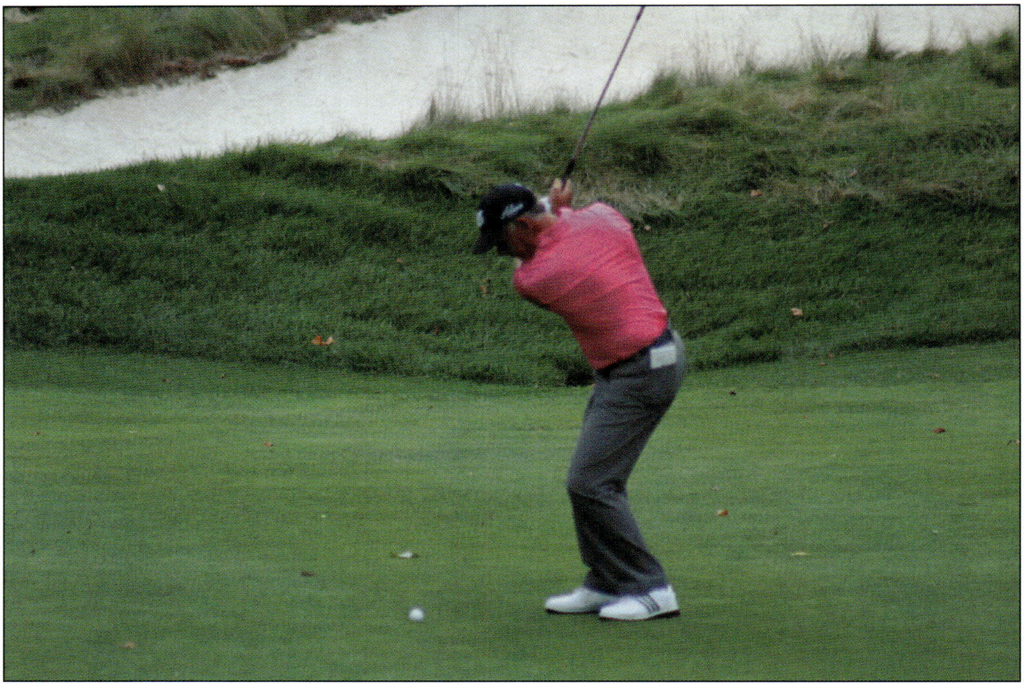

Youthful Talent Wasted. Mike Goodes displays excellent form as he hits an iron shot from the 14th fairway during the 2014 DSGO. Goodes was an outstanding high school golfer who won a partial scholarship to the University of North Carolina, but he did not suit up for the team. He explained to golf.com that he had a lack of discipline for the game in his younger days: "I grew up in a small town, and I wasn't the most mature 18-year-old on Earth."

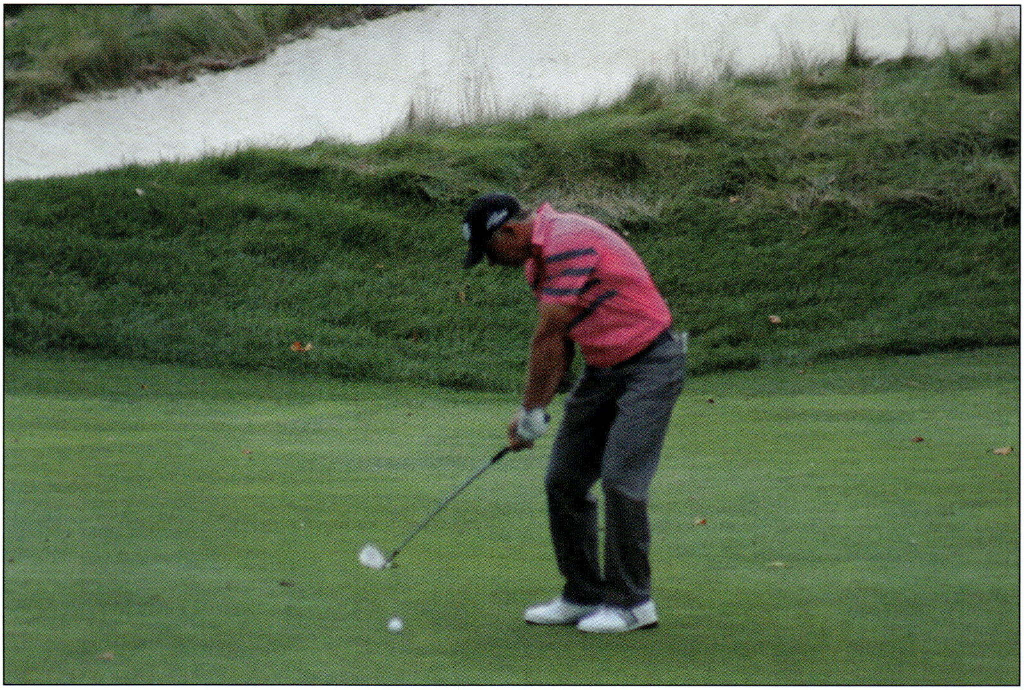

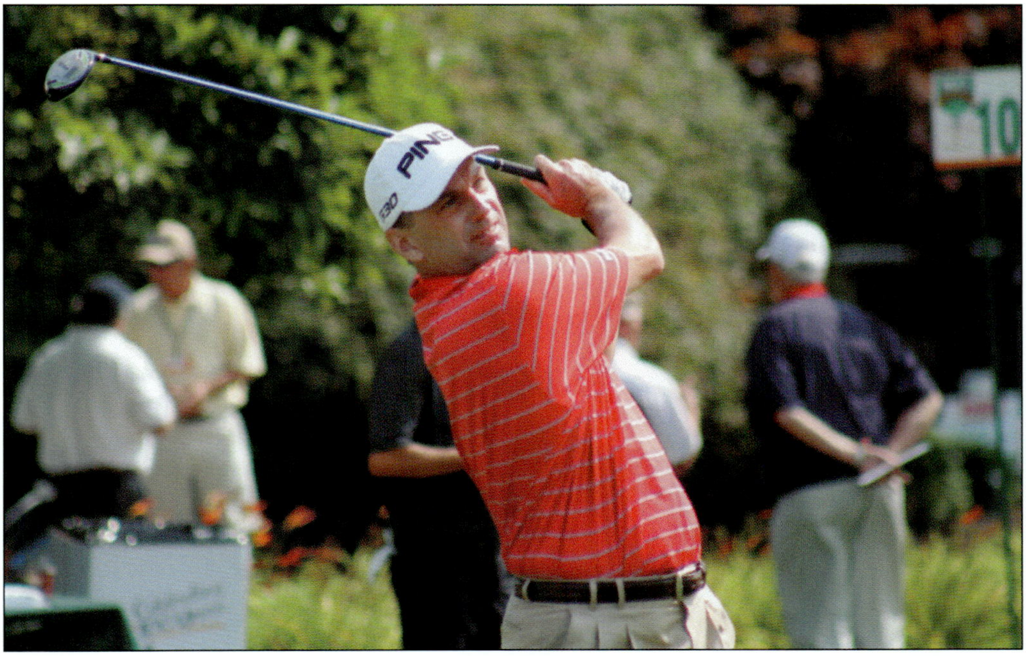

First Shot of 59. One cannot tell from Kevin Sutherland's reaction to his first shot of the day (above) on August 16, 2014, that he was about to make history. Sutherland shot an astonishing 59 on this pleasant Saturday afternoon in Endicott, becoming the first golfer on the Champions Tour to ever score so low. "Man, I wish I had shot 58!" was one of the first thoughts Sutherland had as he walked off the 18th green after bogeying the final hole. Sutherland gleefully explained to the media (below) that one can never be upset over a round of 59, and he knew he had a career day.

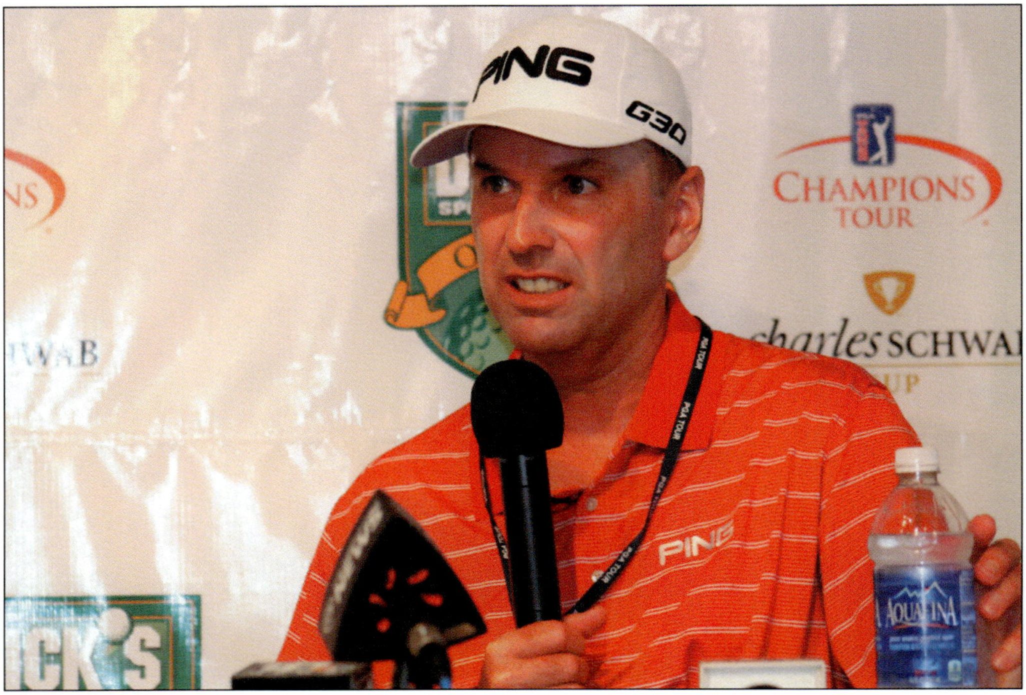

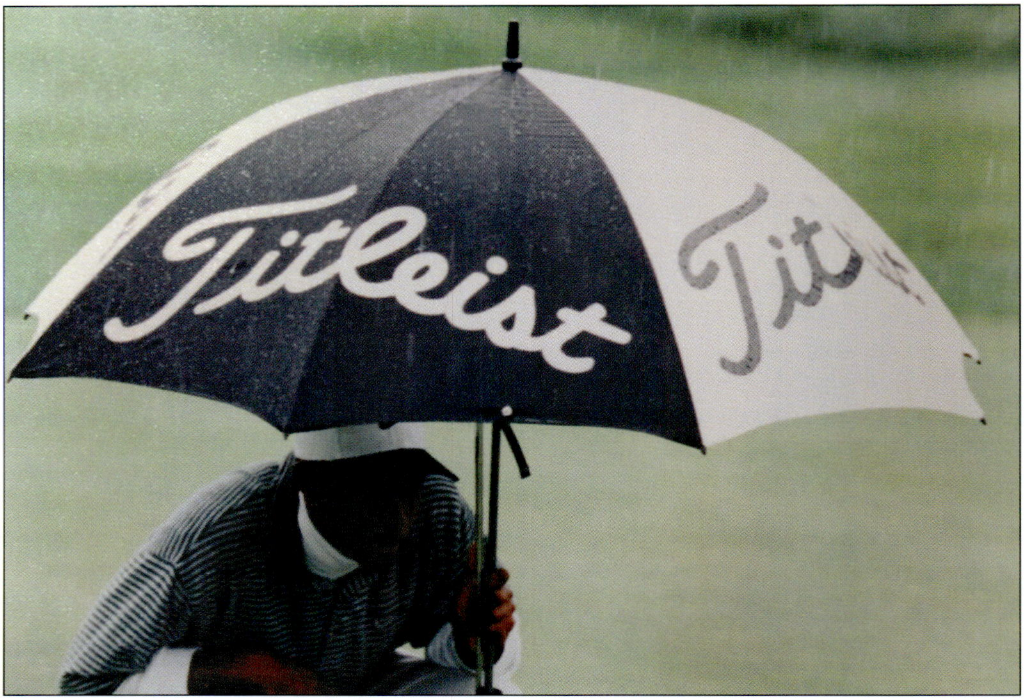

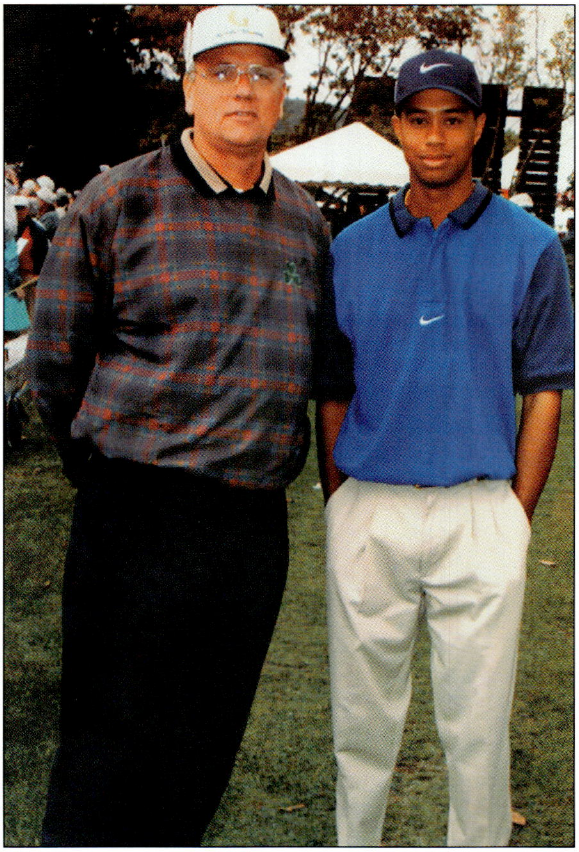

Before the Fame. Above, Tiger Woods lines up a putt in the mist in the 1996 BC Open. Woods shot a 68-66-66 in this rain-shortened tournament, finishing 13 under par for a tie for third place. This placed him three shots from the winner's circle, as Fred Funk won the tournament. At left, Woods poses with the tournament's director, Mike Norman. Woods has been ranked the number one golfer in the world at three different points in his career: from August 1999 to September 2004; from June 2005 to October 2010; and from March 2013 to May 2014.

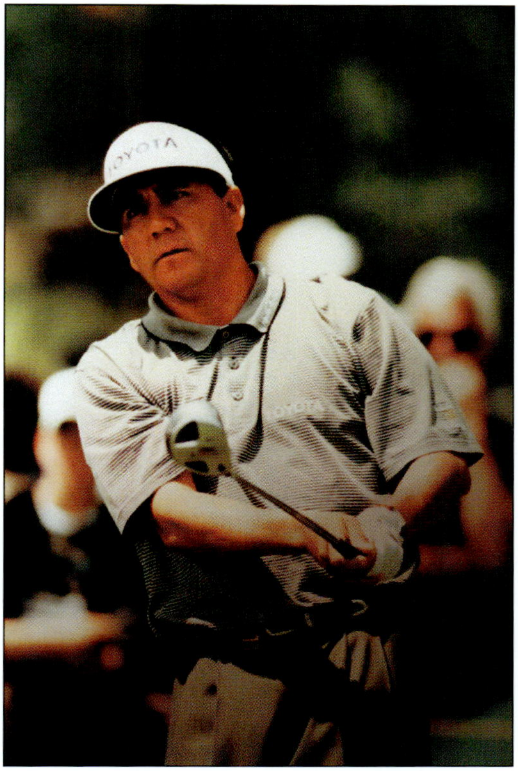

CHASING FAXON. Mexican golfer Esteban Toledo finished second at Endicott in 2000. Toledo and Brad Faxon entered the final day of the tournament in a tie, but Faxon (right) won by a single stroke as he shot a final round of 68. Toledo fell just short in attempting to win his first PGA event. Toledo never did get that PGA win, but he has won twice on the Champions Tour: the Insperity Championship in May 2013 and the Montreal Championship in September 2013. Below, he holds his daughter and waves to the crowd as he receives his second-place check.

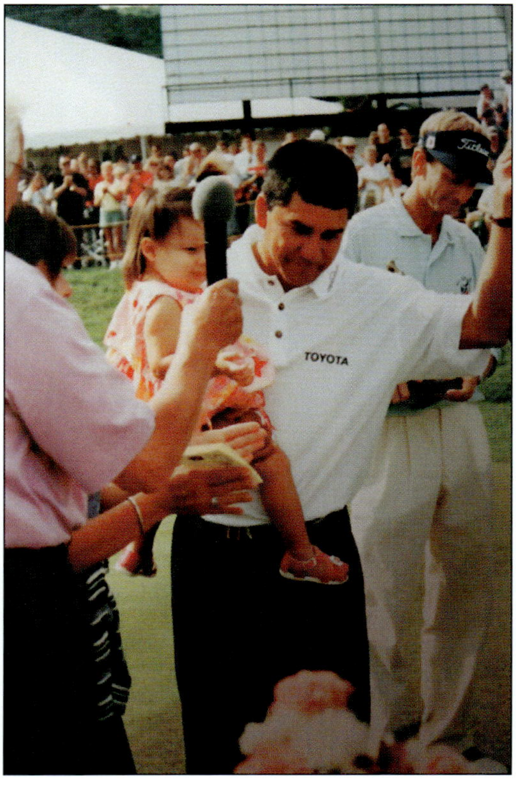

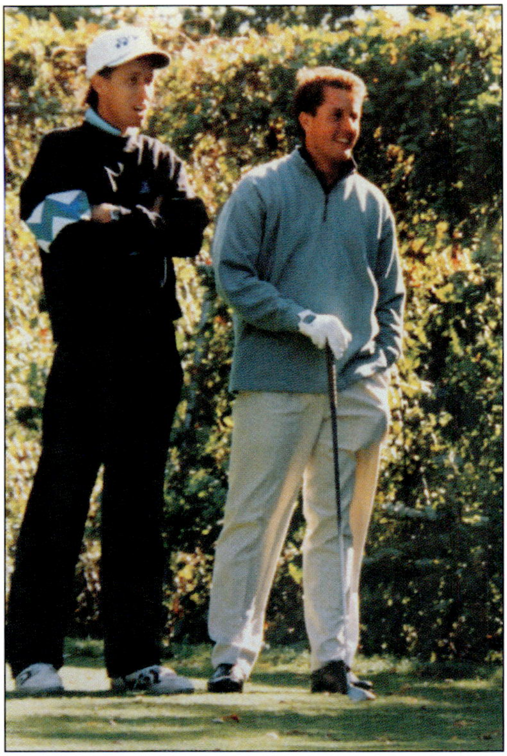

HALL OF FAME DUO. Among the legends of the game who played in Endicott but did not win are Phil Mickelson and Tom Watson. Mickelson (in the left photograph, at right) was born on June 16, 1970. He was inducted into the World Golf Hall of Fame in 2012 and is one of 16 golfers in the history of the sport to win at least three of the four professional majors. The only major that has eluded him is the US Open. Below, Tom Watson surveys the green at the 2012 DSGO. Both golf legends enjoyed their visits to En-Joie. Watson was inducted into the World Golf Hall of Fame in 1988. (Left, courtesy of BCHS; below, courtesy of BCCC.).

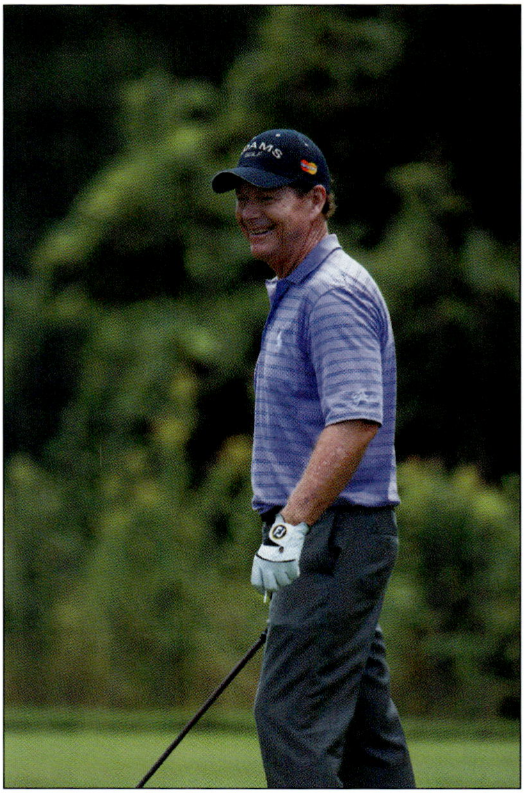

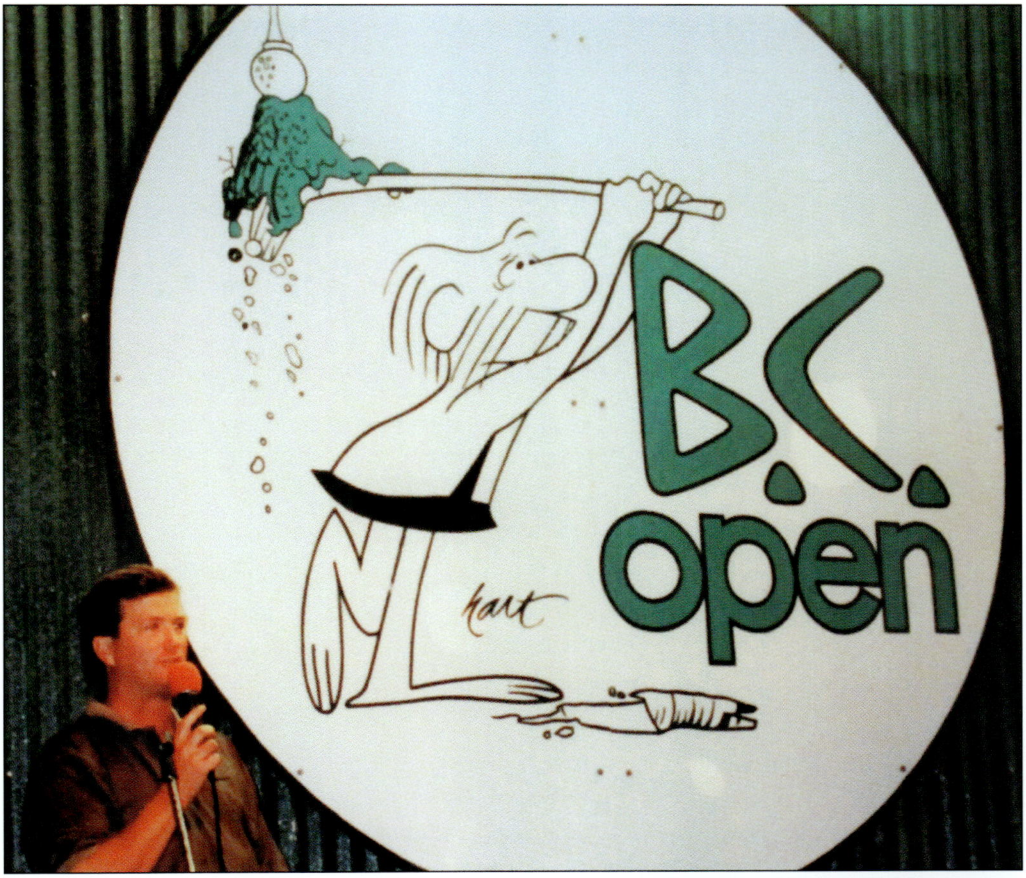

More than Golf. Above, Peter Jacobsen addresses golf fans at En-Joie in front of the BC Open logo. Jacobsen played himself in the movie *Tin Cup* and is also a popular golf commentator, using his sense of humor to good advantage. In the 1980s, he formed a rock group, Jake Trout and the Flounders, which also included Payne Stewart (right), who was an image of sartorial splendor not only at En-Joie, but at every stop along the PGA Tour. Stewart had 11 PGA wins before an airplane crash killed him at 42 in 1999. His Learjet reportedly suffered a loss of cabin pressure en route from Florida to Texas. (Both, courtesy of BCHS.)

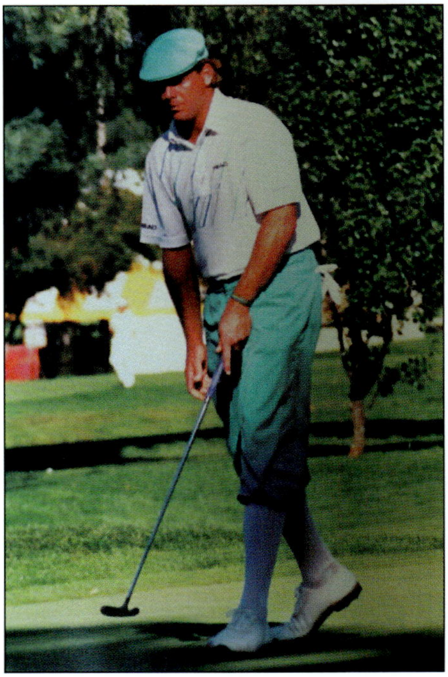

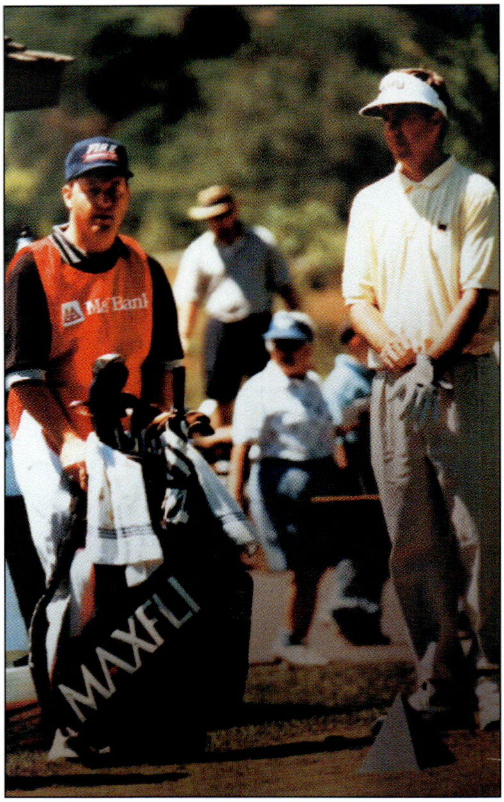

AUTHOR AS CADDY. At left, coauthor Mike McCann (left) caddies for Ted Schultz in 2000. After his PGA playing days were over, Schultz became director of golf instruction at the Cardinal Golf Club in Louisville. Below, Chip Beck shows that even the best golfer can carve up a golf course. Beck spent nearly 30 years on the PGA Tour, winning four tournaments. He has been on the Champions Tour since 2006.

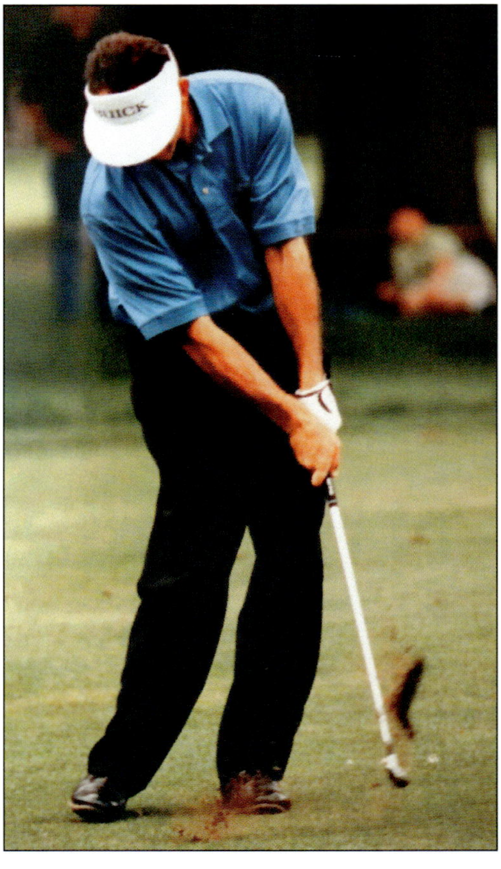

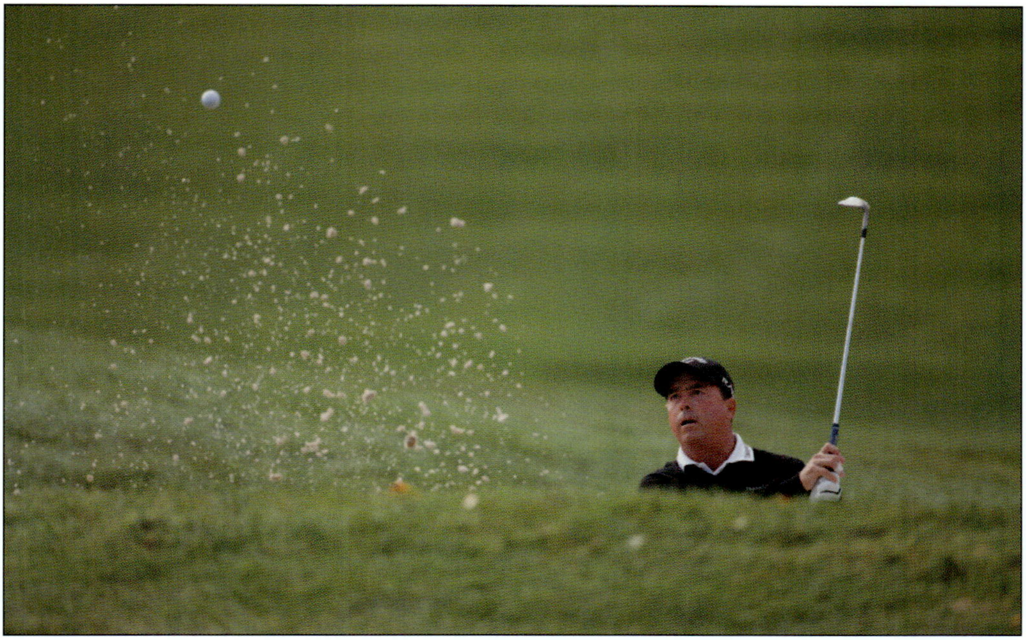

Welcome to the Beach! During the summer, the only people who do not want to be in the sand are golfers. Above, Olin Browne works his way out of a bunker at the DSGO. Browne registered three victories on the PGA Tour and one on the Champions Tour. Below, Kenny Perry looks to get back on course after an errant shot landed in a sand trap. Perry has won 14 PGA events and 7 senior circuit tournaments. In 2013, he received the Jack Nicklaus Trophy for the Champions Tour Player of the Year. (Both, courtesy of BCCC.)

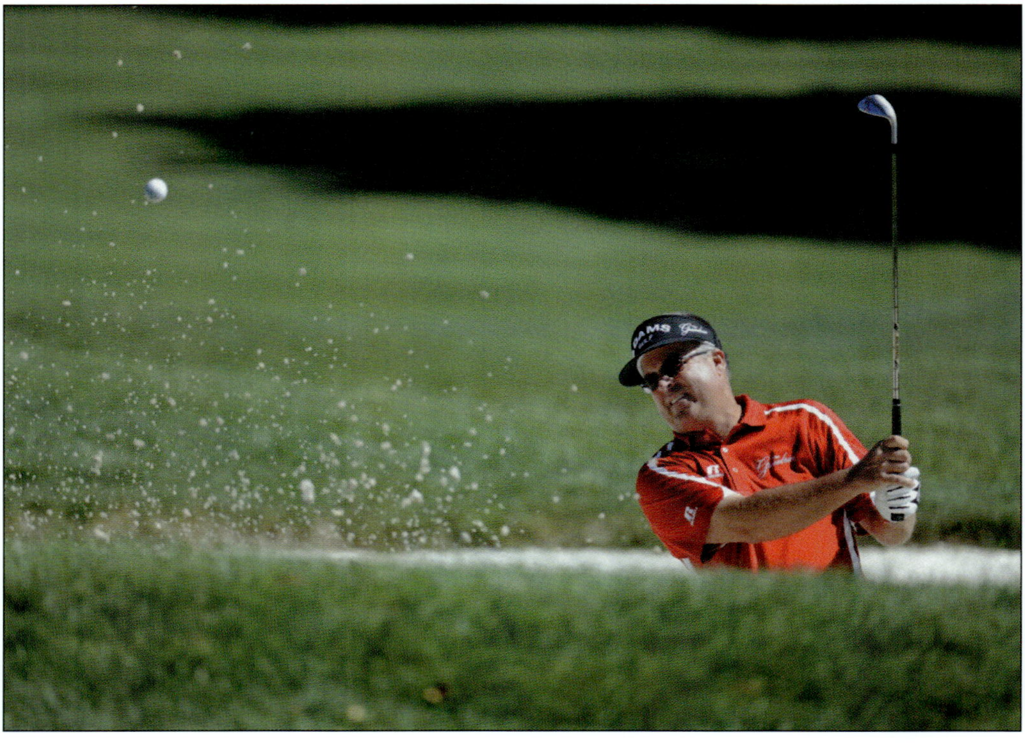

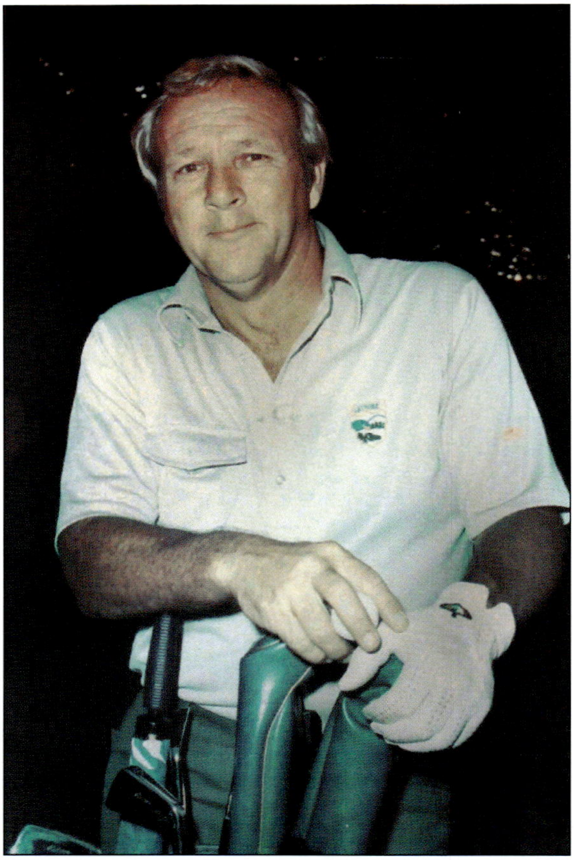

WHAT A CLASS! At left, Arnold Palmer poses for a photograph at the 1977 BC Open. Palmer and Gary Player were part of the World Golf Hall of Fame class of 1974, which included such legends as Ben Hogan, Walter Hagen, Bobby Jones, and Jack Nicklaus. Below, Gary Player's face lights up after sinking a putt during the 1976 BC Open. Noted local columnist Tom Cawley described Player as "looking exactly like the late Rod Serling—deeply tanned, dramatic profile, 5 feet 8 inches, with the wiry look that seems to conceal a coiled spring inside." (Left, courtesy of BCCC; below, courtesy of BCHS.)

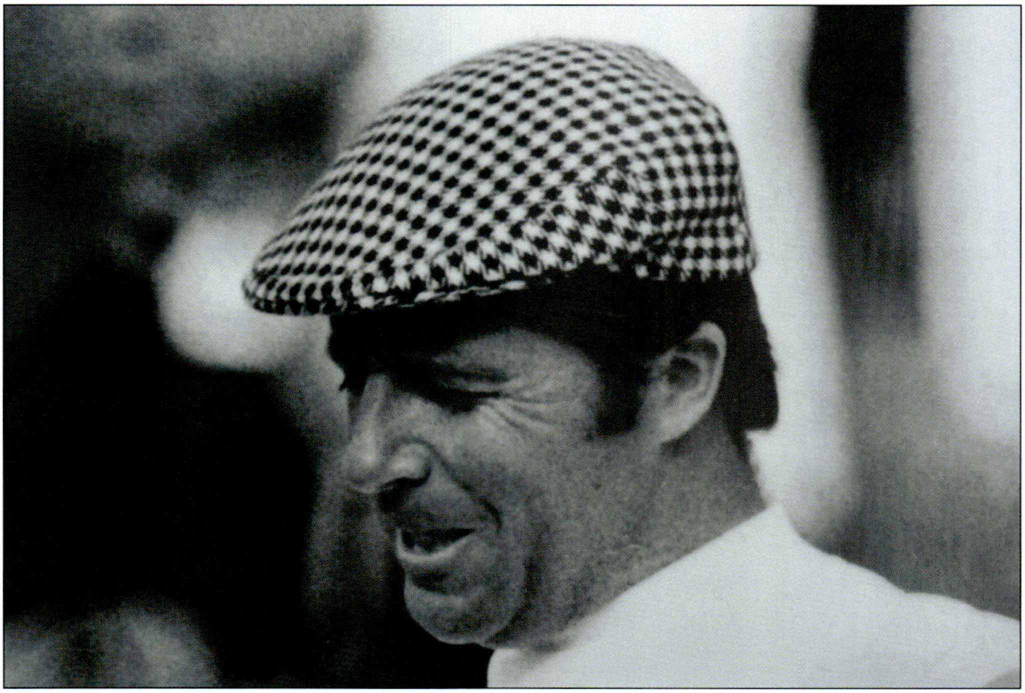

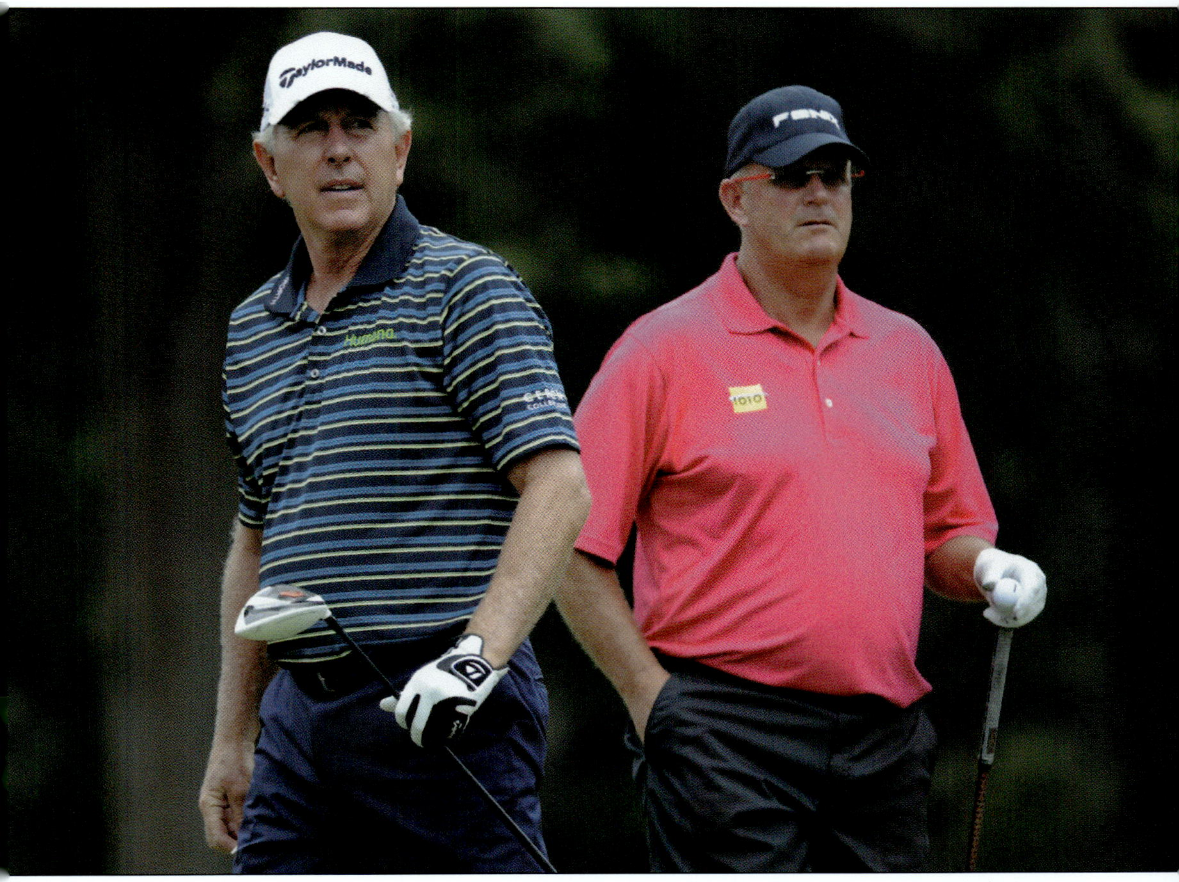

ANYTHING YOU CAN DO, I CAN DO BETTER! World Golf Hall of Fame members Hale Irwin (left) and Sandy Lyle (right) were paired at the 2014 Dick's Sporting Goods Open. Lyle became the first Briton to don the green jacket at Augusta when he finished one stroke ahead of Mark Calcavecchia at the 1988 Masters. He has 29 professional victories, including 18 European Tour and 6 PGA Tour wins. Hale Irwin, not to be outdone, has 87 professional wins, including 20 PGA victories and an unprecedented 45 wins on the Champions Tour. Irwin was inducted into the World Golf Hall of Fame in 1992; Lyle was inducted in 2012. (Courtesy of BCCC.)

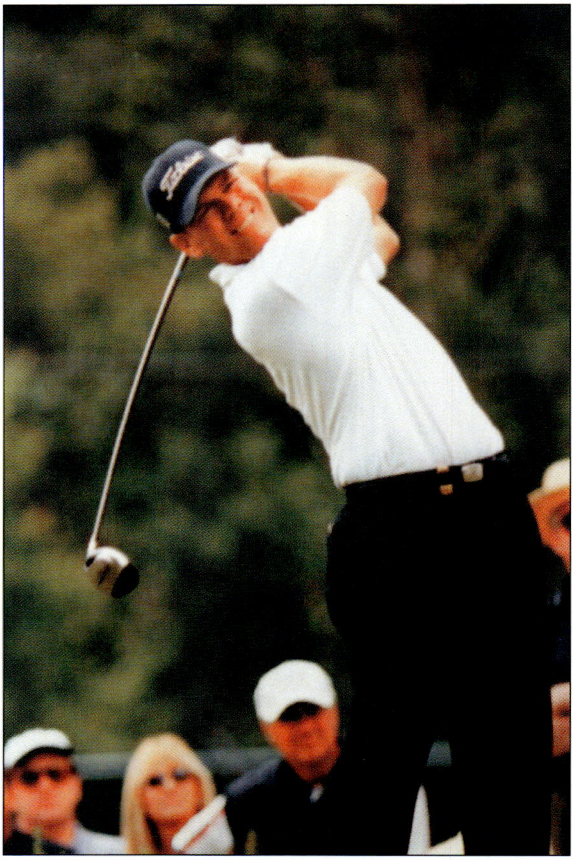

Dad, I Can Hit It Farther than You! Jay Delsing tees off in the 1980 BC Open. His father, Jim, was a major-league baseball player for 13 seasons. Delsing graduated from UCLA, where he was a teammate of fellow PGA Tour golfers Corey Pavin, Steve Pate, and Duffy Waldorf.

An EJ Sponsor. Even today, Bobby Clampett's curly locks make him an easily recognizable figure. Here, he gets ready to putt on the 18th green in the 2014 DSGO. Clampett played on the PGA Tour from 1980 to 1995, leaving the tour to take a job with CBS as a golf announcer, further enhancing his celebrity status. One of Clampett's earliest sponsors was the Endicott-Johnson Corporation.

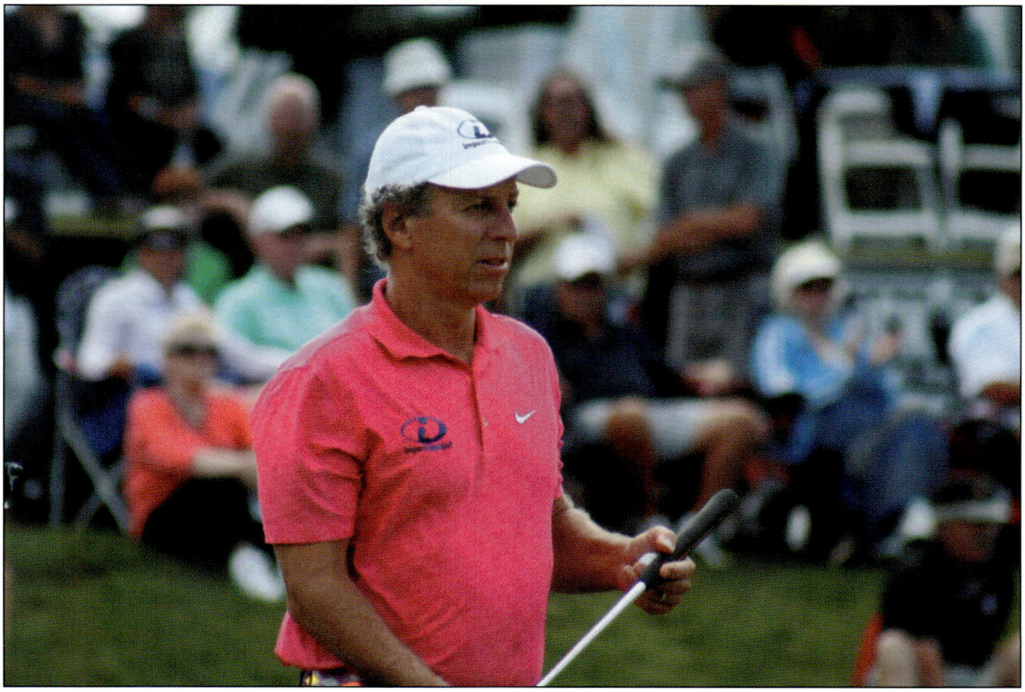

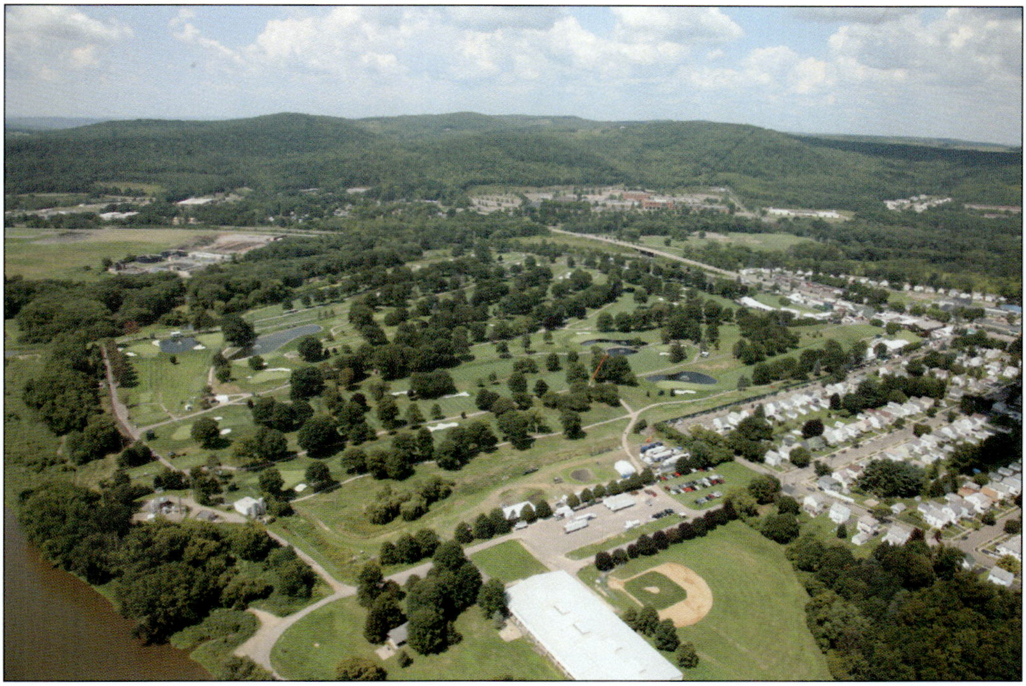

VALLEY OF OPPORTUNITY. One of the nicknames for Endicott and the surrounding community in the early 1900s was the "Valley of Opportunity," due to its being home to such companies as IBM and Endicott-Johnson. The above photograph shows the hills surrounding the golf course, as well as the Tri-Cities Regional Airport (upper left). Many golfers arrive in Endicott via their private jets (below). (Both, courtesy of BCCC.)

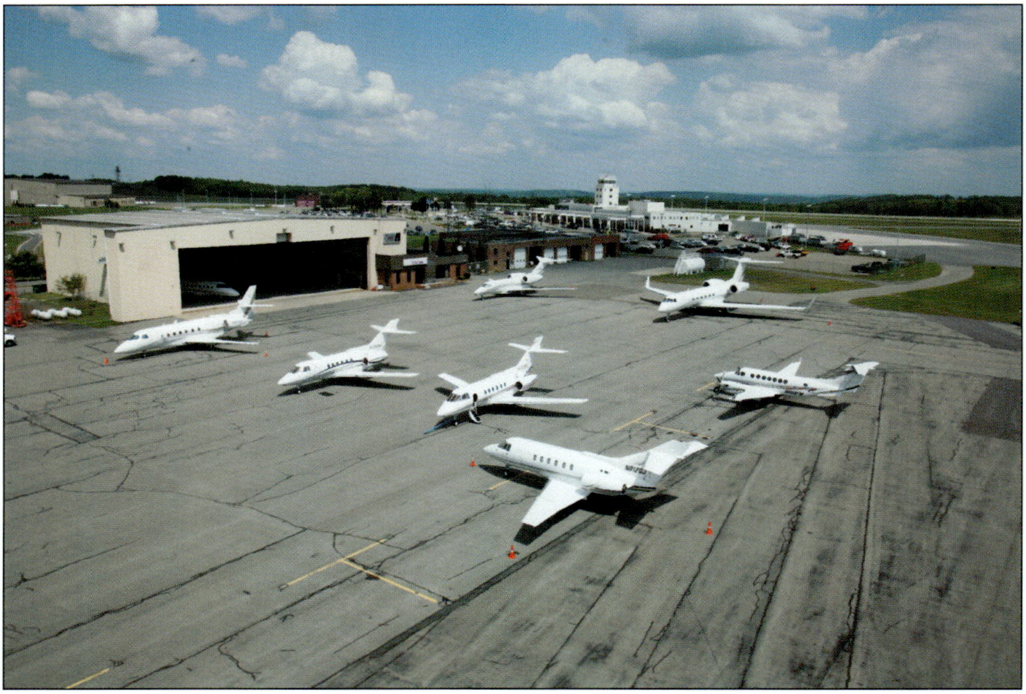

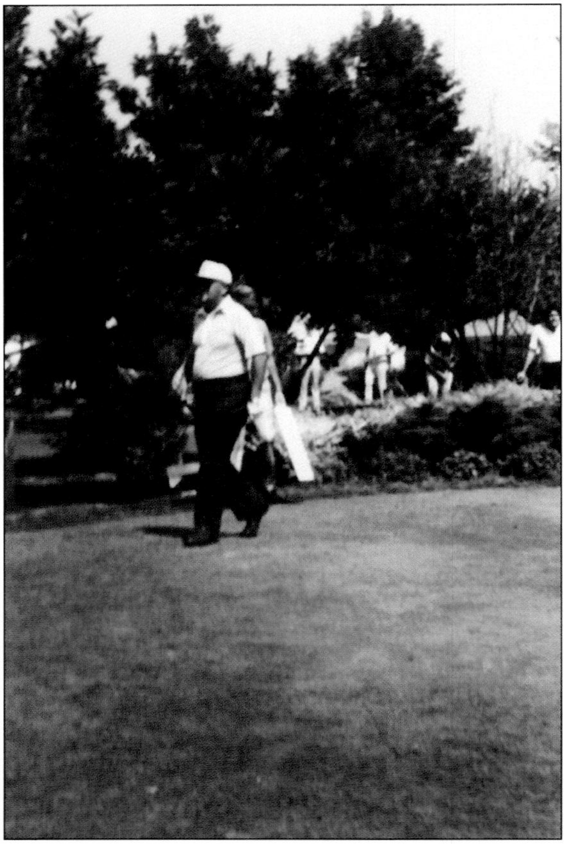

It's Miller Time! Miller Barber, seen walking along one of the holes at En-Joie, enjoyed success on both the PGA and the Senior PGA Tour (now known as the Champions Tour). His career spanned six decades, from 1958 through 2002. He accumulated 11 PGA and 24 Senior titles. (Courtesy of LH.)

Like Father, Like Son. Barry Jaeckel takes time to pose before starting his round at the BC Open in 1980. His father was the highly respected character actor Richard Jaeckel, known for his roles in *Sands of Iwo Jima* and *The Dirty Dozen*. Jaeckel's only PGA win came in 1978 at the Tallahassee Open. (Courtesy of LH.)

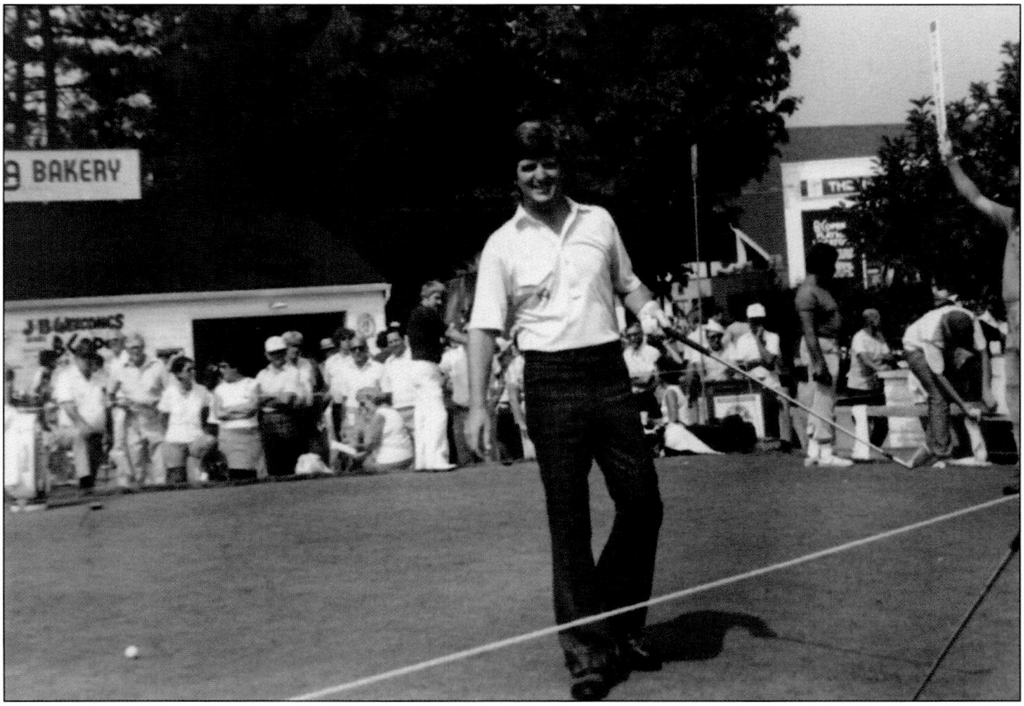

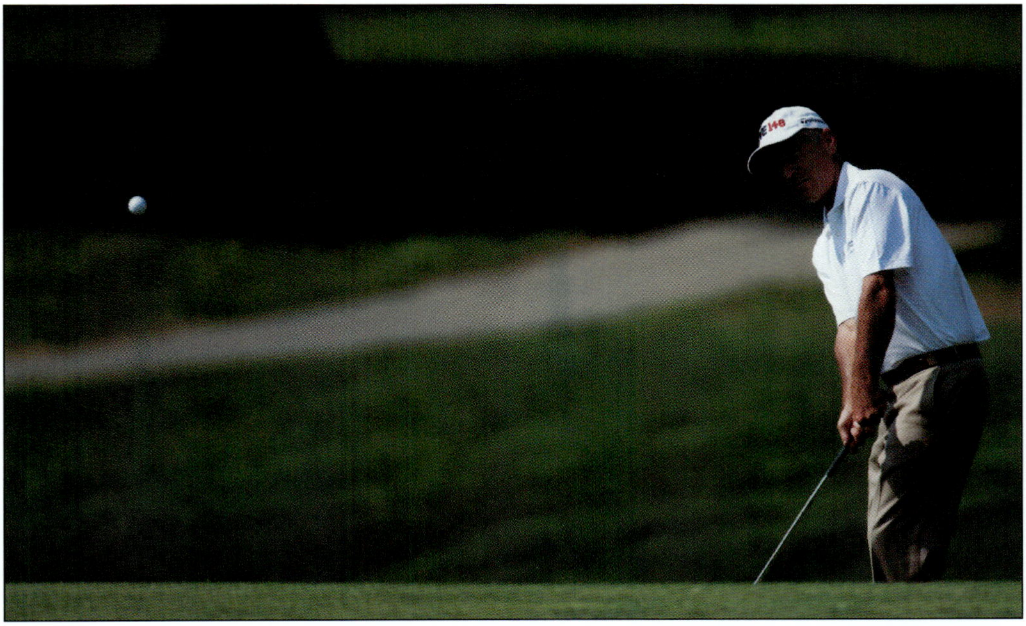

Fifteen and One. Corey Pavin chips onto the green in the 2012 DSGO. He joined the PGA Tour in 1984 and won 15 PGA titles, including the 1995 US Open, beating Greg Norman by two strokes. Pavin has one win on the Champions Tour, the Allianz Championship in 2012. (Courtesy of LH.)

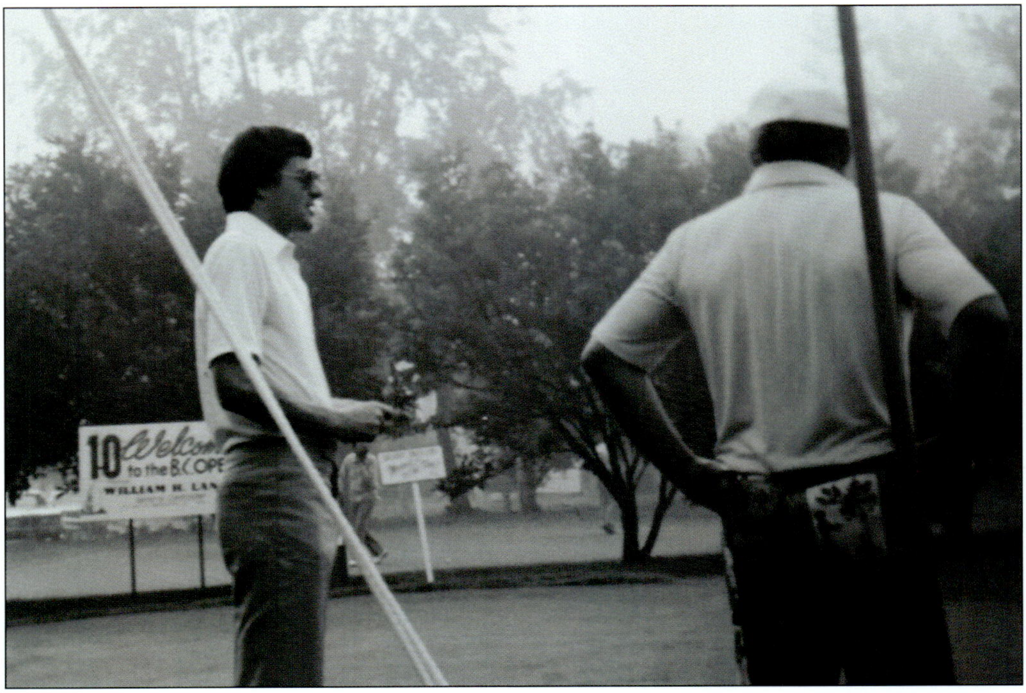

Play It Where It Lyes! Always a fan favorite, Mark Lye enjoyed an 18-year PGA career before retiring due to a torn ligament in his right hand. He became an analyst on the Golf Channel and played himself in the 1996 Adam Sandler movie *Happy Gilmore*. Hand surgery enabled Lye to play in selected tournaments on the Champions Tour. (Courtesy of LH.)

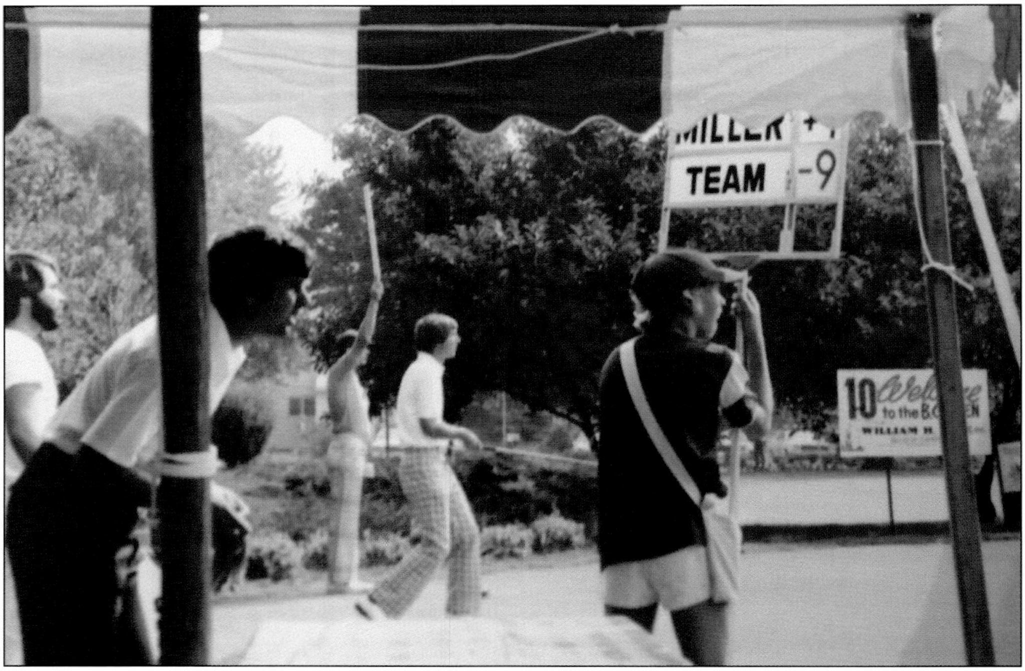

ACTION! The pro-am is always a fan favorite at any golf tournament. Lindy Miller, seen following his drive on the 10th hole, was just getting by at one over when he made this drive. Luckily for him, his team helped bail him out—they were nine under through the first half of the round. Miller later portrayed himself in the movie *Dead Solid Perfect*, which starred Randy Quaid. (Courtesy of LH.)

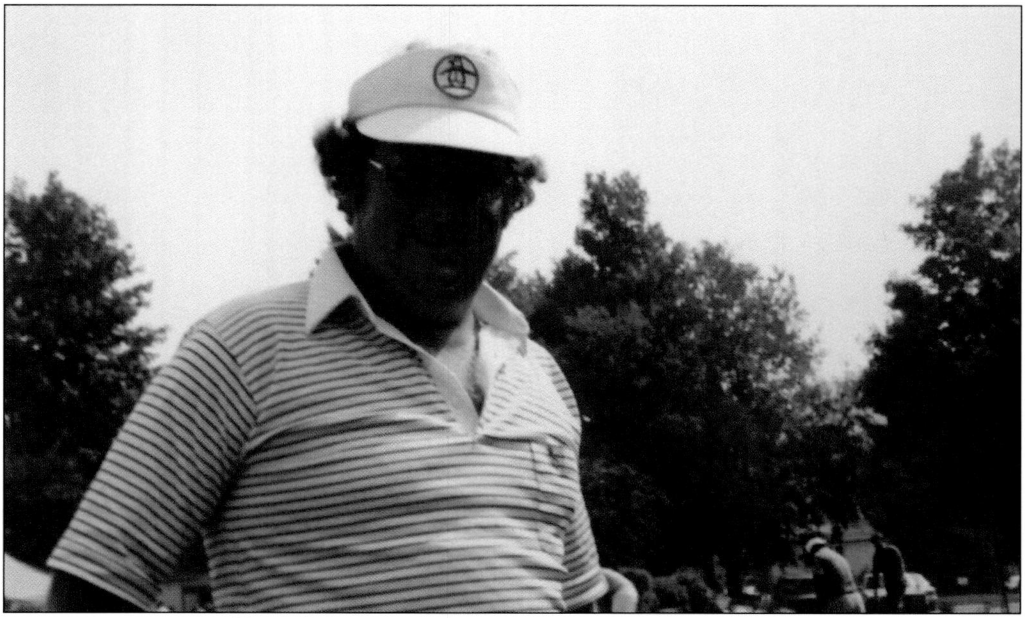

A HAPPY RECAP? Golfer Bob Murphy was a superb high school pitcher, leading his school to a state championship. This was not his only link to baseball, however. He had the same name as the New York Mets' beloved broadcaster, who always followed a Mets win with the words, "Now for the happy recap." (Courtesy of LH.)

Four

Beyond the Golf

Throughout the history of En-Joie, the golf tournaments have involved more than just golf, with a host of special events accompanying the headlining golfers. These special treats have formed an eclectic and varied bouquet of activities, including billiards and pro-am tournaments, as well as shoot outs, in which a group of golfers compete on a hole-by-hole basis. The high scorer drops out until only the winner remains. There have also been charity auctions, women's golf clinics, and drawing workshops by nationally syndicated cartoonists. In many years, the most-anticipated complement to golf has been the annual concert on Friday night, held just off the 18th green.

This chapter features some of these activities, showing the Endicott community during its leisurely hours. These pages provide portraits of En-Joie in its finest colors, whether under the afternoon's cerulean skies or the periwinkle softness of twilight, as thousands wait for the stage's rainbow-colored spectrum of lights at the 18th green.

The chapter begins with some celebrity name-dropping, then continues with special events that foreshadow the concert. Next, the concerts are featured. Following this, the chapter includes an inspirational message or two, before ending with a note of thanks to the staff of the BCCC. The name-dropping starts with guests at the pro-am events, including Joe DiMaggio, Mickey Mantle, Bob Hope, the Smothers Brothers, and billiards player Johnny Archer. The list of performing musicians is also an impressive one.

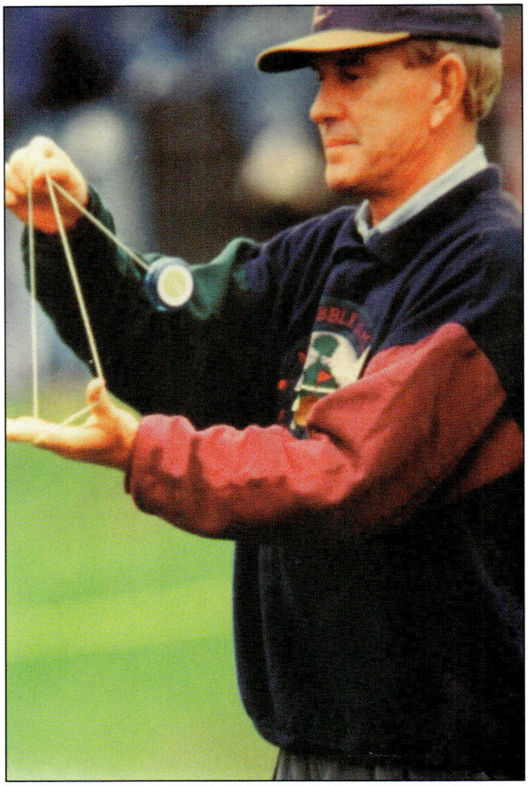

Yo-Yo Man! In 1993, the Smothers Brothers entertained the En-Joie denizens while playing in the pro-am. They took part in two contests at the King is a Fink event, the shoot-out and the short shot. At left, Tommy Smothers works his magic with a yo-yo. When his chip shot fell short of the green, "Yo-Yo Man" took his trusty Duncan out of his pocket and flung it onto the green to within three feet of the hole. Below, he works his Yo-Yo for the crowd during the pro-am. (Both, courtesy of BCHS.)

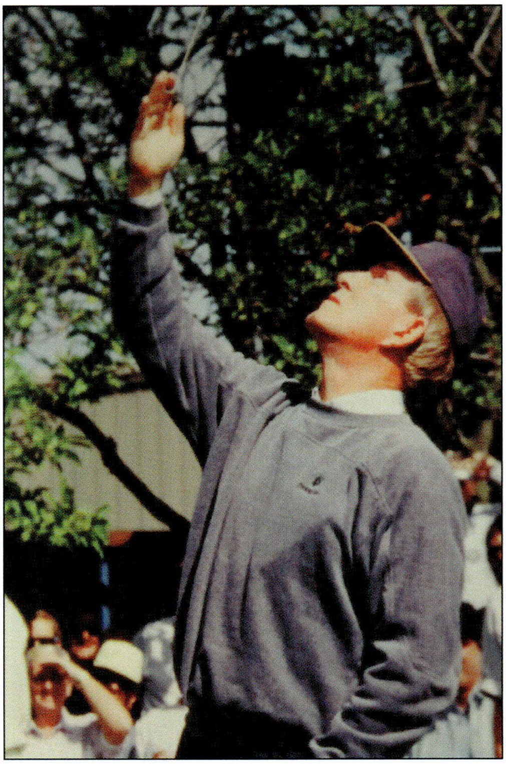

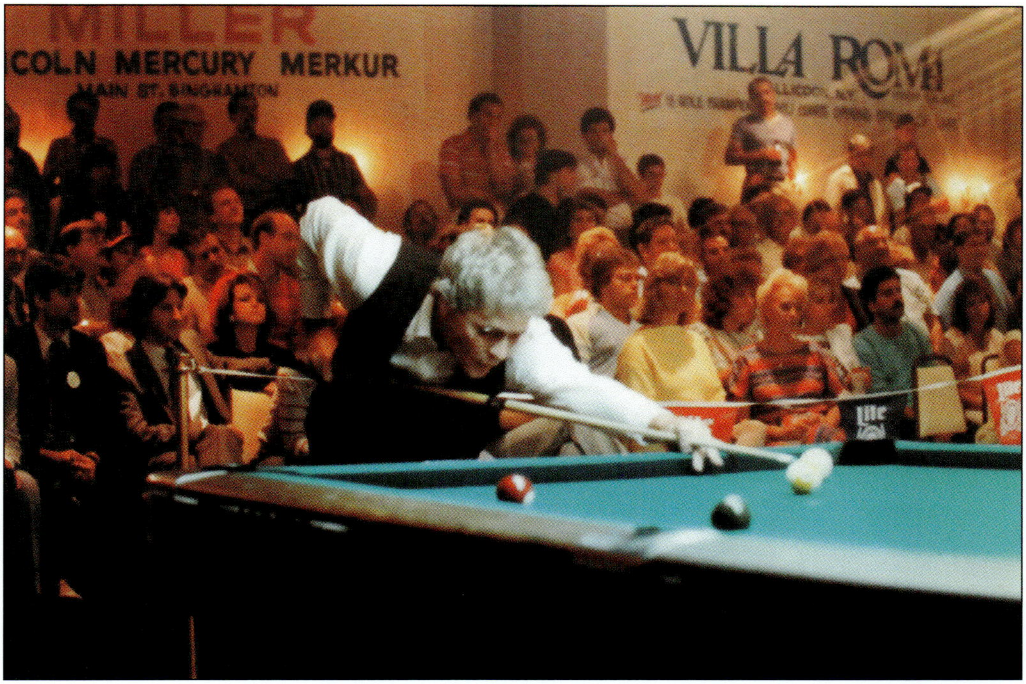

"Hey Thor, 8-ball, Corner Pocket!" Above, cartoonist, golf fan, and Endicott native Johnny Hart lines up a shot during the BC Open 9-Ball Tournament. The event was a regular part of BC Open week from 1985 to 1990. It was usually played at the Holiday Inn Arena in Binghamton and featured famous billiard players. Below, Johnny "The Scorpion" Archer takes aim during a recent 9-ball tournament at the Turning Stone Resort and Casino. In 1989, Archer took part in the annual BC Open 9-ball tournament and helped capture the pro-am division title with PGA golfer Rod Curl. (Above, courtesy of BCHS.)

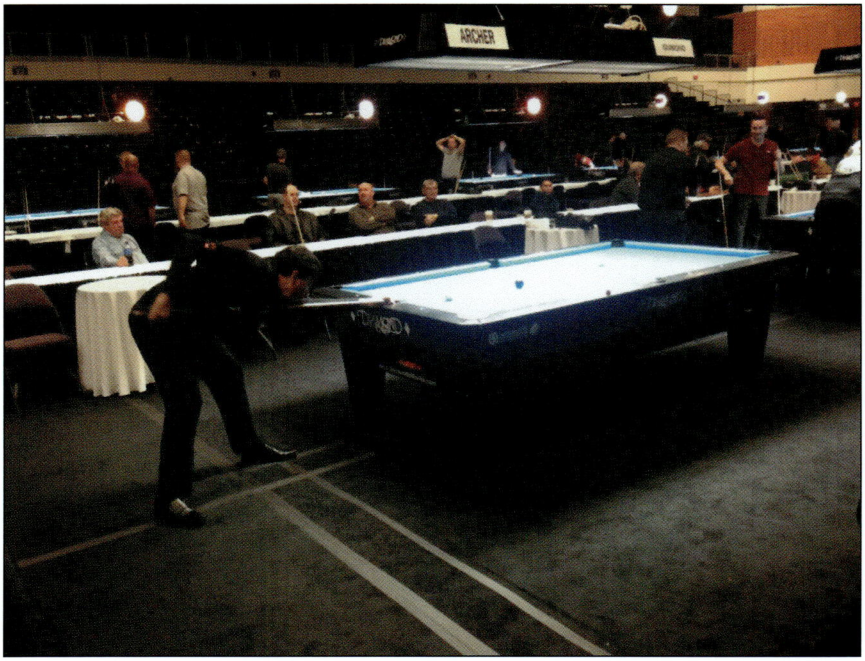

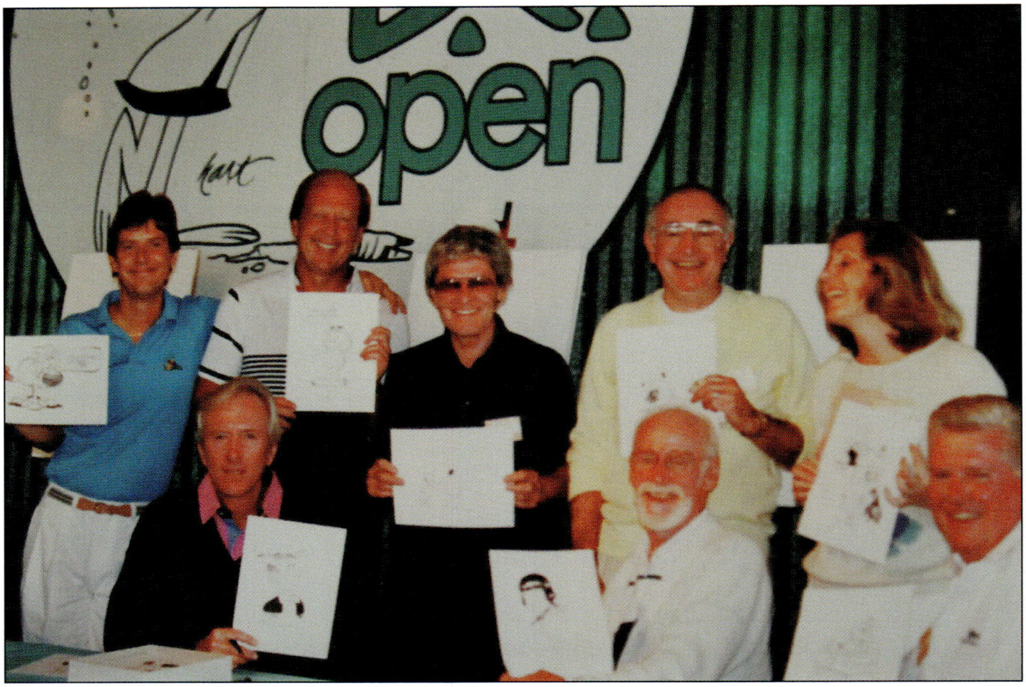

CARTOONIST'S CORNER. Cartoonists often demonstrated their skills as part of the week's activities for the BC Open. Shown here are, from left to right, (front row): Dean Young (*Blondie*), John Cullen Murphy (*Prince Valiant*), and Frank Johnson (*Boner's Ark*); (second row) Mike Peters (*Mother Goose and Grimm*), Jim Davis (*Garfield*), Johnny Hart (*B.C.*, *Wizard of Id*), Brant Parker (*Wizard of Id*), and Lynn Johnston (*For Better or For Worse*). (Courtesy of BCHS.)

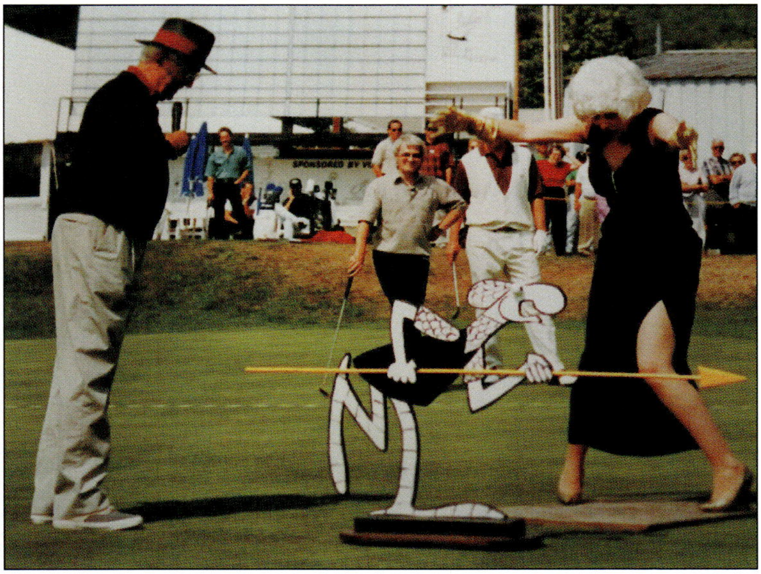

KEEP THOSE HEELS OFF THE GREEN! Nationally syndicated cartoonist Lynn Johnston, creator of *For Better or for Worse*, does her best Marilyn Monroe impression during the short shot contest at the King is a Fink event. Here, Johnston clowns around with tournament director Alex Alexander. (Courtesy of BCHS.)

The Pen Is Mightier than the Club! Endicott native Jack Caprio played every year in the annual shoot-outs. He was primarily a writer for the comic strip *B.C.*, collaborating with illustrator Johnny Hart. Caprio also assisted on the *Wizard of Id* with Johnny Hart, Brant Parker, and Dick Boland. (Courtesy of BCHS.)

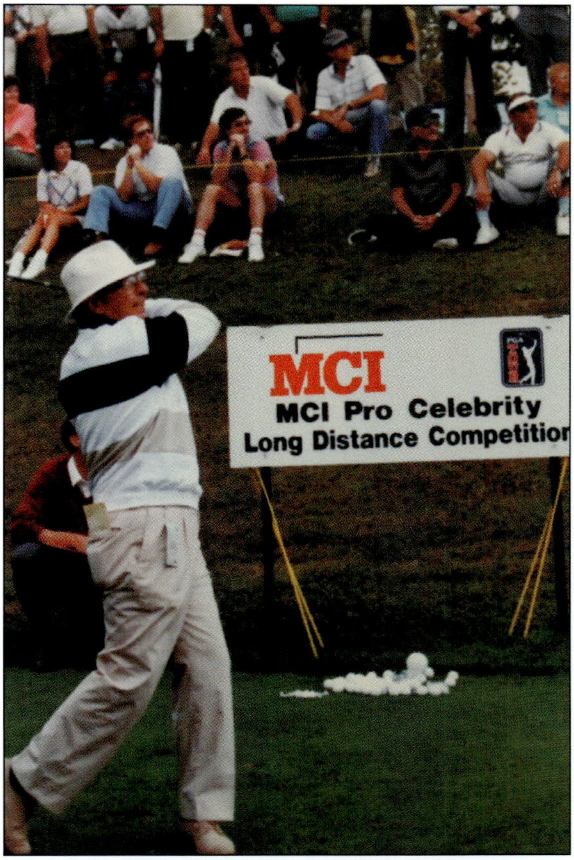

The Prince has Arrived! John Cullen Murphy grew up a neighbor of Norman Rockwell. When Hal Foster decided to cut back his work on *Prince Valiant*, he turned to Murphy to take over the strip. Murphy was a regular at the annual King is a Fink event at the BC Open. (Courtesy of BCHS.)

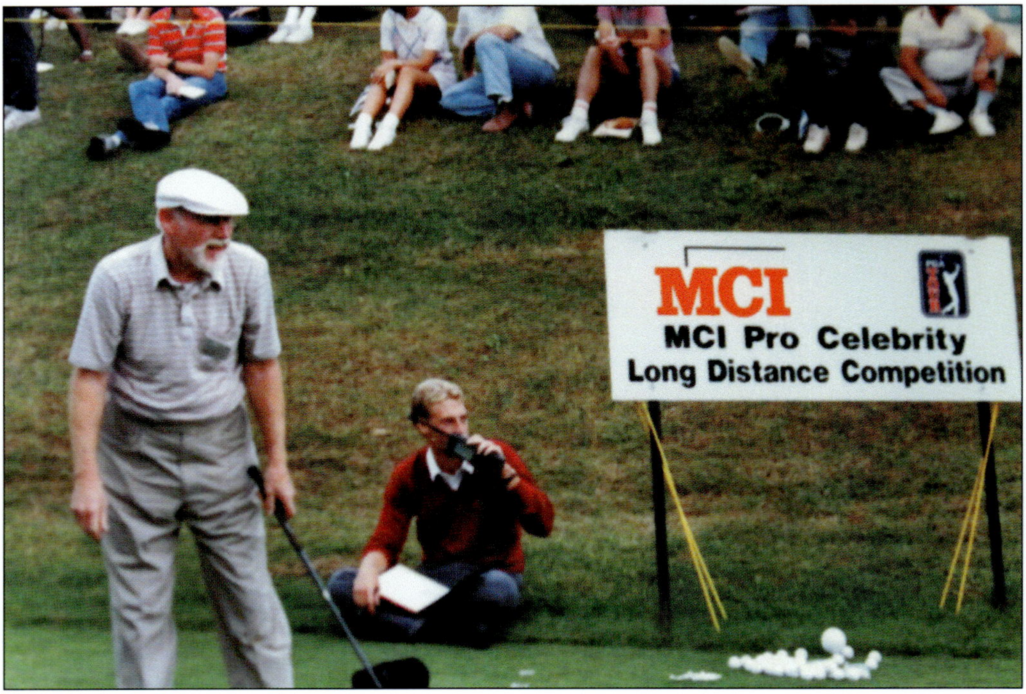

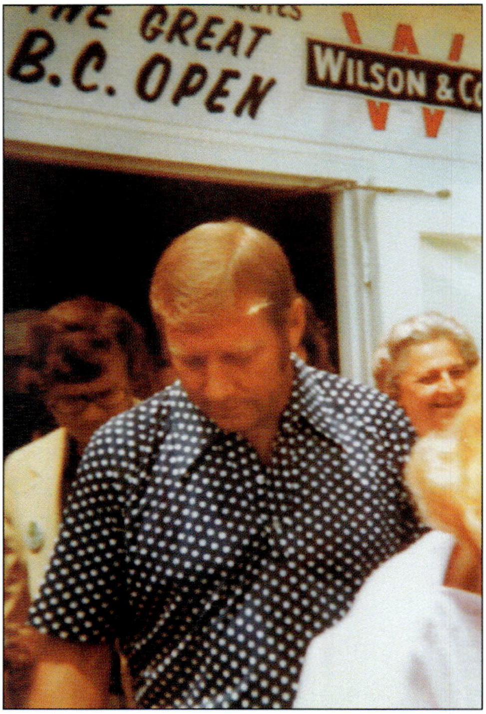

The Mick! En-Joie was graced with the presence of Mickey Mantle and Joe DiMaggio in 1974. (DiMaggio had to cut short his stay due to the death of Dizzy Dean.) Mantle played in the pro-am in the same year he was inducted into the National Baseball Hall of Fame. Here, Mantle works his way through the crowd. (Courtesy of FM.)

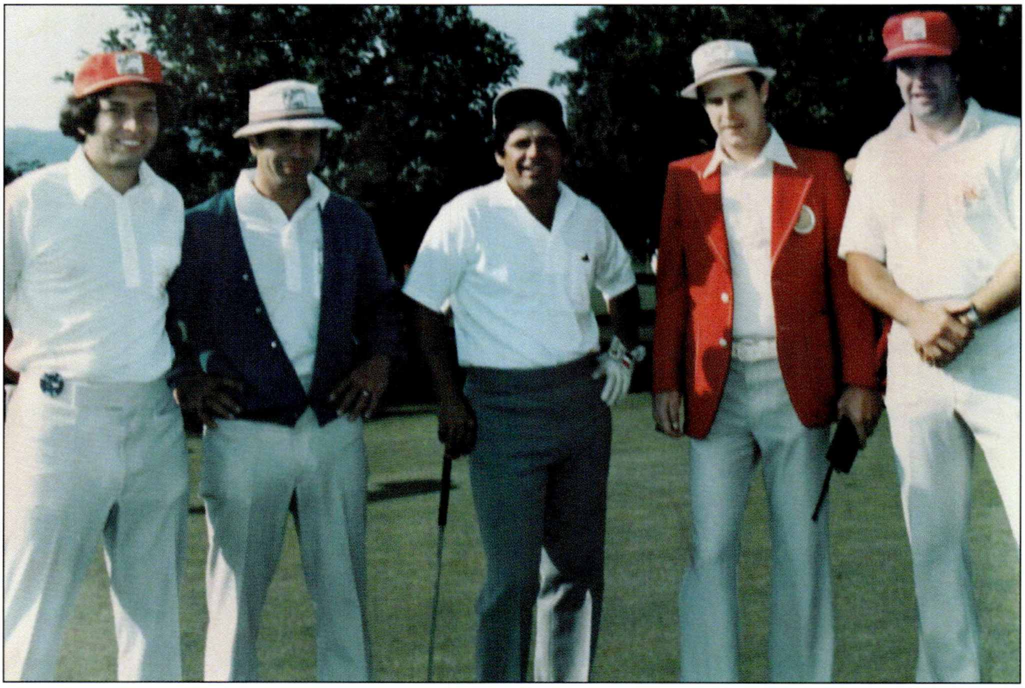

Gallery of Laughter! While playing in one of the BC Open pro-ams, Lee Trevino (center) was paired with Father Quinn from Our Lady of Good Council church in Endicott. When Quinn paused to line up a putt, Trevino said, "Hey, Padre, if you put in a good word with the big guy upstairs to make my back stop hurting, I'll guide that putt in for you!" As expected, the gallery burst out laughing. (Courtesy of FM.)

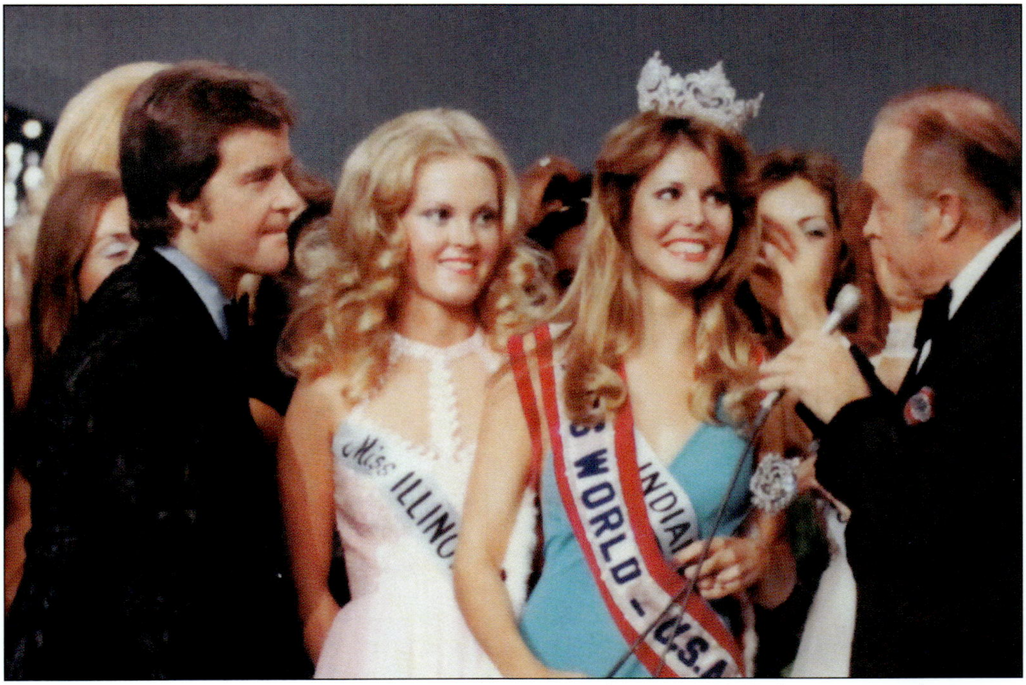

WHERE THERE'S HOPE, THERE'S LAUGHTER! On September 20, 1973, Bob Hope was the master of ceremonies for the Miss USA competition for the Miss World Beauty Pageant, which was held at the Broome County Arena as part of that year's BC Open. Above, Hope has just crowned the smiling winner, Indiana's Marji Wallace, as Dick Clark and Miss Illinois look on. A day earlier (below), Hope posed with some fans at the pro-am, where he played with PGA great Lee Trevino and Bishop Francis Harrison of the Syracuse Diocese. When Hope's approach shot went 40 feet past the flag on No. 11, he asked for help from someone "upstairs" and suggested the bishop use his influence. Hope then drained the long and winding putt and immediately yelled, "It's a miracle!" (Both, courtesy of BCHS.)

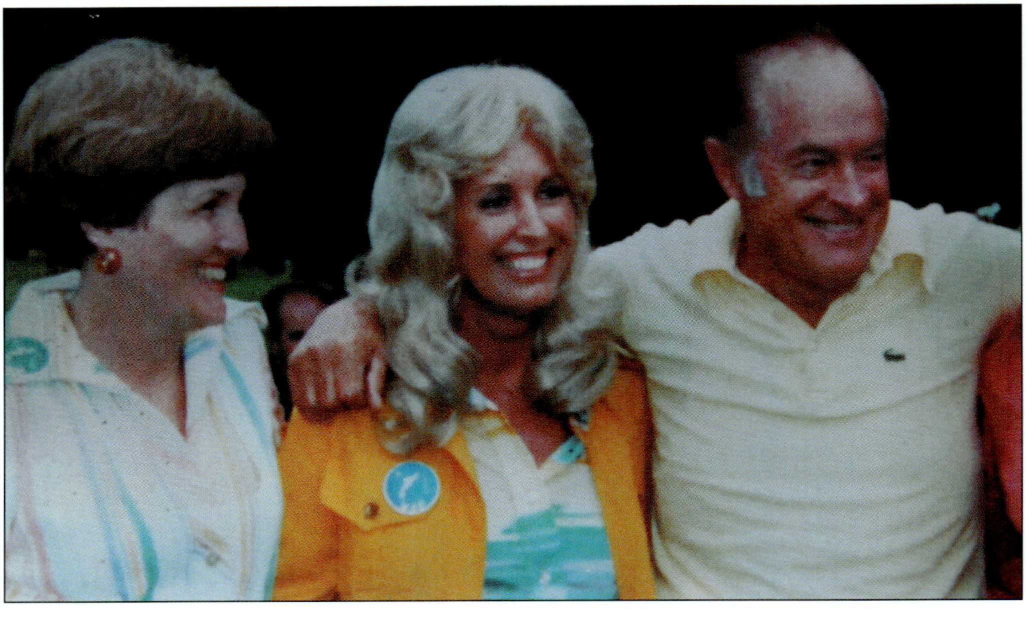

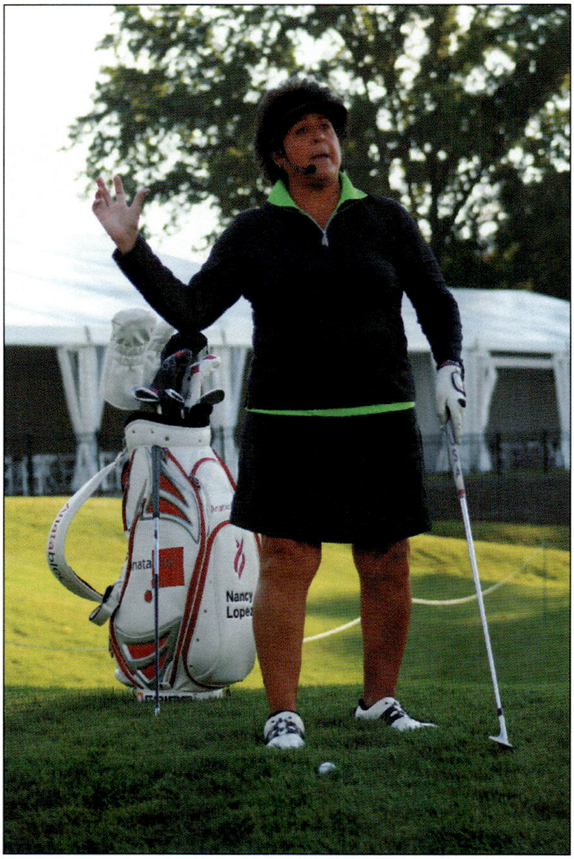

Pearls of Wisdom. For the past several years, Hall of Fame golfer Nancy Lopez has hosted a "Pearls of Wisdom" session for women before the start of the tournament. Lopez provides guidance for life both inside and outside the ropes during this session.

Women in Rapt Attention. The "Pearls of Wisdom" session, typically sponsored by United Health Services, is part of the pretournament package of events. During her session in 2014, Nancy Lopez said she actually gets excited when she winds up in the bunker. "It's all about attitude," exhorted Lopez. "When things are going bad, focus on the upcoming shot and look at it as an opportunity for the good things to come!"

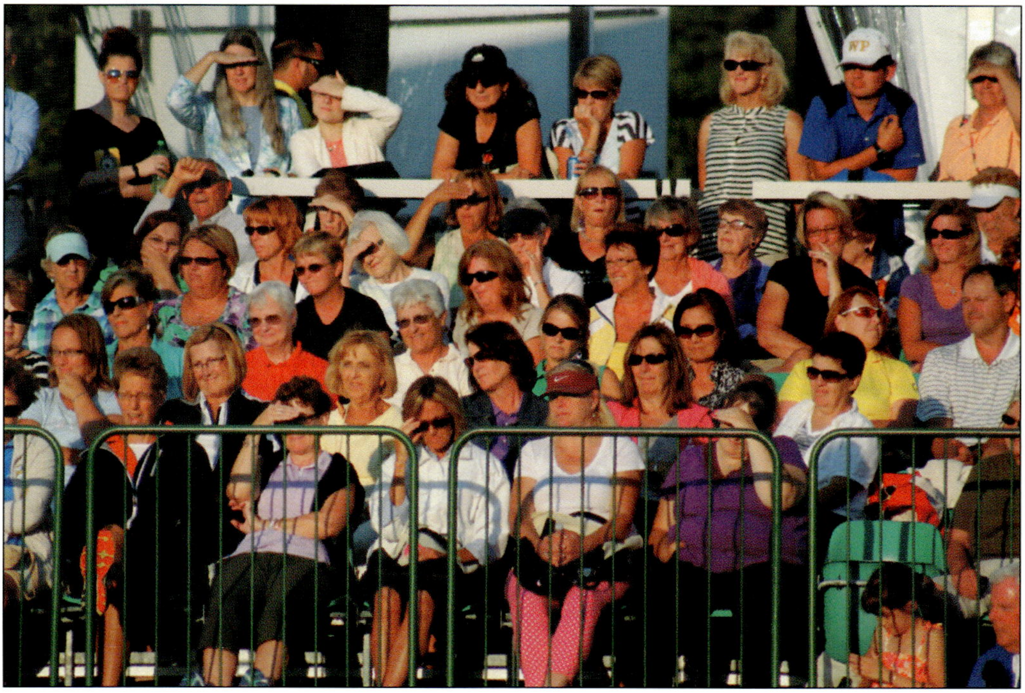

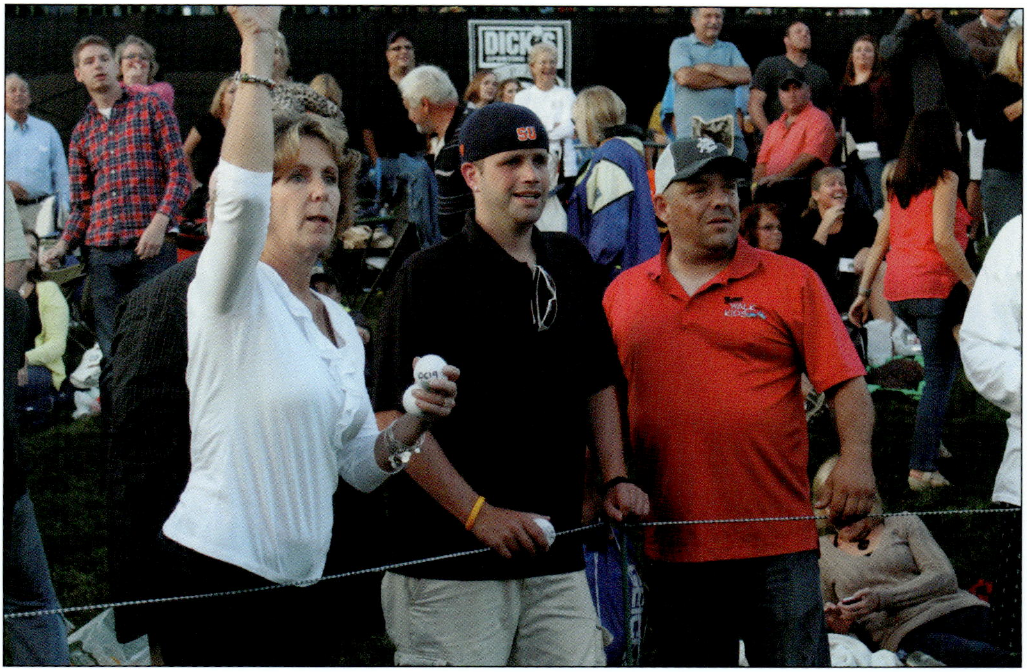

Pitching to Win. Between the first round of golf and the concert on Friday night, the Wendy's Sponge Golf Ball Toss is held on the 18th green. Participants purchase sponge golf balls, write their names or other identifying marks on them, and try to get a "throw in one" into the cup for various prizes.

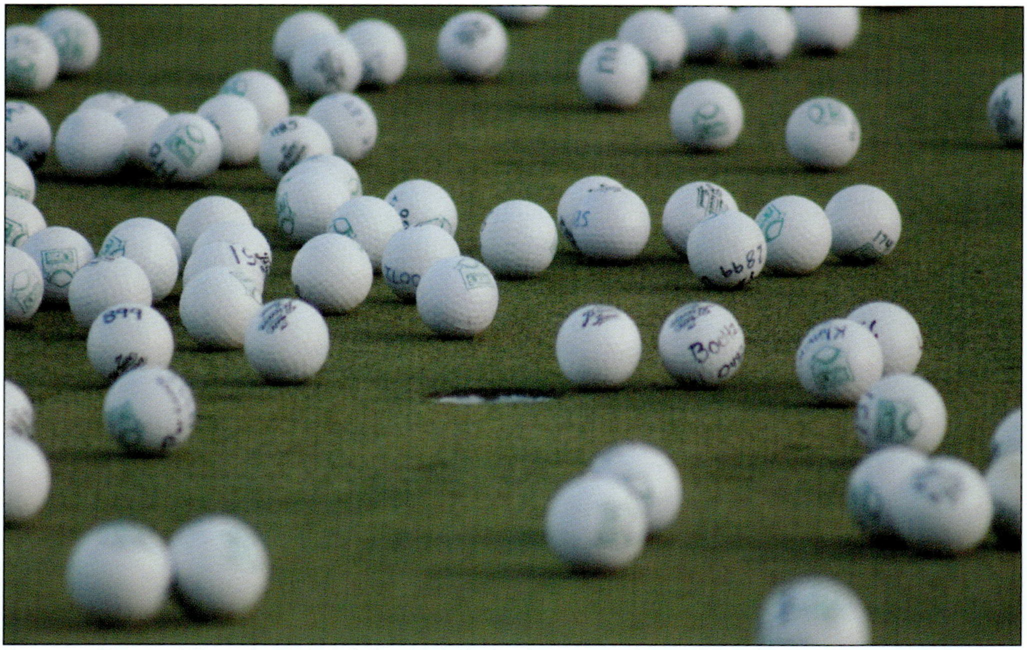

On the Brink. This close-up of the 18th hole shows just how close the tosses get to the cup! The name on the ball that lies in the second-closest position to the cup can be made out. The "rain of golf balls" on Friday night is a great way to entertain the fans as they patiently await the concert.

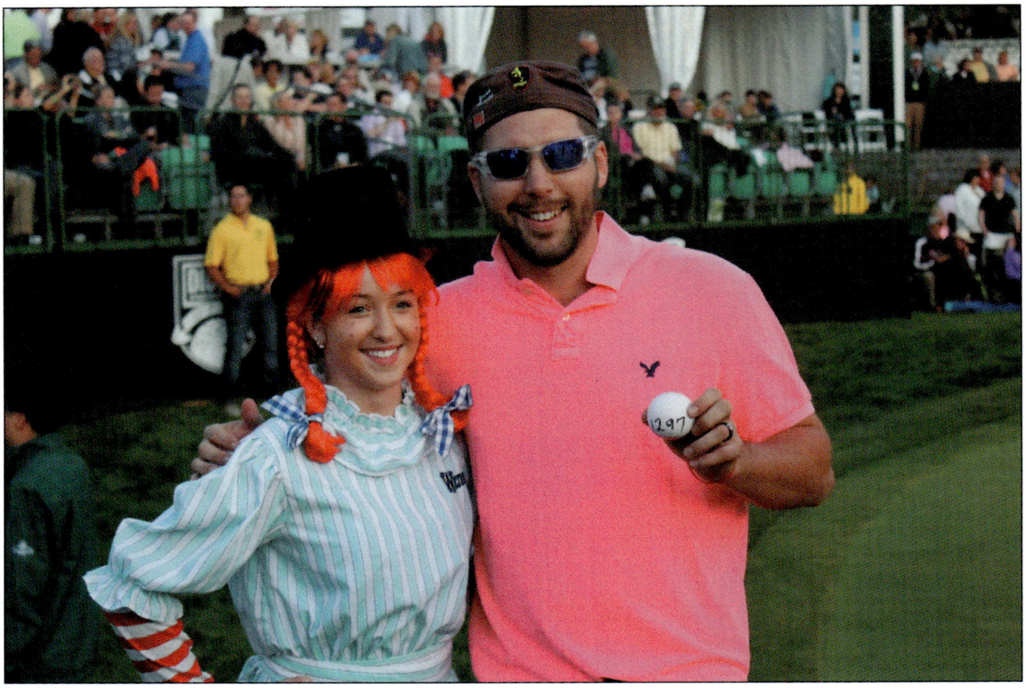

Smiling Wendy's Winners. Above, Chris Hand, from Whitney Point, is all smiles as his toss went right into the cup. His prize was a spot in the 2015 pro-am. Below, Jackie Boeltz from Binghamton won $100. This was an "off year" for her, as, twice before, she won $1,000 in the toss. Boeltz has become a bit of a local celebrity at this event, as participants ask her to toss their golf balls onto the green!

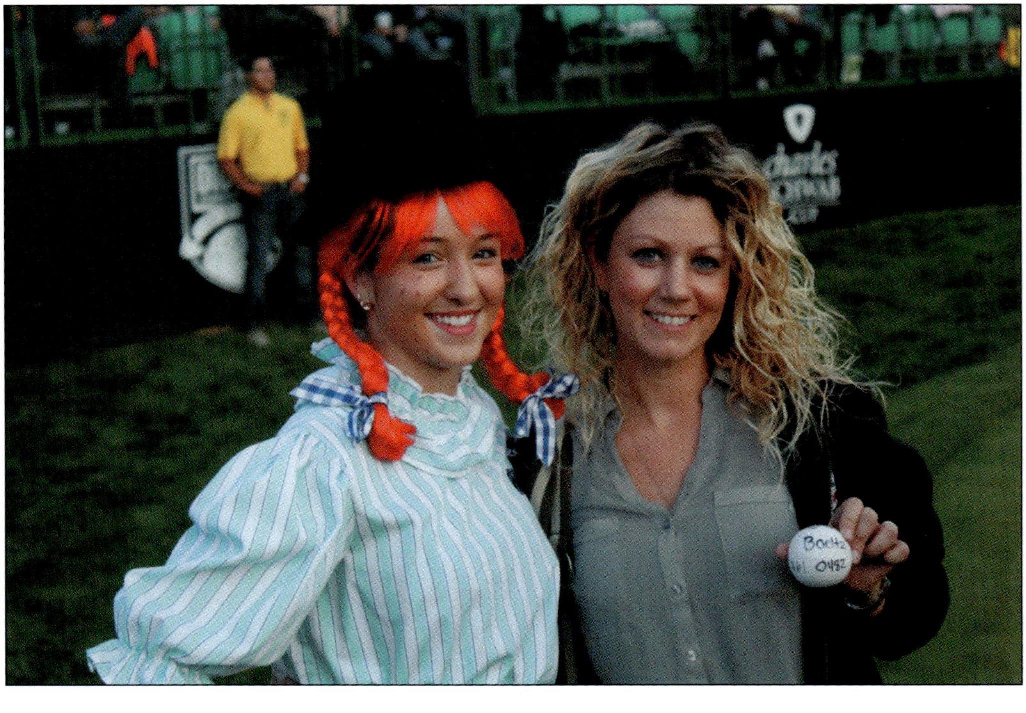

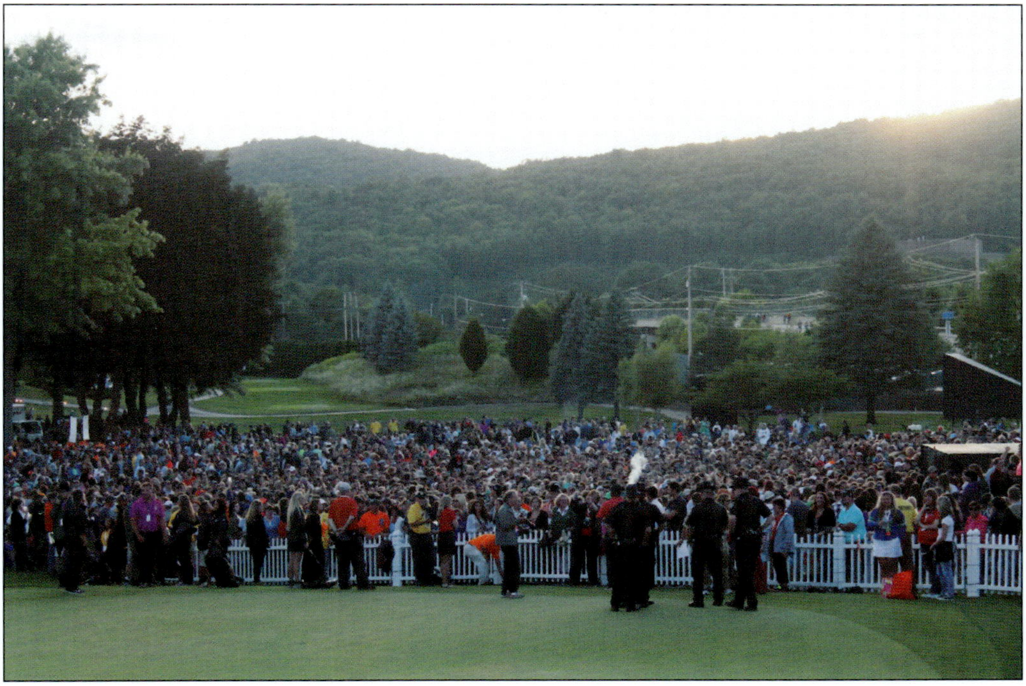

Everyone off the Green. Above, a white picket fence keeps concertgoers off the green as they line the fairway and surround the 18th hole in anticipation of the Zac Brown Band taking the stage. Shown below is a view of the same fairway as it looked throughout tournament play. Michael Allen (left, in red shirt) and Rick Fehr (right, in white shirt) survey the fairway as they and their caddies approach the green.

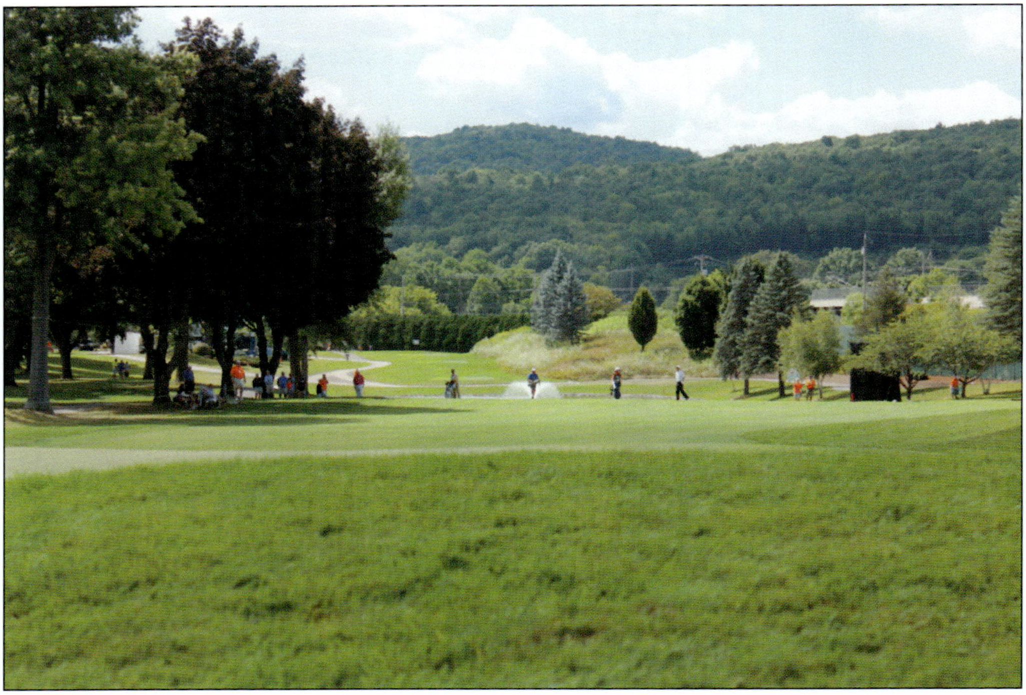

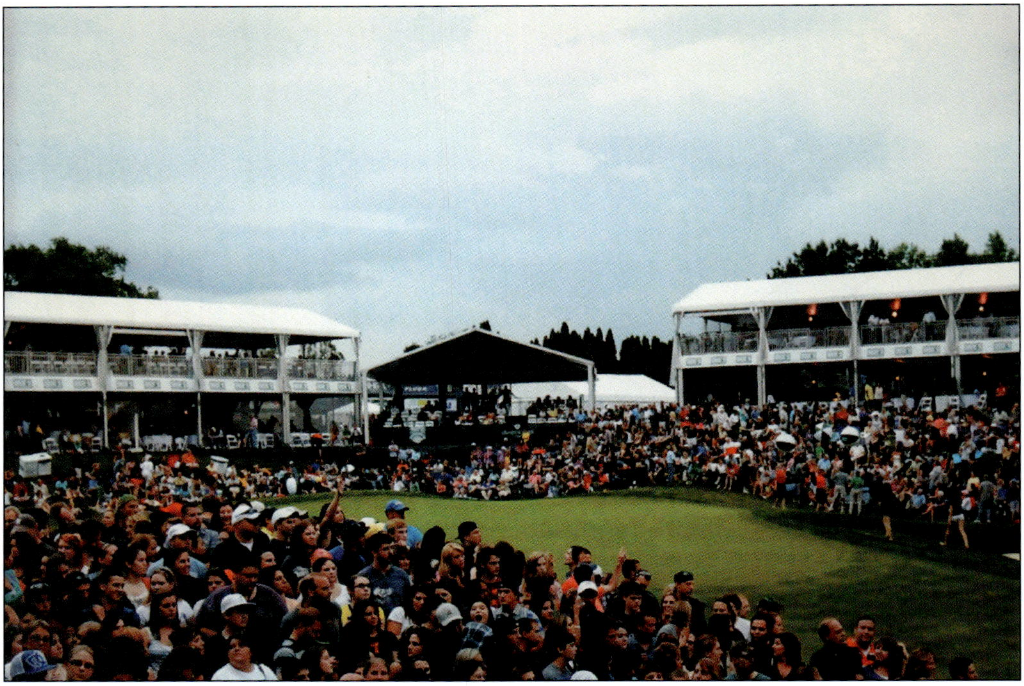

"Exit, Stage Left!" Above, during the day, the crowd awaits the start of the concert. Below, the skyboxes and VIP tents are lit up for fans to enjoy comfortable seating and catered parties. The denizens of the fairway have to negotiate for elbow room and hope the lines are not too long for beer and the bathroom. (Both, courtesy of BCCC.)

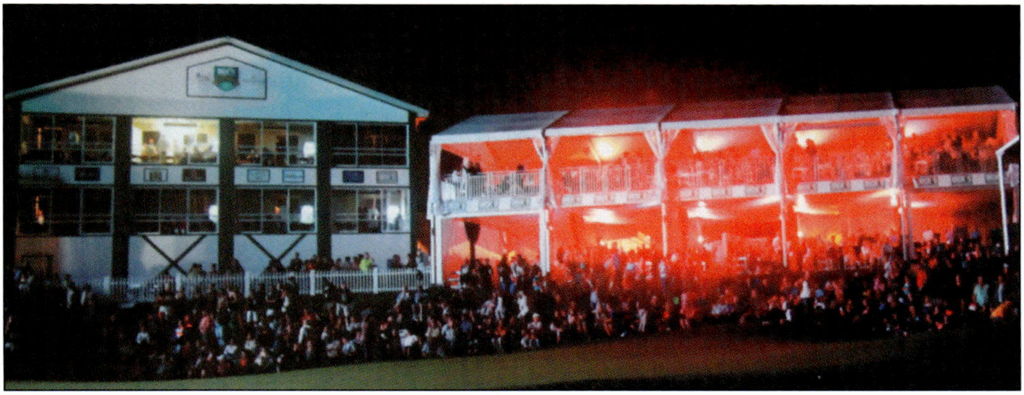

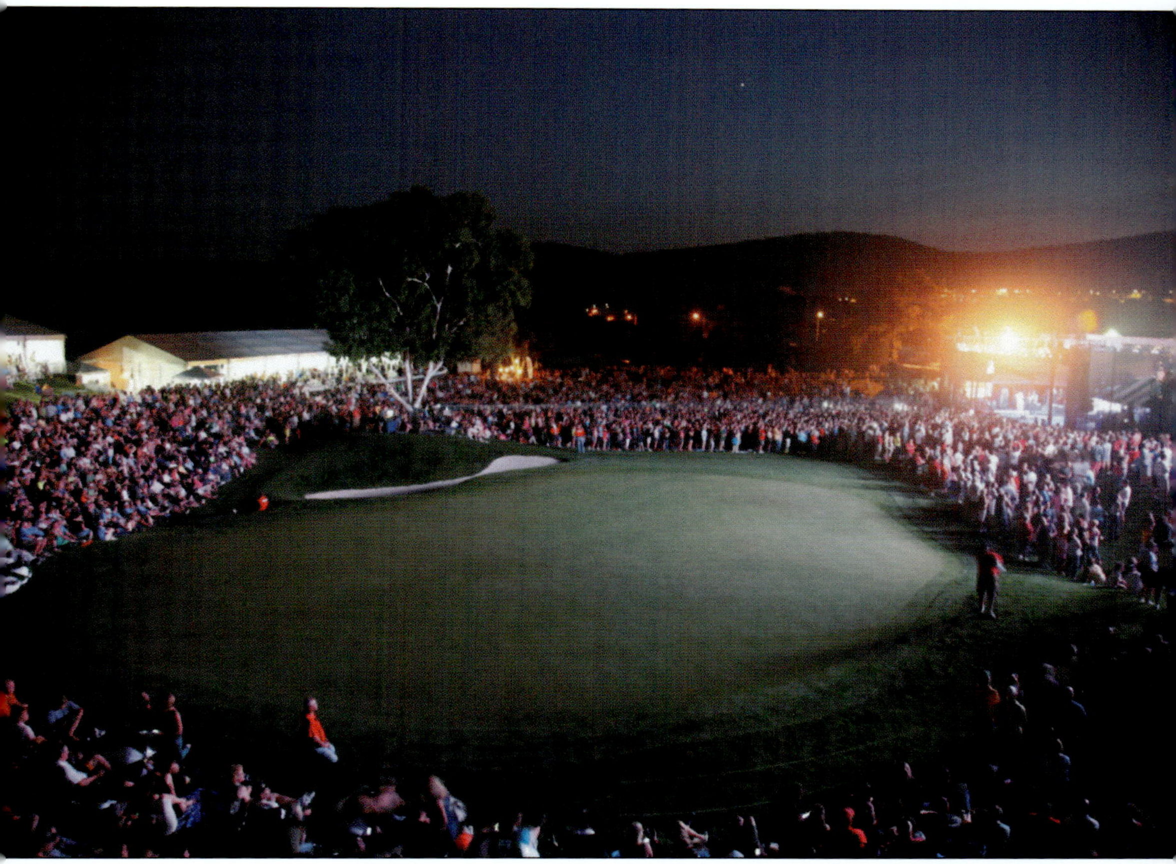

MORE THAN GOLF. This photograph, taken from the top floor of one of the suites on the 18th green, shows that the concert provides an ideal stage for the visual arts as well. The periwinkle sky combines with the lighting to paint a picturesque view of En-Joie as music fills the fairway and pleases the fans. (Courtesy of BCCC.)

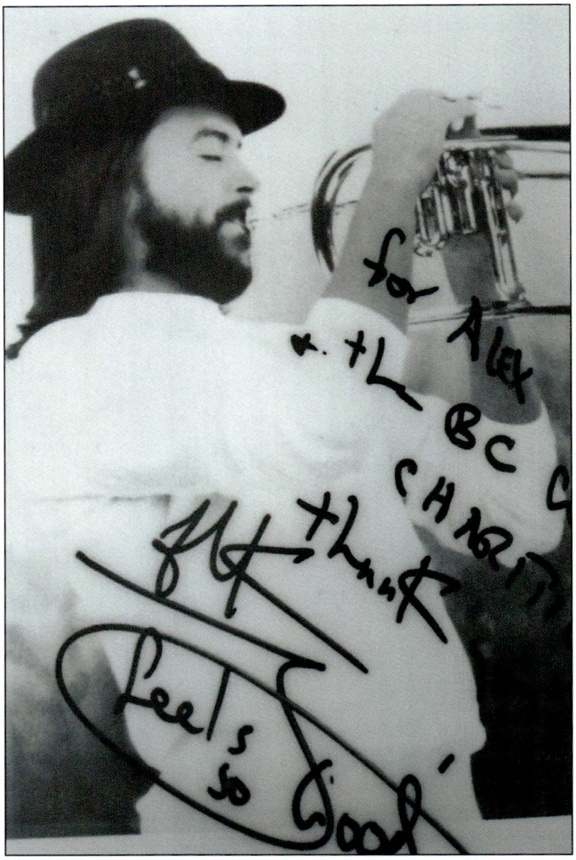

Feels So Good! Grammy-winning Rochester native Chuck Mangione performed several times at the BC Open. His songs have been featured in many movies, including *Cannonball Run*. He even composed the soundtrack for the film *The Children of Sanchez*, starring Anthony Quinn. (Courtesy of BCHS.)

Proud to Be an American! Legendary country singer Lee Greenwood graced the stage at En-Joie in 1996. He is best known for his patriotic song *God Bless the U.S.A.* Greenwood wrote his famous song in 1984, but it became America's proudest song following the events of September 11, 2001. (Courtesy of BCHS.)

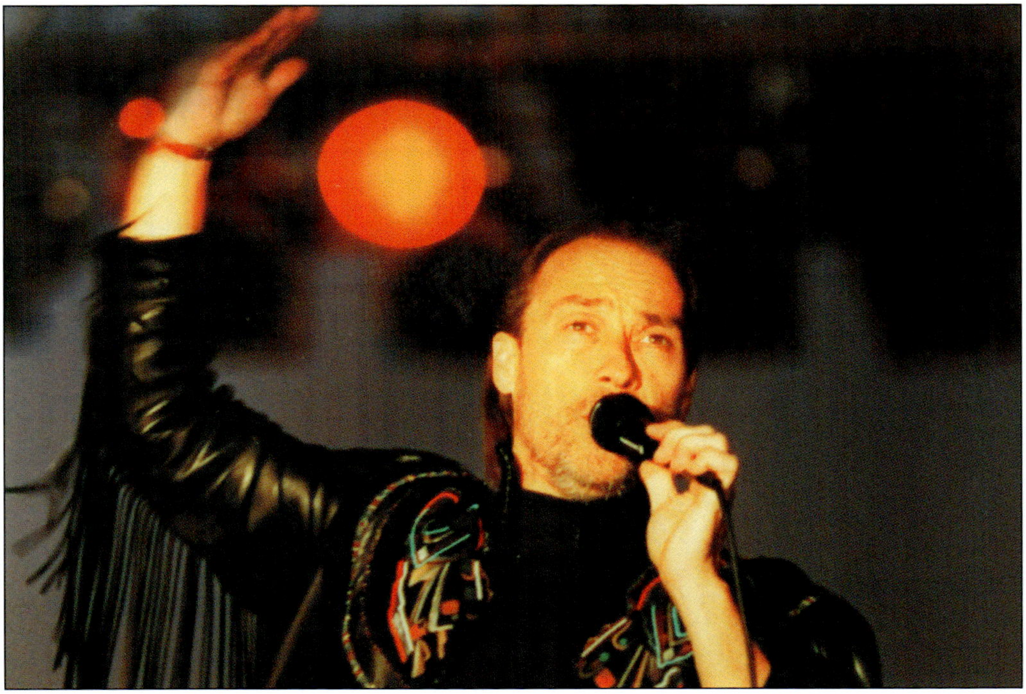

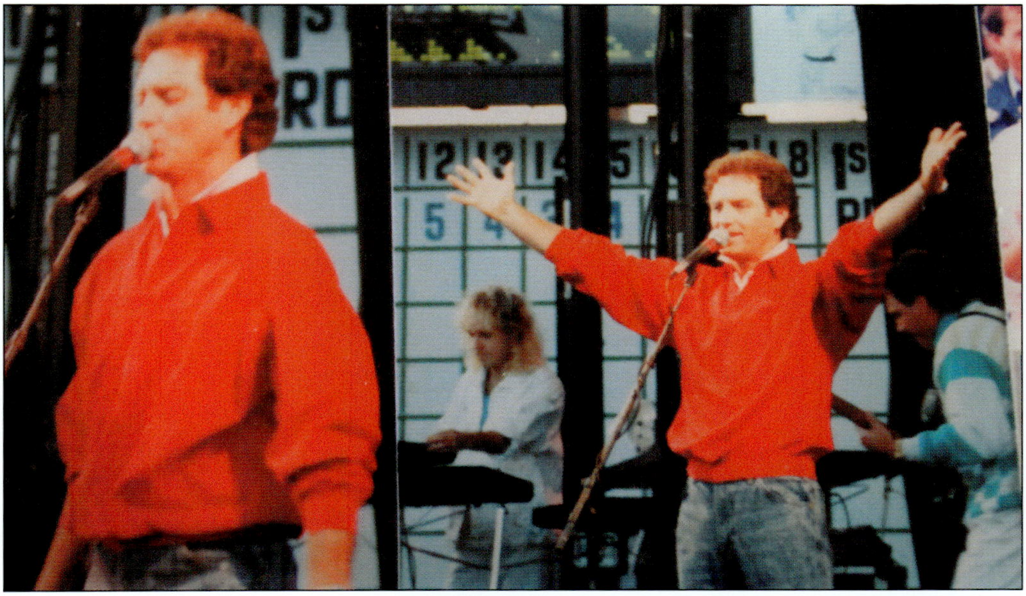

All in the Family. When Larry Gatlin signed with Columbia Records in 1979, he added his brothers to his group, and they became Larry Gatlin and the Gatlin Brothers. In 1988, the Gatlins performed at the BC Open, singing, among other titles, "All the Gold in California" and "She Used to Be Somebody's Baby." (Courtesy of BCHS.)

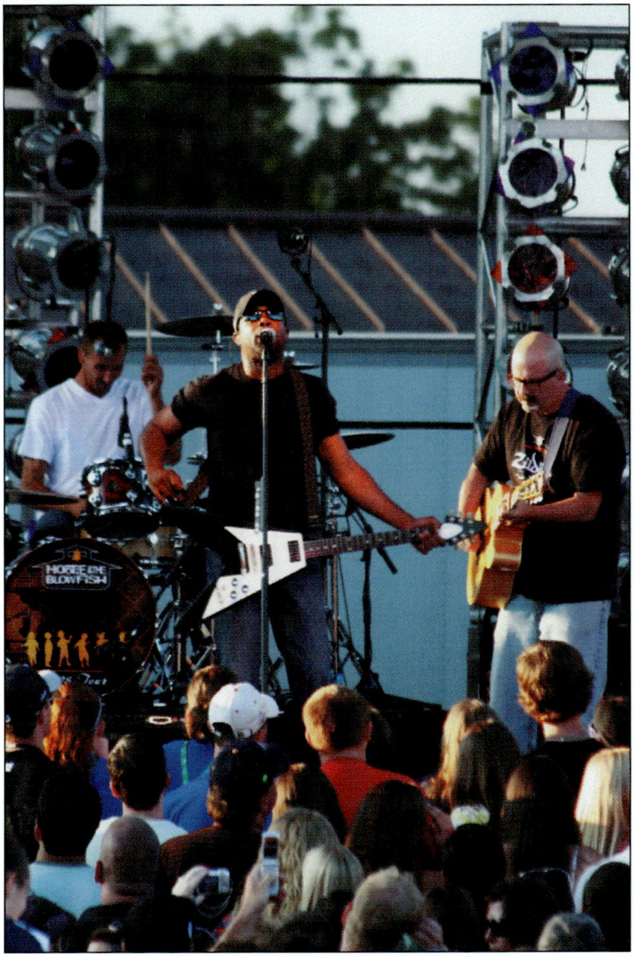

We Sing to Play! Darius C. Rucker, lead singer and rhythm guitarist for Hootie and the Blowfish, belts out a tune in 2008. The band, formed in 1986 at the University of South Carolina, took its moniker from the nicknames of two college buddies. The band members are also avid golfers. (Courtesy of BCCC.)

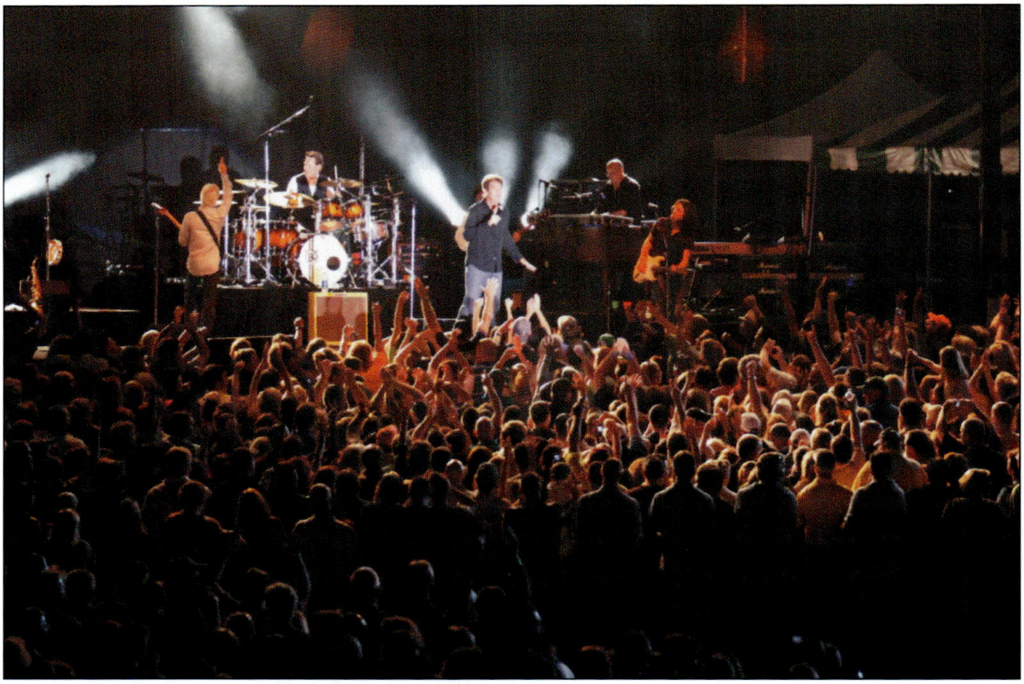

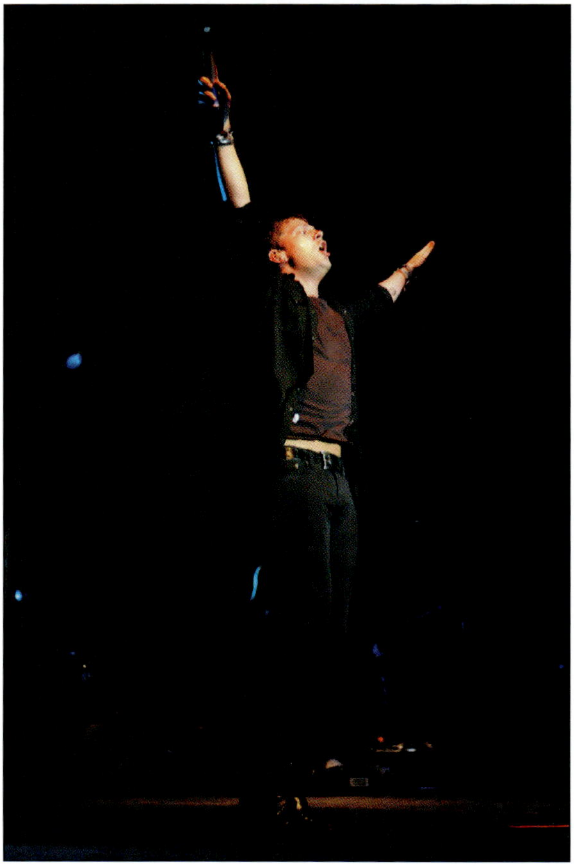

Huey Lewis and the News. Though it has been a while since Huey and his mates have had a hit song, they are still very active. They performed "Take Me Out to the Ballgame" at the 2014 World Series. In the 1980s, the band had 12 top-10 hits, including such No. 1 songs as "The Power of Love," "Stuck with You," and "Jacob's Ladder." (Courtesy of BCCC.)

Hear it, Write it, Sing It. Rob Thomas has had huge success as a musician, whether as the lead singer for Matchbox Twenty, as a soloist, or while collaborating with such musical giants as Santana, Mick Jagger, and Willie Nelson. The singer/songwriter succinctly sums up his gift this way: "I'm a guy who hears songs in his head, and I have to write them down, and I have to get them out." (Courtesy of BCCC.)

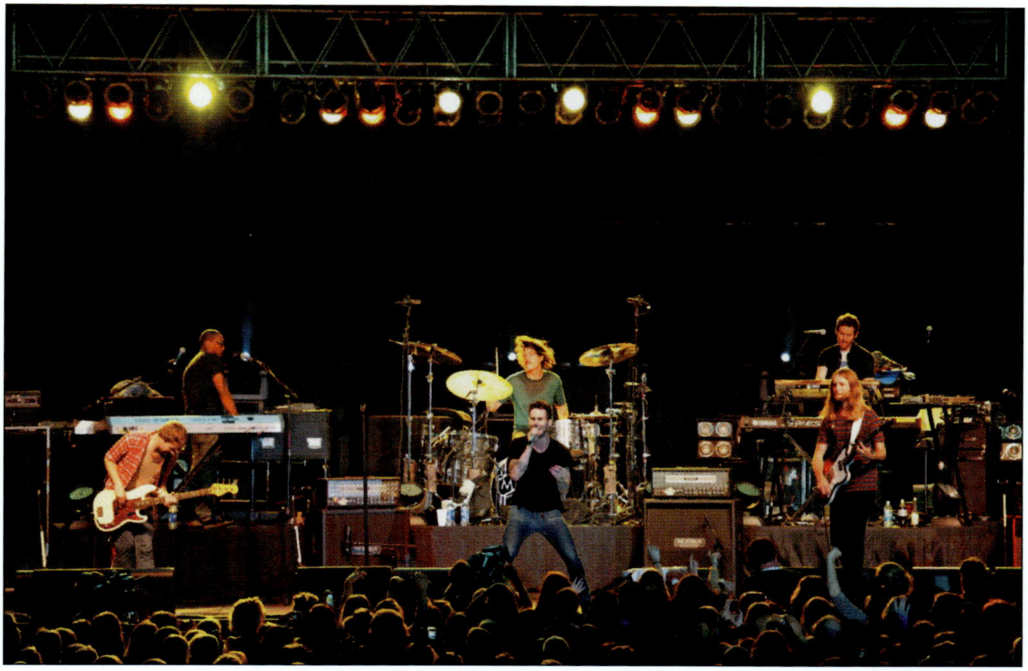

The Voice of His Generation. Grammy-winning band Maroon 5 packed the 18th hole in 2011 (above) as part of their Hands All Over Tour. Coming out swinging, they opened with "Misery" and played through a set list featuring "She Will Be Loved," "This Love," "Makes Me Wonder," and closed with "Sunday Morning." Their front man, Adam Levine, has been a coach and judge on the hit television show *The Voice* since its inception in 2011. Below, Patrick Monahan, the lead singer for Train, reaches out to the crowd. At left is an original band member, lead guitarist Jimmy Stafford. The group started performing in 1993 in San Francisco. (Both, courtesy of BCCC.)

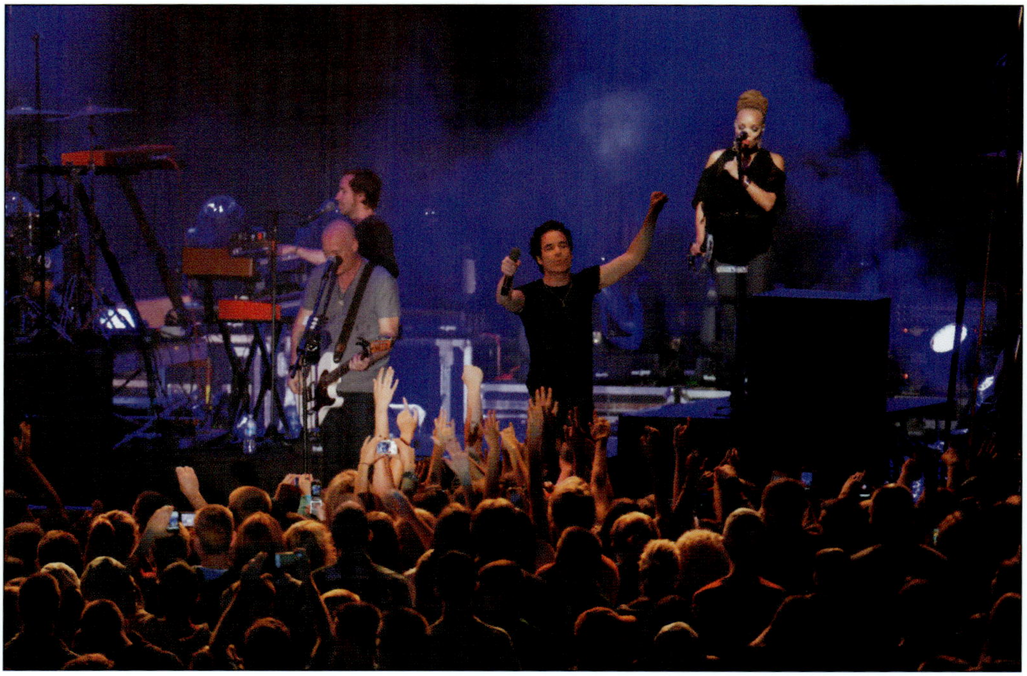

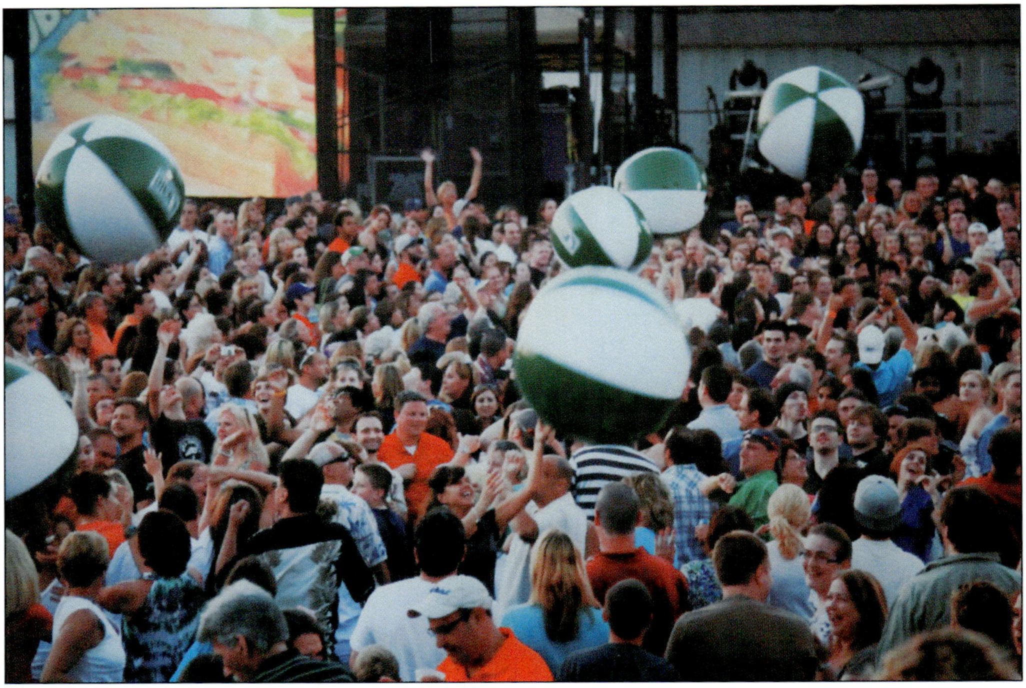

All Aboard! The crowd that showed up to catch Train in 2012 amused themselves by hitting beach balls as they waited under gray skies. The group never missed a beat (below), belting out their award-winning hits "Drops of Jupiter (Tell Me)," "Calling All Angels," and their fan favorite, "Hey, Soul Sister." Train played for over two hours and sent fans home in a great mood. (Both, courtesy of BCCC.)

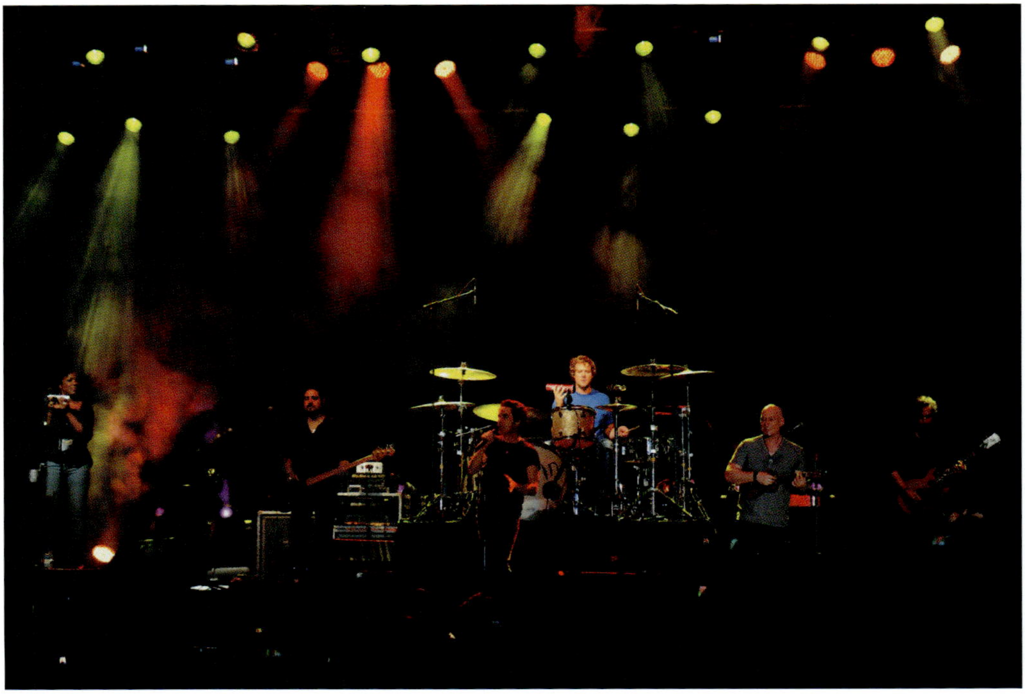

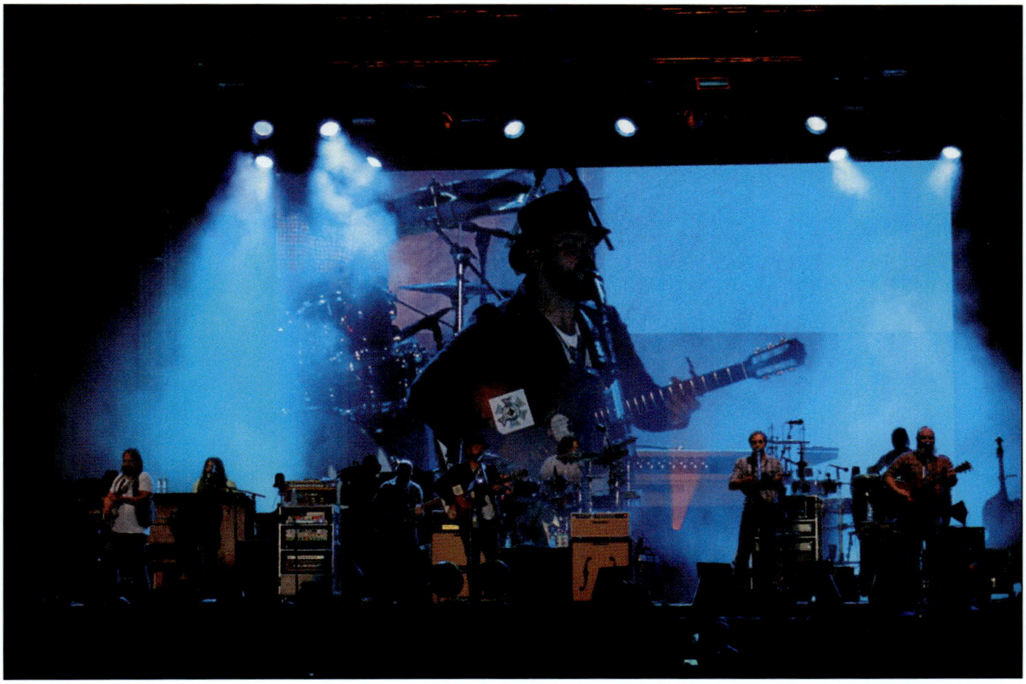

Strummin' Replaces Putting. Zac Brown and members of his multi-Grammy-winning band are all smiles as Brown (above) strums his guitar and sings for the approximately 25,000 fans packing the 18th hole on August 15, 2014. The band's performance on this night included such hits as "Toes," "Chicken Fried," "The Devil Went Down to Georgia," and "Day for the Dead." Below, camera phones capture the performers as they leave their normal stations to do a "sing-along"!

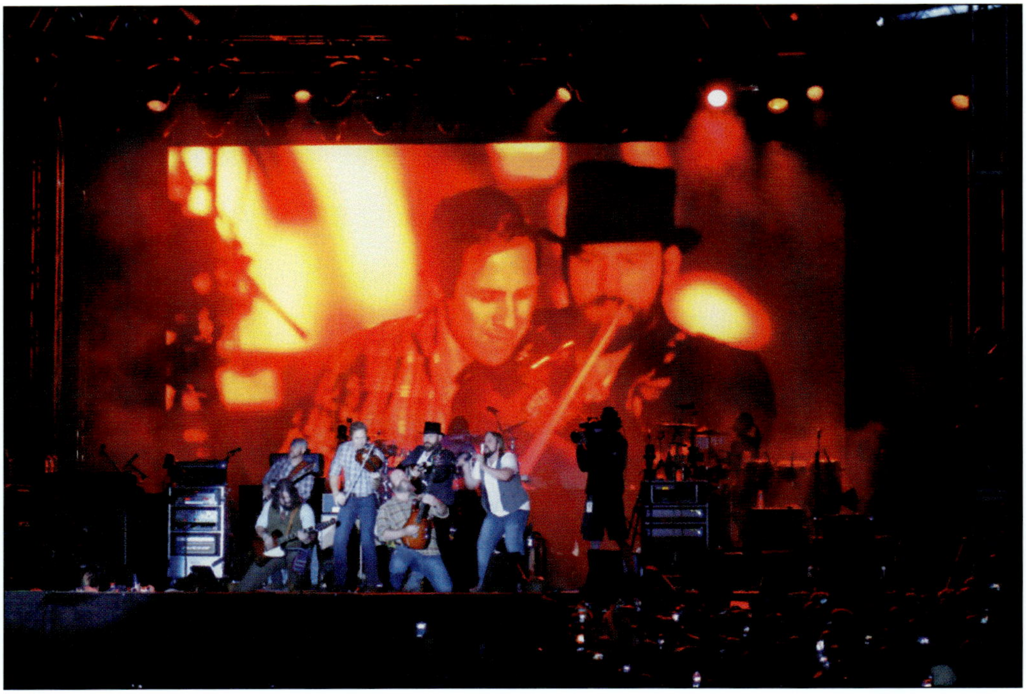

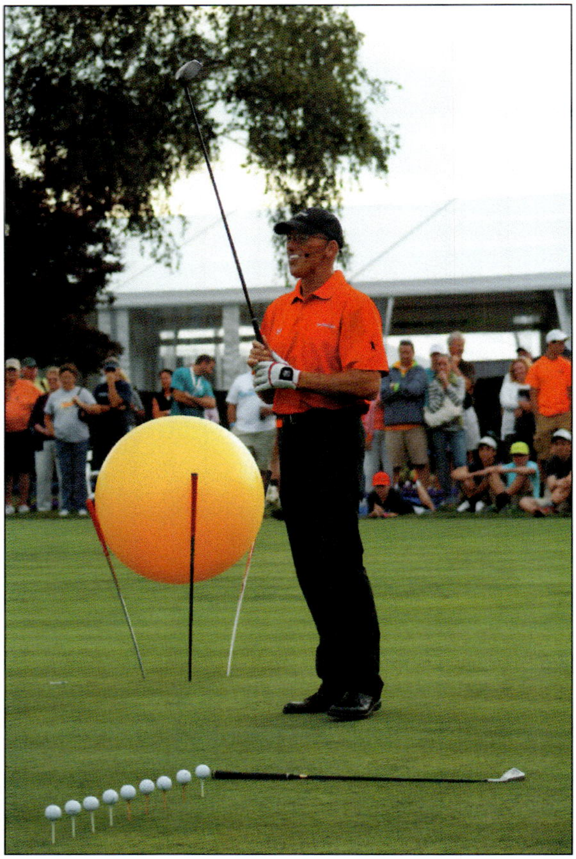

"**Tee it Up!**" Ben Witter is an inspiration for all who hear his story. After earning All-American honors three times in college and two NCAA National Long Drive crowns, Witter was ready to turn pro. However, his pursuit of joining the PGA Tour was cut short with a cancer diagnosis. He defeated cancer and, after multiple facial surgeries, was able to golf again. Although the PGA Tour was in his past, Witter was able to bring his life experiences to the tour in a more inspirational way, becoming a trick-shot artist and motivational speaker. At left, he gets ready to balance on a large orange ball to hit a tee shot! Below, fans surround the first tee area to hear and see Witter.

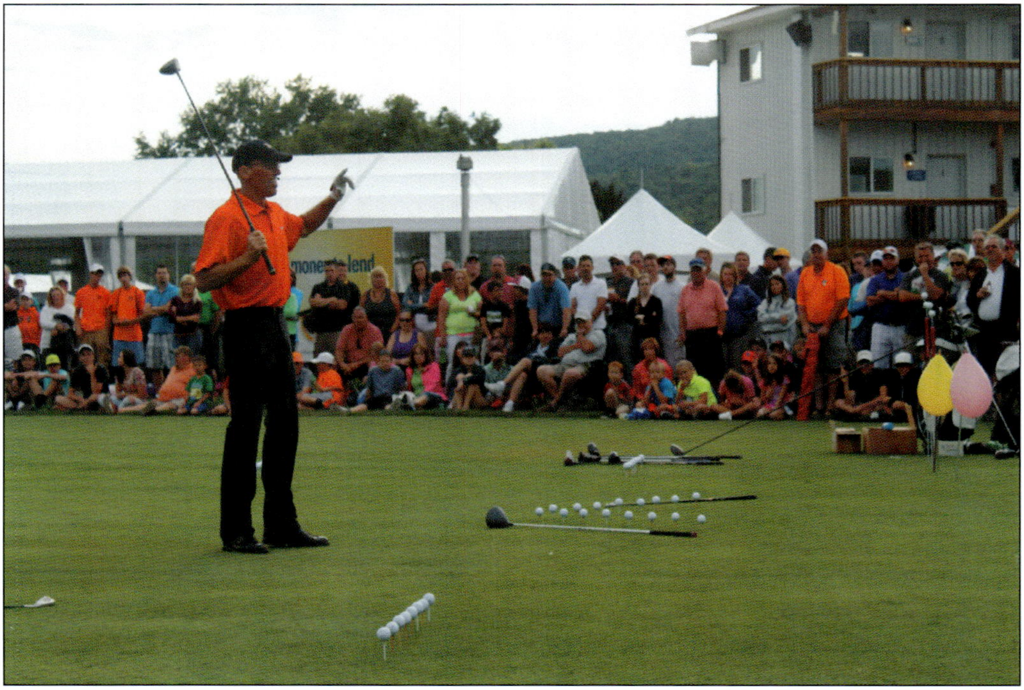

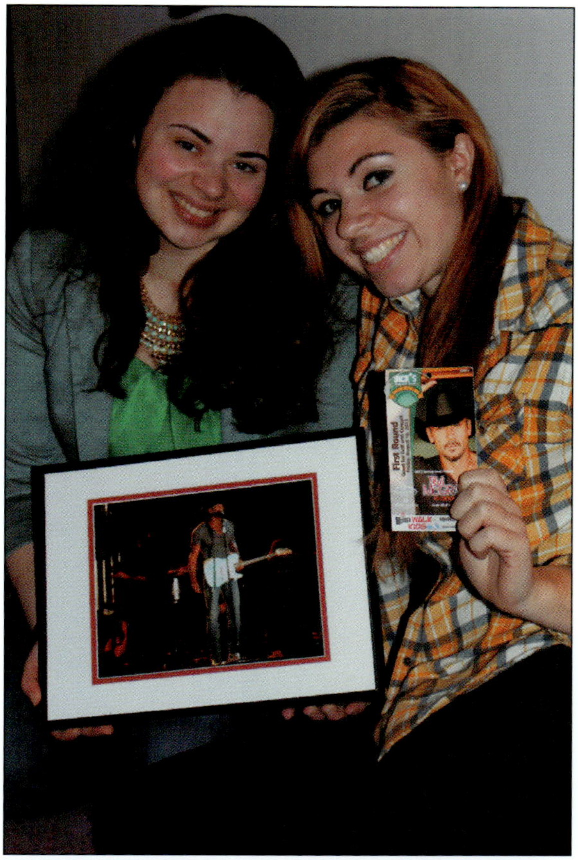

Cherished Memories. At right, sisters Alice and Emily Maggiore show off a ticket stub and a picture of Tim McGraw from his 2013 performance. Indeed, En-Joie's tournaments and special events provide a forum that connects generations. From the stage and tent lights painting a rainbow over the 18th green, to the parents and grandparents who share stories of smiles and frowns along with the birdies and bogeys, En-Joie offers a memory for everyone. Shown below is photographer Chris Condon (center), who was employed by the tournament to freeze some moments in time. (Below, courtesy of BCCC.)

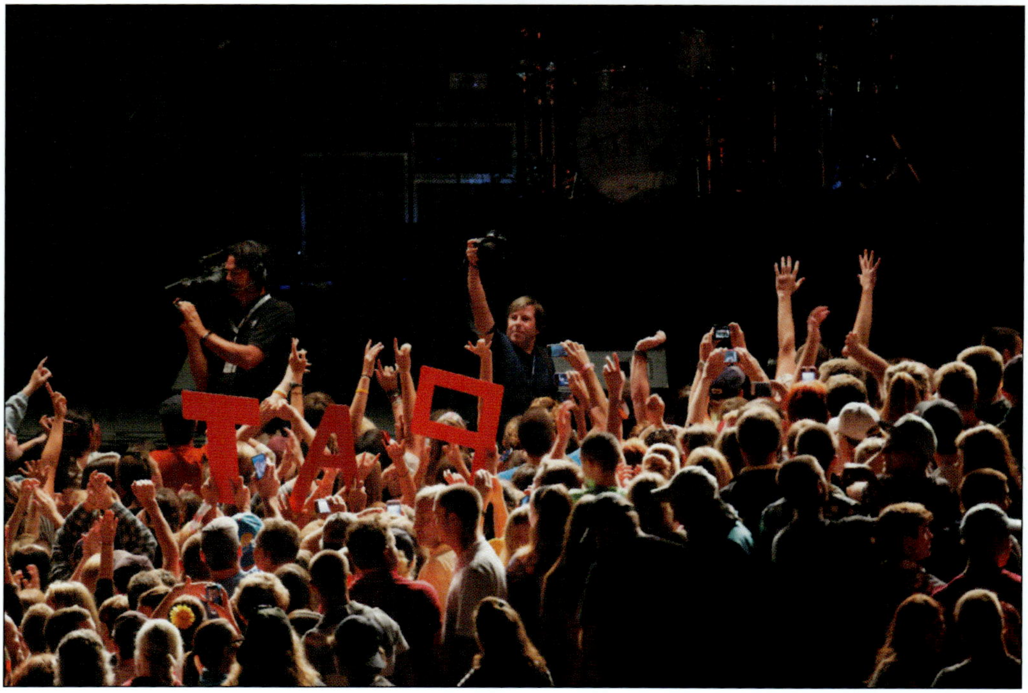

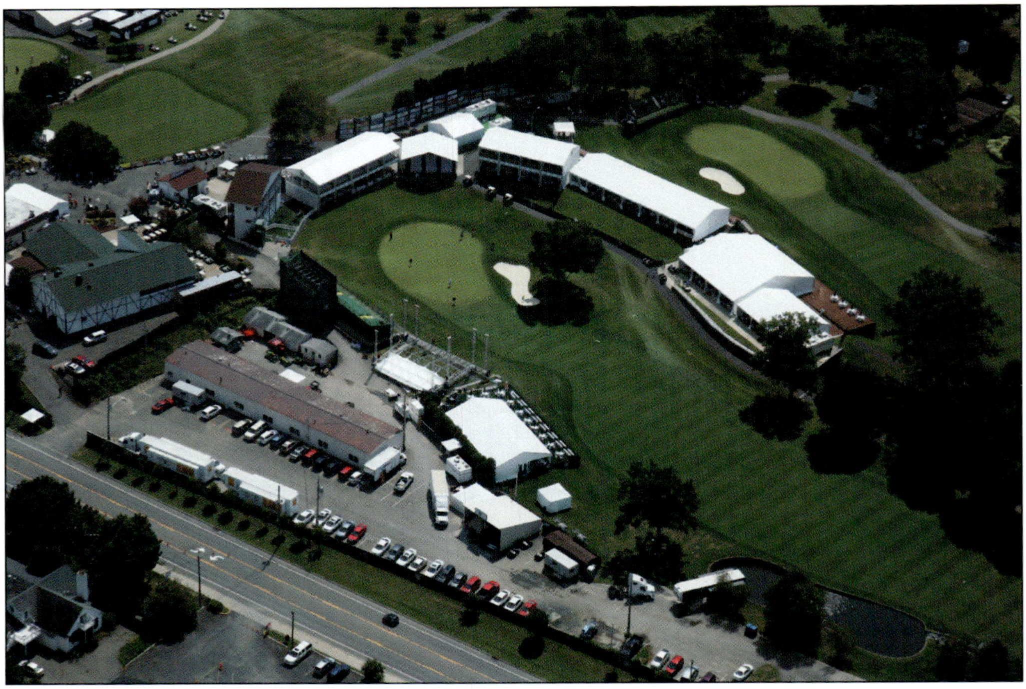

Before and After. The 18th green serves as a focal point throughout the tournament and as a symbol of the vibrancy of the Endicott community. Above, a plane captures the green before the start of tournament play, reflecting a serene stillness. Below, the green in its full splendor as the community waits to crown a new winner of En-Joie. Though this hole has courted many golfers through the years, only the champions of En-Joie can lay claim to having won its heart. (Both, courtesy of BCCC.)

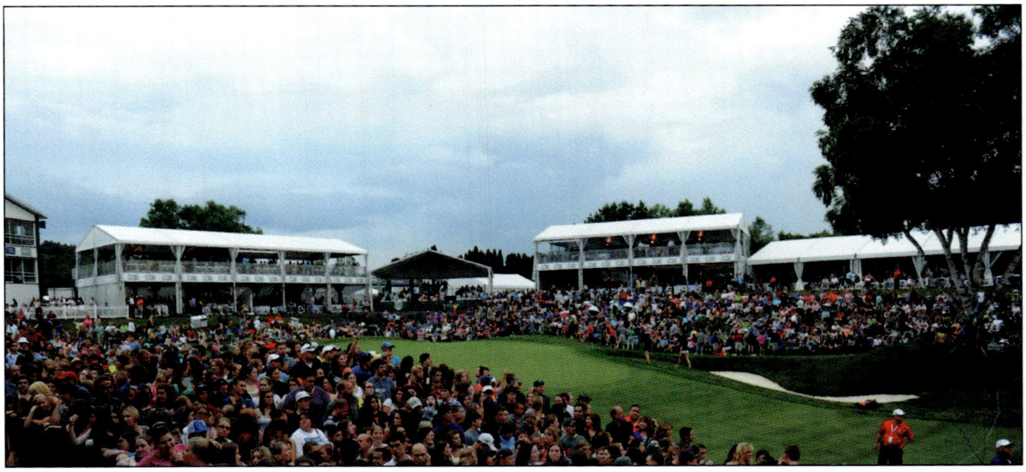

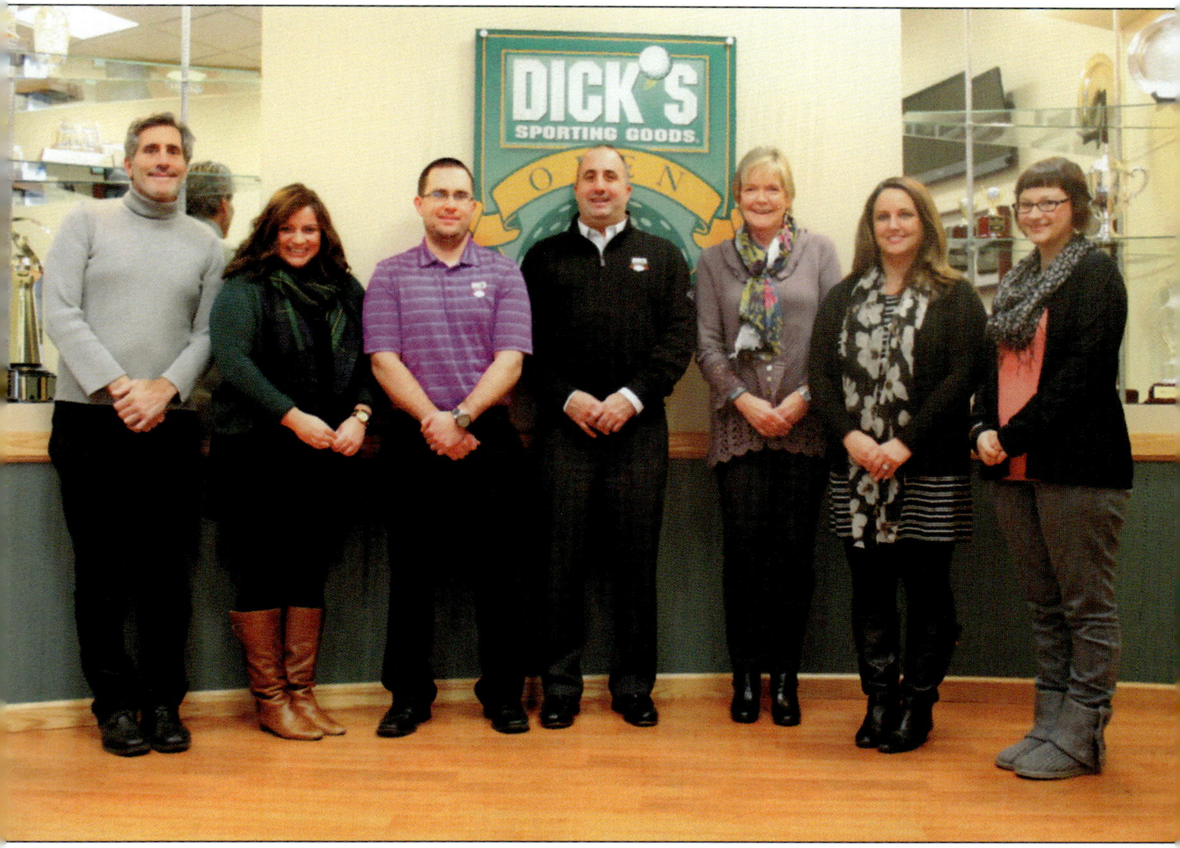

A Carousel of Work. For the final image in this book, it is fitting to include the staff members of the Broome County Community Charities, Inc. They are, from left to right, marketing and communications manager Dave Pessagno, tournament coordinator Tenny Snyder, tournament operations director Mike Schaffer, tournament director John Karedes, office manager Dorn Black, tournament manager Sarah Hutchings, and administrative assistant Liz Klein. The staff of the BCCC, Inc., are symbols of the community that proudly hosts world-class golf every year in Broome County.

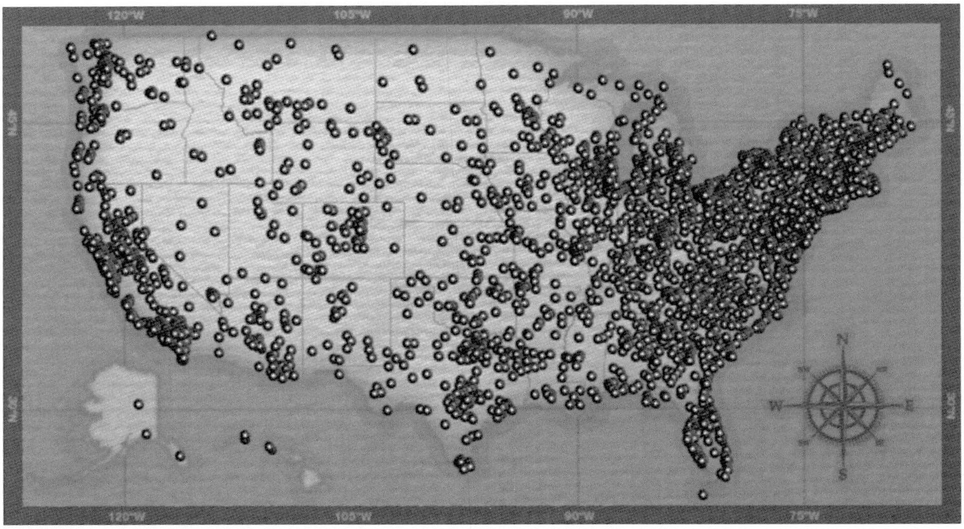